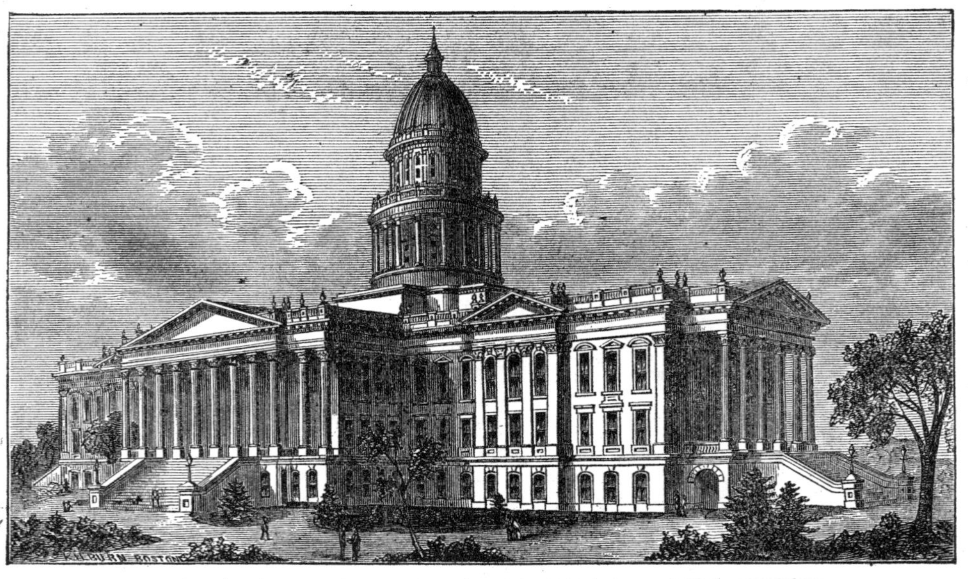

STATE CAPITOL, TOPEKA, KANSAS, ONLY ONE WING ERECTED.

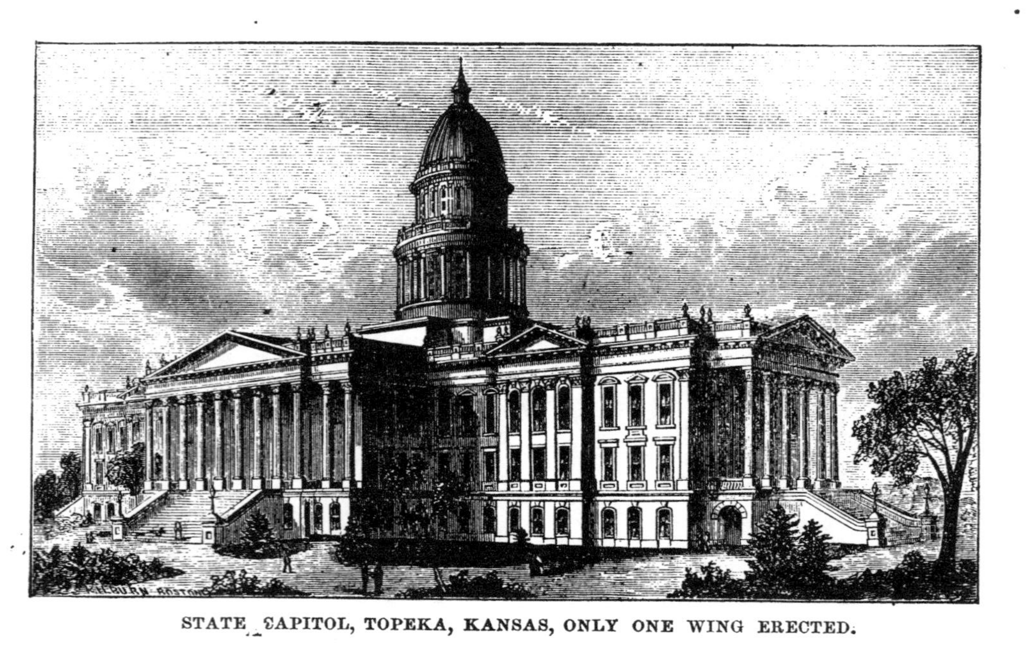

STATE CAPITOL, TOPEKA, KANSAS, ONLY ONE WING ERECTED.

RESOURCES

OF

KANSAS.

FIFTEEN YEARS EXPERIENCE.

BY C. C. HUTCHINSON.

WITH A NEW MAP AND FORTY ILLUSTRATIONS.

"The rudiments of empire here
Are plastic yet, and warm;
The chaos of a mighty world
Is rounding into form."

TOPEKA, KANSAS:
PUBLISHED BY THE AUTHOR.

PRINTED AT THE
COMMONWEALTH" STATE PRINTING HOUSE.

Preface.

THIS little book is designed to anticipate and answer many of the questions which would be asked by persons contemplating a removal from some other region to Kansas. At the same time it has been my purpose to convey information which will be of service not only to Kansas immigrants but to all other immigrants as well. For instance, the articles upon "The Survey of Government Lands," indorsed by the Surveyor General of Kansas; and upon "Acquiring Title to Government Lands," indorsed by the United States Land Officers, are intended to be so explicit that with their help any person may locate Government Land by its corners, and then take proper steps to acquire a title by any of the various methods established by Government.

I have endeavored to be strictly impartial as relates to different localities in Kansas, and have written as if addressing an intimate friend who was entirely ignorant concerning the subjects discussed. It is designed to furnish a hand-book which will be worth all its costs to any person interested in the West.

This book is the outgrowth of experience in relation to the matters of which it treats, and the reader is requested to bear in mind that it is not written by a professional author. It is hoped that upon this ground its many defects will be more leniently regarded.

The map has been drawn and engraved with great care, and everything upon it is from official sources excepting the proposed railroad lines. With this exception it is intended to be strictly accurate, and it is probable that most of the projected roads will be constructed in a few years.

I gladly record my gratitude to the numberless friends who have rendered valuable service in furnishing material for this work, and especially to the members of the Legislature of 1871, which almost without dissent appropriated twenty-five hundred dollars to aid in its publication. Without these kind offices on the part of my friends and those who desire to see the State correctly described, it would have been impossible to sell the work for the small sum at which it is offered.

To Mr. J. G. Haskell, the accomplished architect of the State Capitol, State University and many other buildings which bespeak his taste and skill, I am deeply indebted for assistance in the matter of engravings. Through his introduction I have been able to obtain precisely what was wanted from Mr. S. S. Kilburn, 96 Washington Street, Boston, Massachusetts, whose promptness and accuracy I can commend and whose work commends itself. Two or three coarser engravings were obtained from other sources, but they give accurate views of the objects presented. The views given are only samples of what is to be seen in Kansas. From several towns it happened to be impossible to procure such views as were wanted; and there are buildings, bridges, water powers, etc., in all parts of the State which would interest the reader equally with those given. The engravings are nearly all from photographs, but in a few instances, the buildings are not yet completed, and the views given are from the architect's plans. It is believed that this feature of the book will commend itself to all who desire to know Kansas as it is.

This book points out various means whereby more extended information can be obtained in regard to any particular locality, and the author will also answer all letters addressed to him at Topeka, with stamps inclosed. I shall give especial attention to all changes in the laws, or in the rulings of the General Land Office, in relation to public lands, and will furnish the same at a trifling expense to my correspondents.

C. C. H.

Kansas.

BOUNDARIES AND AREA.

THE parallel of 40 degrees north latitude, which passes eastward a little north of Springfield, Illinois, and Indianapolis, Indiana; and through Columbus, Ohio, and Philadelphia, Pennsylvania, forms the northern line of the State of Kansas.

The southern boundary line of Kansas is the parallel of 37 degrees, which is the latitude of Southern Kentucky and Virginia, passing through Norfolk in the latter State. Westward from Kansas this line strikes the Pacific coast fifty miles south of San Francisco.

Nebraska lies on the north of Kansas; Missouri on the east; the Indian territory on the south; and Colorado on the west.

Kansas is about 210 miles wide and 430 miles long. Its area is about 90,000 square miles, or 57,600,000 acres.

RIVERS.

A considerable portion of the boundary line between Missouri and Kansas is formed by the Missouri river, upon the windings of which navigable stream, the State presents a water front to the east of about one hundred and fifty miles. This river is navigable for steamboats for twenty-five hundred miles above the northern State line, north and westward to Fort Benton, near the Rocky Mountains and British Possessions; and southeastward five hundred miles to the point of intersection with the Mississippi, twenty-five miles above St. Louis. The length of the bridge which spans the Missouri at Leavenworth City, is one thousand feet, but the river is, in places, half a mile wide.

The other principal rivers of the State are as follows: The Kansas or Kaw River, is formed by the confluence of the Republican and Smoky Hill Rivers, near Junction City, and is about one hundred and fifty miles in length.

The Smoky Hill River rises near the Rocky Mountains, in Colorado. It receives the Saline River, which is about two hundred miles long, and the Solomon, about two hundred and fifty miles in length.

The Republican River rises in Colorado, flows through Northwestern Kansas into Nebraska, whence it returns to Kansas, about one hundred and fifty miles west of the eastern line of the State. Its length from its source is more than four hundred miles.

The Kansas River receives on the north, at Manhattan, the Big Blue River, which rises in Nebraska and is about one hundred and twenty-five miles long; and the Grasshopper, about seventy-five miles in length. On the south it receives, near Lawrence, the Wakarusa, which is nearly fifty miles in length. The Kansas River flows nearly due east from Junction City, and enters the Missouri River at a point where the latter, making a great bend to the eastward, leaves the State line. About two-thirds of the State lies south of the Kansas and Smoky Hill Rivers, whence that portion is frequently called Southern Kansas, and the remainder of the State Northern Kansas. The Kansas River is not practically navigable, although steamboats have ascended it, in one instance to Fort Riley, which is on the Smoky Hill, above the mouth of the Republican.

The Marais des Cygnes River, or River of Swans, which Whittier has immortalized in song, rises east of the center of the State, and flowing south of east about one hundred and twenty-five miles, crosses the State line near Fort Scott, and becomes the Osage River of Missouri.

Spring River enters Kansas from Missouri, and flows about thirty miles in the southeast corner of this State, whence it enters the Indian Territory.

STATE UNIVERSITY, AT LAWRENCE.

Old building erected 1865.

The Neosho River rises near the center of the State, receives the Cottonwood and other confluent streams, flows southeast a distance of about two hundred miles, and enters the Indian Territory twenty-five miles west of the southeastern corner of Kansas.

The Cottonwood, which enters the Neosho near Emporia, is much the larger stream at their junction. It is about one hundred miles long.

The Verdigris River flows south nearly parallel to the Neosho, and enters the Indian Territory about one hundred miles from its source. It receives Fall River on the west, which is about sixty miles long.

The Arkansas River rises far up among the Rocky Mountains in the South Park of Colorado, and receives many tributaries in the latter State. It crosses three-fourths of the length of Kansas, flowing east and southeast, and with its tributaries, waters two-thirds of Southern Kansas. It then flows through the northeastern one-third of the Indian Territory, receiving all the remaining streams of Southern Kansas, crosses the State of Arkansas, and enters the Mississippi River midway between Memphis and Vicksburg. Its entire length is more than two thousand miles; its windings in Kansas must amount to about five hundred miles.

The first tributary of the Arkansas, commencing on the north or east side, near the south line of the State, at Arkansas City, is the Walnut, which flows from the north a distance of about seventy-five miles, receiving as tributary, the Whitewater. At Wichita the Arkansas receives the Little Arkansas, a deep flowing river, about seventy-five miles in length, Next comes in the Cow Creek, nearly as long, and at Fort Zarah, on the northernmost part of the Big Bend of the Arkansas, Walnut River enters from the west, it being about one hundred miles long. Beyond are Ash Creek, Pawnee Fork, &c. On the south or west side of the Arkansas it receives the Sha-kus-ka, the Nin-ne-scah or Good River, the Cow Skin and others, from fifty to seventy-five miles long.

In the southwestern corner of Kansas the Cimarron flows a considerable distance in the State and receives the waters of Medicine Lodge, Mule Creek,

Nes-cu-tun-ga, Bluff Creek, &c., each from fifty to one hundred miles long. This region has not yet been surveyed, so that these streams, as well as streams of importance in Northwestern Kansas, are not put down on the map. There are numerous streams from twenty-five to seventy-five miles long, including tributaries of the Republican and Solomon Rivers, which have not been mentioned.

The rivers named above, with their innumerable tributaries, fed by rivulets flowing from never-failing springs, have given to Kansas its reputation of being the best watered region of all the prairie States.

SURFACE AND SCENERY.

To describe the surface and scenery of Kansas so that it can be appreciated by those who have never seen a prairie State is quite impossible, and scarcely less difficult is it to describe it to one who has only seen the flat prairies of Central Illinois. In general it may be called an undulating plateau, the surface of which very gently slopes from the western line, which has an altitude of about thirty-five hundred feet above the ocean, to the eastern line, which is seven hundred and fifty feet above the ocean at the mouth of the Kansas River.

The rise of the first one hundred miles on the Kansas Pacific Railroad from the Eastern State line to Wamego is two hundred and fifty-four feet; for the second hundred miles to Brookville the rise is three hundred and forty-eight feet; the rise of the third hundred miles to Ellis is seven hundred and sixty-nine feet, and the rise thence to Eagle Tail which is near the Western State line is thirteen hundred and seventeen feet.

The interval lands along the water courses, called bottoms, are from one fourth of a mile to three miles in width, but towards the western part of the State are sometimes from five to ten miles wide. None of the bottom land in the State is regularly subject to overflow and when high waters occur on a few streams they subside in three or four days. The ordinary flow of water, in the larger streams, is fifteen or twenty feet below the surface of the bottom lands, almost invariably insuring perfect drainage. The bottoms in the eastern half of the State are about equally divided between wooded and open lands.

Leaving the bottoms, one comes upon the next highest surface called second bottom. This formation is almost entirely absent from many streams of the State, and it varies so much in different places that it can hardly be described. It varies in extent from a narrow belt, to a width of two or three miles, and usually rises gently as it recedes from the stream. The surface is diversified by gentle rolls ordinarily running nearly at right angles with the streams, with their crowns from an eighth to a half mile apart and rising twenty to forty feet above the intervening depressions.

Back from the second bottoms the traveler strikes the bluffs which rise to a hight of from fifty to two hundred or three hundred feet, with a slope of about twenty to thirty degrees. Once upon the summit of the bluff the traveler sees stretching before him what we term the upland prairies, a succession of rolls similar to those upon the second bottom, but with much longer slopes forming a series of earthy billows. Their crests or summits are from a quarter of a mile to a mile apart, and perhaps twenty to eighty feet above the intervening depression or miniature valley. Down many of these little valleys flow rills of clear water, frequently making a narrow gulley as they break through the bluffs and near the streams to which they are tributary.

These rills, which sometimes attain the dignity and

names of creeks are, in Eastern Kansas, usually fringed with timber as they approach the main stream. On the upper front of the bluffs, ledges frequently crop out in bold parapets a few feet high, and along the crests of the large prairie rolls these ledges wind like ribbons around the irregular face.

There is no portion of the State which is flat and and monotonous, or cut up by disagreeable and inconvenient gullies and ravines. The western half of the State is not so much diversified in its scenery, but it has everywhere a rolling and varied surface.

No other such scene is to be found in the United States as presents itself to the traveler who stands upon one of the higher Kansas bluffs. The patient reader, wearied by the formal description we have given of the surface of the country, must now give scope to his imagination else he will not see Kansas as it is. Nature, ever symmetrical in her combinations, is irregular in all her details, and nowhere is this better shown than in the picture we are contemplating. The prairie rolls vary in direction and size nearly as much as the streams and bluffs, and in some localities they are short and comparatively sharp, while in a mile or two they so broaden their extent and lower their surfaces as to appear nearly level to one from a mountainous region. No two streams or bottoms or bluffs or prairies are alike in all this beautiful country. Here is a broad valley miles in extent, and embracing in itself and its surroundings many of the features we have so imperfectly detailed. The bluffs advance and recede at capricious pleasure: on one side of the stream pushing their promontory fronts like the parapets of some vast fortification full into the low lands, or not far away closing nearly together upon either side of the stream, or again with gentle descent approach their grass clad slopes till their harmonious shades mingle with the rich verdure of the forests below.

STATE UNIVERSITY AT LAWRENCE, ERECTED 1870-1871.

Elsewhere, lowlands, bluff and prairie so imperceptibly blend their various characteristics that the features of none can be accurately traced, while here and there the eye rests upon an isolated mound of a few acres in extent, which rises to the level of the high prairies beyond. These views combine the qualities of grandeur in their vast extent and of the picturesque in their loveliness of detail to such a degree that the poet preacher, Rev. Robert Pierpont, upon his visit to Kansas exclaimed: "God doubtless might have made a lovelier country, but it is certain that he never did it."

The landscape, even of the unsettled portions of Kansas carries with it an impression that this is not really a new country, but an old one long since deserted of its inhabitants. Concerning this feature, which immediately strikes all observant travelers, Bayard Taylor remarks: "The counterpart of this region is not to be found in the United States, yet there was a suggestion of other landscapes in it which puzzled me considerably until I happened to recall some parts of France, especially the valleys in the neighborhood of Epernay. Here too, there was rather an air of old culture than of new settlement, only the houses, gardens and orchards were wanting."

Upon the surface of hill and dale which we have described place the artificial groves and hedges, which four or five years suffice to perfect, place here the flocks and herds and growing crops, and you have a scene of pastoral beauty which few countries can equal. Such views are now to be found in the older portions of the State and will in a few years be common throughout its extent.

SOIL.

The soil of Kansas is similar to that of other prairie States. Indeed, this State having been largely settled by Illinoisians, its agricultural resources have always been estimated in comparison with that State—confessedly the Garden State of all the world.

Those of us who have lived in both States and cultivated land in both States, do not object to even this high standard of comparison, and it may be said then, that Kansas soil is as deep as Illinois soil. This opinion is the result of examination with my pocket rule in hundreds of places in both States. Owing to the rolling surface, its drainage is incomparably better, and it will consequently endure the extremes of dryness or moisture much better than Illinois soil. It does not "heave" as much by the action of frosts, and is superior in this, as well as in other respects, for winter wheat.

The vicissitudes of agriculture which are incident to every new country, have severely tried the reputation of this soil for productiveness. Add to this the exceptional occurrence of a dry season, which found a people who were poor when they came to Kansas, now stripped of every resource by the long continued Border war, and it is surprising that the State has obtained so remarkable a reputation for its productiveness.

But since the settlers learned that men must work for a living here as well as elsewhere, and plow and plant in season, and attend their crops as they would attend them in other States, Kansas has made returns that place her in the very front rank as an agricultural State. Formerly men thought that corn needed little or no cultivation here, and were quite indifferent as to the time of putting in crops. With proper cultivation the results satisfy the most incredulous, as may be seen by the following comparative table of products.

TABLE

Showing average yield in bushels per acre in fifteen of the most productive States, copied from the Reports of the United States Agricultural Department. Fractions are omitted.

Report for 1870 not yet published.

PRODUCTS.	Vermont.	Massachusetts.	Connecticut.	New York.	Pennsylvania.	Kentucky.	Ohio.	Michigan.	Indiana.	Illinois.	Missouri.	Wisconsin.	Iowa.	Minnesota.	**Kansas.**
Report for 1865															
Indian Corn.....	43	33	31	24	40	34	41	38	40	35	39	41	42	38	**41**
Wheat	18	17	17	15	12	7	9	15	8	11	12	16	14	20	**15**
Rye..................	16	14	14	15	13	9	12	14	12	16	16	17	18	22	**23**
Oats..................	39	26	35	34	34	24	31	37	29	35	26	40	38	41	**34**
Barley	28	19	23	22	22	21	22	22	22	21	23	26	25	29	**38**
Potatoes...........	164	104	121	107	75	59	83	145	84	117	122	141	120	197	**119**
Report for 1866															
Indian Corn. ...	33	34	33	27	34	31	38	32	36	31	30	28	31	.....	**34**
Wheat	20	14	17	15	11	6	4	13	5	13	16	14	16	.....	**21**
Rye..................	18	17	13	16	13	9	10	15	12	15	19	16	19	.....	**26**
Oats..................	40	29	32	33	33	21	32	34	29	34	30	33	37	.....	**39**
Barley	29	22	23	23	22	13	19	25	19	25	25	25	25	.....	**29**
Potatoes...........	148	139	109	107	99	88	78	110	79	86	92	91	72	.....	**81**
Report for 1867															
Indian Corn.....	36	35	33	30	32	24	28	31	29	23	27	33	33	30	**38**
Wheat	15	16	17	14	12	8	11	12	10	11	12	12	12	12	**14**
Rye..................	15	15	14	15	13	10	13	17	14	15	16	16	19	18	**20**
Oats..................	30	26	27	26	30	18	31	29	10	30	30	35	42	38	**36**
Barley	23	22	23	20	20	17	24	20	21	22	21	25	29	23	**26**
Potatoes...........	116	96	68	84	74	50	75	97	73	60	73	96	108	110	**109**
Report for 1868															
Indian Corn.....	38	37	34	32	35	32	34	33	34	34	30	33	37	33	**18**
Wheat	16	15	15	14	12	8	13	12	11	11	14	13	14	15	**15**
Rye..................	14	16	14	15	13	11	13	18	14	16	18	18	19	20	**20**
Oats	30	24	27	26	27	22	29	30	26	31	32	32	33	36	**25**
Barley	23	20	20	21	21	16	22	23	20	25	24	24	26	25	**23**
Potatoes...........	135	116	117	94	88	80	79	94	88	71	90	77	96	151	**85**
Report for 1869															
Indian Corn.....	34	34	31	27	31	25	30	28	23	23	30	26	33	29	**48**
Wheat	18	18	17	16	14	11	15	15	14	11	14	15	13	16	**18**
Rye..................	16	18	12	14	13	11	14	16	15	14	16	15	16	18	**25**
Oats..................	35	31	33	35	35	19	33	35	29	32	33	36	37	37	**42**
Barley	22	25	23	24	23	19	25	24	22	20	23	25	26	25	**30**
Potatoes...........	160	106	108	114	102	69	112	155	106	103	115	107	123	112	**149**

The bottom lands are usually considered most valuable, but they do not invariably produce the best crops. In a wet season the uplands are most productive. The soil on the bottoms is from two to ten feet deep, and on the uplands, from one to three

JOHN BROWN'S CABIN.

☞ The above cut is from a photograph taken for this book by Barker, photographic artist, of Ottawa, Kansas, who has copies for sale. It is a view of the only building now standing in which John Brown, the Abolitionist, ever lived in Kansas. No less than six of those who fell at Harper's Ferry upon the occasion of Brown's raid into Virginia, had eaten and slept in this cabin. The figure with uncovered head is the venerable James Hanway, and the other Mr. Wasson, who were neighbors, companions and friends of Captain Brown. The former at one time lived in this cabin, when it was that Old John Brown wrote his famous "Parallels" under its roof. (See Redpath's "Life of Brown," page 218.)

Through the doorway, and against the open space made by the falling of the huge old fashioned chimney, may be seen the ends of ox-bows suspended to dry. These tell the story of "the piping times of peace" which have come since the days when John Brown threw himself into the jaws of death to rescue an oppressed people. The cabin, now rapidly falling to decay, stands in Franklin county, about two miles from Lane post-office.

feet deep. In the eastern half of the State, it is a black, sandy loam, intermixed with vegetable mold, and the soil of the entire State has in its composition what is lacking in many prairie soils, an abundant supply of mineral constituents. It is for this reason that many practical men who are familiar with the entire west believe that Kansas soil will prove to be permanently rich, when other soils now very productive will be exhausted.

Lime is everywhere abundant in this soil, and gypsum or land plaster is found over a very large extent in the central and western portion of the State, intermingled largely with the soil, as well as existing in ledges, ready to be used as a fertilizer at a trifling cost.

Under date of March 31, 1871, Professor Wm. H. Saunders, M. D. of the State University, furnishes me with the following analysis of average prairie soil, the specimen being taken at the depth of seven inches below the surface:

Organic matter	11.05
Silica	69.83
Alumina	8.66
Sesqui oxide of iron	2.05
Potassa	1.05
Soda	a trace
Lime	3.28
Magnesia	2.00
Chlorine	0.00
Sulphuric acid	a trace
Phosphoric acid	2.08
	100.00

The Professor says:

"From the above it will be seen that we have a a soil rich in all the chemical elements necessary for the vigorous growth of vegetation, and thorough, intelligent cultivation will certainly bring the most gratifying reward."

There are to be found, occasionally, small isolated tracts, where a stiff sub-soil comes near the surface, and which at first only produces light crops, but greatly improves by cultivation. The common grass of the prairies is of tender, rapid growing varieties, covering the earth like a mat, but the grass growing on these "patches" is short, wiry and scattering. It is called "buffalo grass," but is distinct and totally different from the nutritious grass with its long curled leaf, which covers the western half of Kansas, and upon which vast buffalo herds feed and fatten.

Not one acre in a thousand in Kansas is of the objectionable "buffalo land" character described above, and even this land with deep plowing (it is very heavy plowing the first time), or by the application of a little manure to give it "life"—eight or ten loads per acre—produces excellent crops of all kinds. Lime is also beneficial to such soils. It is confessedly capital wheat land. There is rarely more than one to ten acres of it in a body, and sometimes a few square feet only. It is not found on one farm in ten in the State, but settlers who, in the early history of the State, happened to cultivate a patch of it, at once jumped to the conclusion that Kansas was a barren region. This land is sometimes improperly called "alkali land." The unerring certainty with which it is detected by the grass, and the insignificant amount of it in the country, almost makes it inexcusable to devote so much space to the subject; but I desire to state the facts about Kansas, whether favorable or unfavorable, so that strangers need not be deceived when purchasing land.

After the above went to press, I learned that Prof. W. H. Saunders had made an analysis of this soil, and upon application for his opinion of its qualities

I received the following letter, under date of April 6th, 1871:

"I have the following reply to make in answer to your letter of inquiry respecting the nature of 'alkali spots' on 'buffalo wallows.' Any one can easily detect them in cultivated ground by the color, which is much lighter than the surrounding soil, especially after a spell of dry weather, when a white, efflorescent powder forms on the surface of these spots.

"The composition of the soil, which is an exceedingly tough and compact clay, is chiefly silicate of alumina, containing a little organic matter, a little sesquioxide of iron, and occasionally a little lime. This soil has become strongly impregnated with sulphate of magnesia, (epsom-salt,) which is the white powder seen on the surface. This salt in small quantity, is valuable as a fertilizer, but when in excess is very destructive to vegetation, hence the barren nature of these spots.

"Of more practical interest, however, is the question: what can be done to render these spots fertile? This, fortunately, admits of easy solution. After the soil is well loosend, a top-dressing of quick-lime, applied just before a rain, will decompose the sulphate of magnesia, and form sulphate of lime, (gypsum,) a valuable fertilizer, while the magnesia will soon absorb carbonic acid and be converted into carbonate of magnesia, which being insoluble in water, will be much less injurious to vegetation. Lime should not be thus applied when a crop is on the ground, for the caustic action of the lime and magnesia would destroy it. This method is liable to the objection that it simply converts the noxious agent into a less injurious form, but does not assist in removing it from the soil.

"A much more effectual and better way is simply to thoroughly pulverize the soil as deeply as possible at least once a year. The magnesian salt, being very soluble in water, will be leached out by the rains, and the soil thus permanently freed from its presence; fertilizers then applied will render the soil productive. The experience of those who have tried this method confirms me in the belief that it is the best way to treat this soil. The popular notion, that these spots contain an alkali and that the soil has been rendered hard by the wallowing of the buffalo, is erroneous. The soil contains no alkali, and its hardness is owing to its chemical composition, but the buffalo have discovered the salt taste of the soil impregnated with the sulphate of magnesia, and, by long repeated licking and tramping, have worn considerable depressions in places, which during the wet season are filled with water."

Occasionally sandstone soil is found in tracts of a few square miles. This is confessedly the best fruit land in the State, and is highly regarded by many persons for purposes of cultivation, owing to the fact that it is ready for spring work sooner than limestone soil, and can be more readily cultivated during a wet time. Many of the limestone ledges lie higher than the sandstone formation, and it is probably from this cause that there is a good deal of lime to be found even in sand stone soils, but if this is lacking it may be cheaply supplied, because lime is everywhere present, either in the form of limestone (lime and carbonic acid), or gypsum (lime and sulphuric acid).

There is less waste land in Kansas than in almost any other State in the Union. In fact there is really no waste land at all, because there are neither swamps nor sloughs, and the entire State can be cultivated, excepting those portions covered with timber or where rock prevails.

The latter feature is fully described elsewhere, and it will be seen that the rock of Kansas is of immense value to the State. It is only necessary to say here that there is probably not one acre in five hundred in the State where rock is so exposed as to make cultivation impossible, and even this is not waste land, for it affords excellent pasturage with a plenty of springs and running water.

Bayard Taylor says: "I consider the country within one hundred and fifty miles of the Missouri River in Kansas, to be the finest unbroken tract of farming land in the world."

HUMBOLDT BRIDGE.

The above is a King's Wrought Iron Bridge of 1[illegible]0 span. It cost about $13,000.

The soil of the western half of Kansas is very different in appearance from that of the eastern half of the State. While the latter is black, the former is usually light colored, or reddish toward the southwestern part of the State, excepting upon the larger river bottoms, but the soil of western Kansas is the deepest, running from two to ten feet. Perhaps upon no point is there a greater lack of knowledge concerning Kansas, even by some citizens of the State, than in relation to this western Kansas soil. This soil has mingled with it very little vegetable mold or humus—that deposit of decayed vegetable matter which gives to the soil of eastern Kansas its dark color.

The attentive observer will notice a perceptible difference in this respect however, even at the extreme western State line, between the surface and the soil two feet below. In some localities, especially on bottom lands, the surface is quite dark, and gradually grows lighter as you penetrate the earth.

This is called by geologists, "The Bluff Formation," so named by Professor Swallow, because it forms a large proportion of the bluffs which are so conspicuous and unique in the scenery about Council Bluffs, Iowa, and in general all along the Missouri River bluffs above the mouth of the Kansas River. This formation occupies the surface of a considerable portion of western Iowa, extending east in the north part of the State a distance of forty or fifty miles. Its eastern limit seems to run in a southwesterly direction, and it forms the surface of nearly all the State of Nebraska, and of the western half of Kansas. It also *underlies* a good portion of eastern Kansas, but is here largely affected by the character of the subjacent rocks. This accounts for the fact, which has often been remarked with wonder, that the sub-soil in many places upon being thrown to the surface, and exposed to the action of the air and frost, produces as good crops as the surface soil.

Its analysis by the Missouri State Survey, gives, when dried at 212° Fahr., 77 per cent impalpable sand; 11 per cent alumina (clay); 3¼ per cent, lime; 5½ per cent pottassa, magnesia and carbonic acid, and about 3¼ per cent of water and loss. This analysis proves its agricultural value; but that point is sufficiently demonstrated by long experience.

The best of crops grow upon this soil in Iowa and Nebraska, as I can personally testify. Its sand is so fine that no grit is perceptible to the touch, and those who cultivate it in Iowa, call it a fine light clay, but it has none of the physical characteristics of a stiff clay soil. It never bakes, is ready for cultivation in a few hours after a rain, and with *deep plowing* will keep crops in a thriving condition with very little rain.

As the reader well knows, it is not essential that a soil be black in order that it be productive. With the single exception of corn, as good crops are raised upon much of the red land of Virginia and Tennessee as is ever grown upon the blackest soils of Illinois or Kansas, and deep plowing is all that this red land needs for Indian corn.

Having seen the luxuriant crops that are grown in northwestern Iowa about Sioux City, upon the light colored soil which we have described, as well as the heavy crops upon newly cleared red lands of Virginia and Tennessee, I have learned not to condemn land until it is tried, whether its color be black, white or red.

In Kansas this soil has not been largely cultivated, (although it is held in high esteem by those western settlers who have tilled it,) because there are at least twenty million acres of rich black soil unoccupied in the State. But no man appreciates Kansas as he ought, until he realizes that it not only ranks pre-eminent as a grain producing and blue grass State, but that within its limits and within one or two days drive of its rich farms, are to be found the finest of pasture fields now open and easily accessible to the public. Here is free grazing upon the buffalo grass and winter grasses which grow on the rich soil we have just described. Not only this but with *deep plowing*, and *deep and early drilling of the seed*, this is to be the great winter wheat *storehouse of the nation.* It is not too far north or south; its altitude gives it a superb harvesting season, while there is rain enough for growing the crop during the cool season, The admixture of lime and gypsum, with all this soil, is a matter of the utmost moment. That gypsum is almost universal, admits of little doubt, for it is seen in ledges in many places, and it is found crystalized in the form of thin semi-transparent sheets, wherever geologists have explored western Kansas. The blue-stem, a tall variety of prairie grass, chiefly used for hay in eastern Kansas, and which only grows on rich corn land, is rapidly extending westward upon this soil, and taking the place of buffalo grass.

Finally, the bottom lands of the Kansas and Arkansas Rivers, are largely made up of the wash of these western regions, and there is no better soil in the world than these valleys afford.

CLIMATE.

Many flowing sentences and well rounded periods have been framed in the endeavor to describe the climate of Kansas. It has been called "Arcadia," but more frequently travelers who have been around the globe, and enraptured citizens who write to their friends in the East, call it an "Italian clime." In truth, it is neither Arcadia nor Italy—at least it is *not* one unbroken round of golden days and halcyon nights, but it is quite certain that there is no region in the United States, east of the Rocky Mountains, where there is more bright, sunshiny days than we have in Kansas. The winters are more mild than in the same latitude east of us, and the thermometer rarely sinks below zero. During midsummer the heat at noonday sometimes ranges for several days from 80 to 100 degrees, but the air is so dry and pure that one scarcely realizes the range of the mercury, while the nights are invariably cool and refreshing. Men work on buildings and in other exposed situations, with safety, at a temperature which would be fatal in the eastern States.

The soil is so fruitful that farmers never feel obliged to expose themselves to severe weather, summer or winter. Especially is our climate held in high esteem by those who escape to it from the extremes of northern frigidity, or from the torrid heats of southern latitudes.

It must not be forgotten that Kansas is a State of great extent and of various climate. Sometimes there are two or three inches of snow in the north-eastern part of the State, which lays on the ground three or four days, and at the same time there will be no snow at all on the southern border of the State; at other times a light fall of snow may cover the State for a week, but there is no preparation made for sleighing, because there is rarely more than one such snow during a winter. Ice usually forms in December or January from four to eight inches in thickness, but rarely thicker than six inches, and two or three winters have occurred when no ice formed thick enough to store in ice houses. Farmers can plow during ten months of nearly every year in this State, and some years every month. I have seen masons laying stone and mortar during every month of the year, although not in every month in any one year, perhaps, because after building has generally ceased, and the hands are discharged and tools scattered, it is not customary to commence again until spring opens, which here occurs in February.

Still there are cold days here and people ought to come prepared for them; but there are also bitter cold days in Tennessee or Texas, and taking our average climate, it is mild and agreeable. Whenever, as during the past winter, it is very cold here, the telegraph always announces that it is colder in the same latitude east, and much colder north of us. During the past winter, 1870–71, we had three considerable snow storms; the first six inches deep, of light snow, and each of the others about three inches deep. This was accompanied by almost continuous cold weather, sufficiently so to keep the ground covered with snow for four or five weeks. It has been, by far, the severest winter I ever experienced in the State, and it is the universal testimony of the "reliable old settlers" that the snow never before laid on the ground so long.

The extraordinary clearness of the atmosphere strikes all strangers as worthy of mention. Non-residents can form no conception of this peculiarity of our climate, but one may here distinguish objects at a long distance, which could hardly be seen at all, if the same distance away in the east. The vision is thereby strengthened, and man's natural powers increased, giving greater zest to the pleasure with which one rides across our prairie swells.

The most disagreeable feature of our climate is the wind, but none complain of the cool breezes which healthfully agitate the atmosphere during the summer months. Besides, all prairie regions are subject to more winds than timbered countries. The winds are no more severe here than in other prairie States, and the groves and hedges, which may be speedily grown, will abate their force and break up their currents.

One of the greatest blessings of our Kansas climate, is the cool nights which invariably follow even the hottest days. These nights are so well described by the Lawrence Daily *Journal*, that I quote as follows:

"The cool nights of Kansas refresh and invigorate everything. No sooner does old Sol conclude to bathe his burning forehead in the sea of night, than the whole atmosphere changes and everything is lovely.

"We recall with a twinge of agony, terrific summer nights spent in the northeastern States, when the thermometer indicated the same degree of heat at twelve midnight as at twelve noon, but nothing could be more agreeable than our Kansas climate in this respect. However hot the day, the night is

ADAMS HOUSE, MANHATTAN.

cool and bracing. A day in which a man is reminded of Sydney Smith's desire to 'get out of his flesh and sit down in his bones,' is followed by a night in which long before daybreak a fellow finds himself feeling sleepily around the foot of his bed for his blanket. After such a night one arises refreshed for the labors, and fortified against the heat of another day."

As the records of scientific observations are the true criterion by which to judge of any climate, I solicited from Prof. F. H. Snow, the following tables, for which I am under special obligations to him, as well as for other records which are presented elsewhere:

TABLES

Compiled by Prof. Frank H. Snow, of Kansas State University at Lawrence.

TABLE of Mean Temperature of twenty States for five years, from January 1st, 1865, to January 1st, 1870, compiled from Reports of the Department of Agriculture:

STATES.	SPRING.	SUMMER	AUTUMN.	WINTER.	YEAR.
Kansas	52.2	75.5	54.3	29.1	52.8
Maine	40.7	66.4	46.6	19.8	43.4
New Hampshire	41.7	66.7	46.6	20.4	43.8
Vermont	40.4	66.1	45.6	18.4	42.7
Massachusetts	45.0	68.6	49.7	25.5	47.2
Connecticut	45.0	69.1	50.4	25.8	47.6
New York	43.9	69.7	50.0	24.9	47.1
New Jersey	49.8	72.3	54.3	30.3	51.7
Pennsylvania	47.3	71.7	52.0	28.1	49.7
Maryland	51.7	74.2	55.6	32.4	53.5
Kentucky	54.4	74.5	55.7	35.2	54.9
Ohio	49.4	72.6	52.7	29.1	50.9
Michigan	42.4	67.8	49.1	24.2	45.9
Indiana	50.4	74.2	53.2	29.7	51.9
Illinois	47.6	72.9	52.0	25.8	49.6
Wisconsin	41.8	68.6	47.8	20.5	44.7
Minnesota	39.4	67.8	45.3	14.0	41.6
Iowa	44.5	71.2	48.9	20.3	46.2
Missouri	52.5	75.5	55.0	30.7	53.4
Nebraska	45.9	73.4	51.0	22.9	48.4
Mean for 20 States	46.3	70.9	50.8	25.4	48.3

Meteorological Summary for 1870 *by Prof. Snow.*

The following table gives the mean temperature, the extremes of temperature, and the rainfall for each month of the year 1870:

MONTHS.	MEAN.	MAXIMUM.	MINIMUM.	RAINFALL.
January	29.43	56.5	—1.0	0.67
February	35 42	69.0	—4.0	0.03
March	37.69	71.0	1 0	1.86
April	56 84	91.0	19.0	1.08
May	68.00	90.0	44.0	2.46
June	73.71	102.0	44.0	1.83
July	80.27	99.0	55.0	5.58
August	73.54	98.0	53.0	6 69
September	67.88	88.5	53.0	2.82
October	56.50	79.0	29.0	6.96
November	44.92	72.0	17.0	0.57
December	28.70	64.0	—10.0	0.72
Year 1870	54.50	102.0	—10 0	31.32
Year 1869	50.36	96.0	—5.0	38.51
Year 1868	53.36	101 0	—16.5	37.48

Face of the Sky.

"Mean cloudiness of the year, 47.94 per cent. of the sky. Mean at 7 A. M., 50.67 per cent.; at 2 P. M., 52.94 per cent.; at 9 p. m., 40.21 per cent. In the morning and at midday the sky was less cloudy than in 1869, but cloudier at night."

"The number of clear days was 152, counting as clear those days on which less than one-third of the sky was covered with clouds; half-clear days 93, including under this designation those days on which between one-third and two-thirds of the sky was covered; cloudy days, 120, when two-thirds or more was covered. The clearest month was July, mean cloudiness 30.64 per cent.; the cloudiest month was September, mean cloudiness, 68.66 per cent."

Barometer.

Mean hight of barometer, 29.097 inches, being 0.006 less than in 1869. The mean hight for the two years, 1869 and 1870, was 29.100. Upon this basis, the hight of the instrument above the level of the sea is 884 feet.

Mean hight at 7 A. M., 29.121 inches; at 2 P. M., 29.074 inches; at 9 P. M., 29.096 inches. Maximum hight, 29.764 inches, at 7 A. M., January 8; minimum, 28.191 inches, at 12:45 P. M., January 16, giving a range of 1.573 inches for the year. The highest monthly mean was in December, 29.192 inches; the lowest in May, 29.005 inches. All the barometer observations were reduced to the freezing point.

Relative Humidity.

Mean for the year, 68.4. Mean at 7 A. M., 80.4.; at 2 P. M., 49.9; at 9 P. M., 74.8. Air saturated with moisture, 48 times; number of fogs, 13. The driest month was April, relative humidity 54.7; the dampest month was September, relative humidity 82.8. The air was driest at 2 P. M., February 18th, when the relative humidity was only 2, this remarkable condition of the atmosphere being followed by a sudden change of temperature within twenty four hours."

Force of Vapor.

Mean for the year, 0.344 inches; mean at 7 A. M., 0.337; at 2 P. M., 0.342; at 9 P. M., 0.352; greatest, 0.863, at 2. P. M., July 10; least, 0.008, at 2 P. M., February 18.

Frosts.

"An important fact in regard to the long period of *entire* absence of frost, ought, perhaps, to be mentioned. There was no frost in 1868, from April 10 to September 17—one hundred and sixty days; in 1869, from April 13 to September 26—one hundred and sixty-six days; in 1870, from April 18 to October 12—one hundred and seventy-seven days. The interval between the latest and earliest *severe* frosts would be considerably longer—one hundred and ninety-seven days in 1870."

RAINFALL AND CHANGE OF CLIMATE.

One of the most interesting facts in relation to the settlement of this country, and yet one of the most difficult to illustrate and explain, is the change of seasons which is here taking place. I do not allude especially to the increased rainfall which is evident in all the region west of the Missouri, wherever there are settlements and railroads, because the meteorogical records show that the mean annual precipitation of moisture in Eastern Kansas, has always been sufficient for agricultural purposes, if we except the single year of 1860. Being desirous of knowing whether such a drouth might be expected to occur again, I took occasion, when visiting Washington on the succeeding winter, to examine the records at the Smithsonian Institute, having the aid of one of the assistant officers of the Institution, and found that the rainfall was as great during the seventeen years preceding 1860, at Fort Leavenworth and Fort Scott, Kansas, as in Illinois or Missouri.

From the many tables which have been since published, and from those elsewhere given in this book, it is evident that the *mean annual* rainfall of Kansas has always been quite sufficient. But it is a fact patent to all "old settlers" that we have more showers than formerly, more rainy, drizzly days, more occasions when one can carry an umbrella in a rainstorm. The word "storm," which is almost

TOPEKA BRIDGE.

invariably applied to a rain in this country, shows the character of those events. Ten or fifteen years ago few people kept umbrellas in Kansas, because "when it rained it poured," and the wind blew with such force that an umbrella could hardly be carried. The rains were indeed storms, severe but short, a heavy fall of rain occuring in a few hours. It is not only my experience, but the universal testimony of all who have been here ten or more years, that the rain storms are less severe, and the rainy days more frequent, than of old. I have endeavored to collect statistics upon this point; but not many observations are recorded as to the number of rainy days.

Prof. F. H. Snow writes me under date of January 16, 1871:

"My records at this place cover only three years. From these it appears that rain fell in 1868, on 64 days; in 1869, on 92 days; in 1870, on 97 days. In the absence of positive proof from records, it certainly would be legitimate to cite the testimony of many of our "old settlers" to the fact that the rain fall is more evenly distributed now than ten years ago, coming at shorter intervals and more gently, and that single storms, or showers, extend over more hours than formerly. This belief I have often heard expressed by our most intelligent citizens."

It is not a new or startling theory to claim that a change of seasons is taking place in Kansas. California is a marked illustration of the changes in climate, which succeed settlement. Especially is this shown also in the vicinity of Salt Lake, Utah.

Here is a region once comparatively destitute of rain, but where now almost enough falls to supply the growing crops. Great Salt Lake, which is more than one hundred miles long and forty or fifty miles wide, is said to have risen twelve feet since the Mormons commenced the settlements, and the water has a smaller proportion of salt.

Illustrations of the ill effects to climate, resulting from clearing away the forests of timbered regions, are too well known to call for recital. But without taking the reader to Europe and Asia, where the most disastrous consequences have occurred, these effects may be traced in all the older northern States. During the year 1870 a drouth of alarming severity occurred in New England, which is ascribed, as have been many lesser drouths of the last quarter of a century, to clearing off nearly all the timbered land.

The effect of railroads and telegraphs, is undoubtedly to cause more frequent showers, perhaps by promoting a more even distribution of the magnetic forces. From some cause it is certain that thunder storms are less severe than formerly, in Kansas.

A. D. Richardson, after returning from his last trip across the continent, informed me he was convinced that railroads and telegraphs do have an effect upon the climate and cause an increased and more frequent rainfall. It is quite well understood also that trees and hedges, in various ways tend to increase the fall of rain, and the planting of these objects is the cause usually indicated for our change of seasons.

But I think the main cause remains to be stated. When rain strikes upon the compact surface of our rolling prairies, it almost immediately runs off, very little settling into the ground. Having no ponds or swamps in the State, and our streams all being rapid, the rain soon runs away. But with the settlement of the country, every piece of cultivated land becomes a reservoir, or cistern, wherein is collected and retained for a considerable time, most of the water which falls upon its surface and sinks into the mellow soil. A portion of this rainfall gradually finds its way to the surface in lower places, causing living springs to appear where before there was no sign of water, while another portion of the rainfall caught in the plowed land evaporates from the field. Thus the atmosphere is charged, to a degree, with moisture, and a very little addition in this respect is often sufficient to produce rain. Sometimes we say "it almost rains," yet there is lacking in the atmosphere a very few degrees of humidity, and in consequence of this lack no rain falls. It is plain that at such times, the slight change in the atmospheric conditions caused by the evaporation of water retained upon tilled land would cause rain. In this State the entire process of subjugating the country is precisely opposite to that which takes place in a timbered country. In the latter case the trees which, with their foliage, protected the ground from the direct rays of the sun, are cut down. The logs and sticks and withered leaves are removed, which caught the rain and retained it in little pools or bogs. Fallen trees are cleared out of the streams, and in every way the water is given free course and more rapidly finds its way to the sea. On the other hand, in settling a prairie country more water is retained, as already explained, and the ground is shaded during summer months by growing crops, while newly planted trees and hedges add their influence to the causes which produce a climate continually growing more humid. Upon the contrary the climate of a timbered country continually grows less humid as the country is cleared of timber, and the springs and streams dry up.

There are in Kansas to-day thousands of springs where there were no springs a few years ago, and other thousands of springs which formerly were dry in the summer, now flow continually. It is for this reason, in part, that there is now so much greater value attached to the water power of the State than there was a dozen years ago, as the streams are continually increasing in power and regularity. This process will go on, and all one has to do to induce springs upon his land is to break up and cultivate his soil.

In the western portion of the State especially, and generally in all the country called "The Plains," the ascent towards the Rocky Mountains is very rapid, and the falling rain runs off almost immediately. The rise in the western half of the State and in Colorado is ten to fifteen feet per mile. Consider that the fall of the Missouri river, one of the most rapid of large rivers, is less than one foot per mile, and it will be seen that the streams upon the plains must be very rapid, while the entire face of the country is also considerably undulating, carrying off the rain from the compact surface with extraordinary rapidity. Add to this influence the increased rapidity of evaporation arising from the increased altitude, and we discern at once one of the causes why "The Plains" are not covered with a deep layer of vegetable mold like Eastern Kansas.

TABLE showing the average rainfall of Kansas, in comparison with that of other States, for the five years from January 1, 1865, to January 1, 1870. By Prof. F. H. Snow:

STATES.	SPRING.	SUMMER.	AUTUMN.	WINTER.	MARCH 1, TO OCTOBER 1.	YEAR.
Kansas	10.82	18.06	9.79	5.42	34.15	44.09
Maine	13.74	10.55	13.33	9.99	28.23	47.61
New Hampshire	10.40	10.49	12 66	7.85	25.40	41.40
Vermont	10.31	10.44	11.82	7.32	25 01	39.89
Massachusetts	13.46	11.17	11.72	10.20	28.71	46.55
Connecticut	13.01	13.34	13.11	10 54	30.88	50.00
New York	11.16	11.19	12.41	9.92	26.85	44.68
New Jersey	13.18	13.88	12 53	11.39	31.81	50.98
Pennsylvania	12.04	12.46	11.17	10.01	29.05	45.68
Maryland	13.67	13.95	12.39	11.22	32.05	51.23
Kentucky	15.18	13 77	9.88	12.50	33.92	51.33
Ohio	12.34	11.73	9.80	8.09	29.24	41.96
Michigan	8.32	9.90	11.00	6.47	23.19	35.69
Indiana	14.35	12 84	10.32	9.27	32.94	46.78
Illinois	11.53	12.07	8.14	6.02	27 92	37.76
Wisconsin	8.92	13.23	8.16	5.87	25.53	36.18
Minnesota	6.09	13.39	8.42	3.78	24.43	31.68
Iowa	10.57	16.72	8.86	6.38	32.14	42.53
Missouri	12.67	13.34	9.29	6.42	30 74	41.72
Nebraska	8.76	12.56	6.25	5.09	24.93	32.62
Average rainfall in 20 States for 5 years.	11.52	12.75	10.55	8.19	28 86	43.01

FROM A CHARCOAL SKETCH BY PROF. WORRALL, TOPEKA, PHOTOGRAPHED BY J. LEE KNIGHT.

2*

Concerning this table, Professor Snow writes as follows:

"Twenty States were included in the comparison, those States engaged in the rebellion being omitted because the returns from them during the years 1865, '66, '67, were too meager to afford trustworthy results. From the comparison it appears that the total annual rainfall for Kansas, during the five years, was greater than that of the following States; New Hampshire, Vermont, Ohio, Michigan, Illinois, Wisconsin, Minnesota, Iowa, Missouri and Nebraska. (10 States out of the 19). I have also calculated the amount of rain in each of the twenty States for each of the four seasons. The result shows that while Kansas has less rain in the winter months than any other State on the list, except Nebraska, she has more rain in the remaining nine months than any of the other States, except Connecticut, Maryland, New Jersey and Kentucky. *It also appears that for the seven months from the first of March to the first of October, when rain is needed for the germination and growth of crops, Kansas stands at the head of the list, having more rain than any of the nineteen States with which the comparison is made.*"

Mr. Watts Beckwith, of Olathe, Kansas, who reports meteorological observations for publication by the Agricultural Department at Washington, has kindly furnished me with the following table, which also illustrates the last statement of Professor Snow, given above, and shows the heavy rainfall that takes place in Kansas during the growing months of the year:

TABLE showing the rainfall in Kansas during each month for six years, from 1865 to 1870 inclusive, from recorded observations by Mr. Watts Beckwith:

MONTHS.	1865	1866	1867	1868	1869	1870
January	2.5	2.6	0	6	3.9	3
February	4.9	6	3.4	1		0
March	3.6	2.0	2.9	7.7	1.9	2.
April	6 6	3.0	4.1	4.9	5	6
May	7.9	4.3	8.4	4.9	5.6	7.1
June	15.8	10.6	3.	5.8	11.7	2.7
July	13.7	9.8	5.7	6.7	17.7	6.5
August	13.1	1.4	2.2	16.2	4.9	7.0
September	8.1	16.6	2.	5	5.3	2.2
October	2.9	5.6	2.	2	2.3	6.1
November	0	3.8	1.5		1.7	5
December	1.8	3.4	1.3	3.5	9	5

Mr. Beckwith also says:

"I think of late years we also have less thunder and lightning, but this I have not recorded as carefully as the amount of rainfall."

It should be noted that all the records from which the foregoing figures of rainfall in Kansas, have been collated, were made in the eastern half of Kansas. Unquestionably less rain falls in Western Kansas, than the tables indicate, but the increase in that portion of the State is very noticeable.

HEALTH.

To write upon this subject so as to be understood, we must compare this with other States. Although the climate of Eastern Kansas is somewhat less bracing and vigorous than that of States farther north, it is much more so than the same latitude anywhere east of us and west of the Alleghanies, and it is conceded that Kansas will eventually be reckoned as the most healthful of all western States.

In northern latitudes it is to be observed that people usually build close houses, so constructed that no fresh air can enter. Shutting themselves up in small rooms, heated by that modern barbarism, an iron stove, or hot air furnace, they hibernate during the long winter months. This seems to be a necessity of all that damp, inhospitable winter climate, which is found north of our latitude and east of the Mississippi River, but the hydra-headed diseases which seize so many victims in those regions are largely induced by this housing process. In Kansas people live more out of doors. Dwellings may safely be constructed with less care to keep out fresh air, and during many winter days, doors and windows are left wide open. There is no place in the world which is best adapted to all persons, but regions like Kansas, which occupy an admirable mean between the extremes of latitude, are best suited to the constitution of a majority of mankind.

It is not true, as many suppose, that Kansas climate is uniform in temperature. This cannot be truthfully asserted of any portion of the United States east of the Rocky Mountains, but the remarkable *dryness of our climate* so mollifies the influence of the sudden changes to which, in common with other States, we are subject, that their effect is much less injurious here than elsewhere. The rains of Kansas chiefly fall during the summer months, causing the fertile soil to yield a vegetation almost tropical in its luxuriance, but during the cooler seasons we have little rain, and the air is dry and bracing. Damp air causes damp clothing, and moisture is a good conductor of heat. In the humid atmosphere of more eastern States, clothing is at times ineffectual towards keeping the body warm, and at these times sudden changes are fatal to many, and dangerous to all. But in the dry, elastic Kansas atmosphere, woolen clothing completely protects the person, and thus protected, sudden changes are sustained with little danger to health. An atmosphere so pure and dry that it will preserve fresh meats in hot weather, without salting, must be a healthy and invigorating atmosphere. This is the case in the extreme western portion of the State. "Jerked meat"—layers of lean meat, jerked off by tearing the fibres, and then cured in the sun—keeps through the season, and after August, quarters of beef, buffalo, venison, etc., suspended a few feet above the ground, keep perfectly sweet. In this atmosphere, Kansas offers great advantages to all consumptives, or persons with asthmatic or bronchial difficulties. In this, too, there is great room for choice in location.

In the three degrees of latitude which Kansas occupies, we will find a very considerable difference in temperature between the northern and southern extremes of the State, but to a greater extent will the careful observer note a difference between the eastern and western limits of Kansas. This difference arises from two causes. It is a well known fact that the Rocky Mountain range induces a heavy precipitation of moisture upon their western slopes, leaving their eastern slopes, and a belt of considerable width stretching eastward therefrom, and known as "the plains," that has but little rain. The western limits of Kansas trench upon this region, and the dry air which passes over these plains is vastly beneficial to invalids, whether suffering from pulmonary complaints, or from general debility, indigestion or nervous exhaustion. The second cause to which I refer is the altitude to which one may attain in Kansas. As already shown the State rises gradually from its eastern to its western boundary, attaining an altitude of 3500 feet above the level of the sea. The height of the Cumberland Mountain plateau, in Tennessee, is only 1000 feet above the miasmatic bottoms of the Tennessee River, which flows at its base, and its average altitude above the ocean about 1800 feet, which is less than the average altitude of Western Kansas above the same level. The former is famous as a resort for invalids—the latter will be more famous whenever its advantages are fully known. The entire State is so favorably situated in these regards that little attention has been paid to the relative claims for healthfulness of its various portions. "Burleigh," the well known correspondent of the Boston *Journal*, (Matthew Hale Smith), write thus under date of November, 1870:

"Before I speak of Topeka, the Capital of Kansas, I will mention a few peculiarities of the State. The name given to the atmosphere is that of 'champagne,' from its exhilarating properties. It is very elastic and invigorating. Its effect on diseased, debilitated and worn out systems, is very remarkable."

It may be mentioned as illustrative of the peculiar properties of the atmosphere of Kansas, that horses are never known to contract the "heaves" in this State, that disease which is so common and fatal to horses in States east of us.

Kansas also occupies a favorable mean in relation to two distinct types of diseases which are found—the one in very low miasmatic regions and the other in elevated and mountainous localities. Concerning the former complaints, they have not extensively prevailed in Kansas, excepting in unfavorable situations during the early settlement of the country, and it is confidently asserted that in no country east of us did the early settlers experience less sickness. It is a fact also worthy of mention that all localities most subject to fever and ague have been settled for some years, and this disease is consequently disappearing with the improvement of the country, while the newer and more elevated portions of the State are not subject to its attacks.

Concerning the class of rheumatic and acute febrile diseases which prevail in all mountainous regions, Kansas is almost entirely exempt from them; Vendors of "liniments and "Poor Man's Plasters,' are not advised to come to Kansas.

WATER.

The water of springs and wells in this State is pure and good. There are small isolated tracts, embracing two or three farms each, where good, clear water is not easily obtained by digging; but the

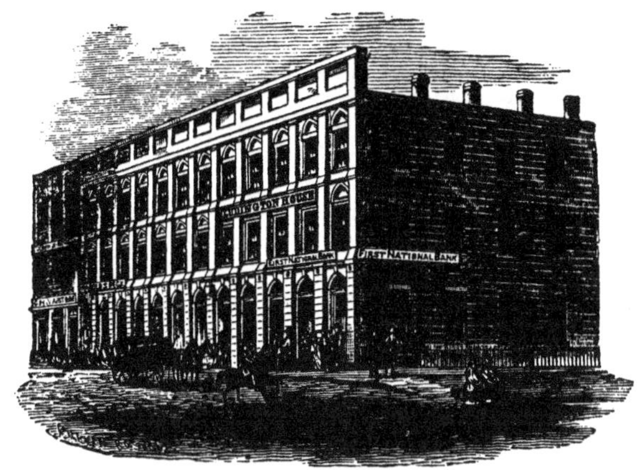

LUDINGTON HOUSE, OTTAWA.

settlers here, like the settlers upon large tracts of country in Missouri, Iowa and Illinois, where the well water is uniformly turbid and unpalatable to the taste, must drink rain water caught in cisterns. This is healthful, and by use becomes agreeable. It is probable that on some of the high divides between streams in the western portion of the State, it may not be easy to find water by digging. In fact, the Kansas Pacific Railroad failed to obtain water by digging at two or three of their stations near the western State line; but of the many emigrants, buffalo hunters and others who have traversed all the western portion of the State, none say that they have much difficulty in finding water, either flowing from springs or by digging a few feet in favorable localities. It is a peculiarity of some streams in the extreme western portion of the State, that they suddenly sink into quick sands, and appear again a few miles below.

One of the first things for a settler to do here, as in any country, is to provide good pure water. *Dig a well at once*, unless you are near a spring, and *do not* drink surface or creek water. This custom of western settlers, I believe to be the cause of more sickness than any other, or prehaps all other bad habits or unnecessary exposures of western life. Of all the eastern half of the State, a tract of country two hundred miles square, and—if we except the inhabitable portions of Maine—as large as all New England, it can be truthfully stated that it is abundantly watered with springs and streams for stock purposes, and that clear, healthful drinking water is universally obtained from springs, or by digging from twenty to sixty feet. It is a peculiarity of the country, that water is often found upon the high prairies at a less depth than on the low lands. The water here is not, as in other western States, uniformly hard. Settlers can locate where they may have soft or freestone water if they prefer, as in a small portion of the State the sandstone formation predominates, which furnishes soft water.

All the streams in the settled portion of the State are larger than when the country was new, and many brooks and creeks flow continuously, which were formerly dry several months in each year. Not only is this well known to all early settlers, but there are thousands of springs on the prairies where there was formerly no indication of one. This phenomenon is owing to causes to which we have more fully alluded under the head of Climatic Changes.

The editor of the *Chicago Railway Review*, spent several weeks of 1870, in a thorough examination of Kansas, as he had previously examined the other Western States. In his paper of October 27, 1870, he says:

"The readers of our previous articles must be convinced that eastern Kansas is anything but a region destitute of streams. *No country in the world is better watered.*"

In the early settlement of the country all the principal roads were laid out on the divides, winding about between the sources of the streams, because bridges could not at once be erected, and roads cut through the timber growing on their banks. From this fact many early travelers in Kansas, following the principal roads, concluded that there were few streams in the country. The railroads, however, take a direct course across the country, and bridging is an expensive part of the work. A report of the bridge contractors of the Leavenworth, Lawrence & Galveston Railroad, was published in the *Ottawa Journal* of December 16, 1870, and this report shows that in a distance of one hundred eight and one-half miles south from Lawrence to Thayer, there were constructed sixty-seven bridges and trestles, (besides culverts,)—being nearly one to every mile and a half of the road. More than three million feet of timber was used in the construction of these bridges and trestles. A glance at the map will show that this railroad does not follow the windings of one or two streams. The line is directly across the country over divides from the Kansas River to the Marais des Cygnes, thence to the Pottawatomie and thence to the Neosho. A few trestles are reported as over unimportant ravines, in which probably there is not a constant stream of water flowing, but the general evidence of this report is, that Kansas railroads are pretty well bridged for a country "destitute of stock water," as she has been reported to be.

TIMBER.

In the eastern half of Kansas there is a sufficiency of timber for practical purposes. It is found along the streams and in adjacent ravines, sheltered from the ravages of prairie fires by high rock-capped bluffs. The following is a list of the trees and shrubs of this State, prepared by Dr. C. A. Logan for a State document on the sanitary relations of Kansas:

White Oak, Red Oak, Burr Oak, Black Oak, Black Jack Oak, Water Oak, White or American Elm, Red or Slippery Elm, Black Walnut, White Walnut or Butternut, Cottonwood, Box Elder, Hackberry, Honey Locust, Willow, Shell Bark Hickory, Pig Nut Hickory, Pecan Nut Hickory, Sycamore, White Ash, Sugar Maple, Red Mulberry, Linden or Basswood, Crab Apple, Wild Cherry, Coffee Tree.

Of shrubs and vines he gives Elder, Sumac, Green Brier, Gooseberry, Hazel, Pawpaw, Prickly Ash, Raspberry, Blackberry, Prairie Rose, and Grapes of several varieties.

The streams, with their attendant timber belts, varying in width from two or three rods to as many miles, so cut the prairies in every direction that few farms of Eastern Kansas are more than one or two miles from timber, and cordwood sells from four to six dollars per cord in our towns. This wonderful advantage over most prairie States is appreciated by the writer at least, for my first experience in western farming was in Illinois, forty miles from Chicago, when every rail and fence post and stick of firewood, or whip stock even, was hauled ten miles. Many splendid farms have been opened in that State, by hauling timber twenty miles.

Kansas really needs less timber than any other western State. Nowhere else is there as much good stone available for building purposes, while coal is abundant and good. Yet I think that in no other prairie State, is there a fair supply of timber so evenly distributed. The mild climate of this State and the comparative dryness of the winter months, really makes the demand for timber less imperative than in localities subject to excessive cold weather, or where cattle need continued shelter from cold rains. In the latter respect the timber in this State is distributed in exact proportion to the wants of the country, for on the western and comparatively treeless prairies there is very little precipitation of moisture during cold weather.

In the older settled portions of the State, considerable of the best timber has been cut, but railroads are already constructed in every county in this region, bringing pine at moderate prices (which are given elsewhere) from the upper Mississippi and Michigan pineries. Two or three lines of Kansas railroads are also soon to penetrate the pineries south of this State. By these roads pine will be furnished at low rates. It now sells at the mills in the pineries of the Indian Territory, Arkansas and Texas, at ten dollars to fifteen dollars per thousand feet. The hard pine of southern pineries is unsurpassed for fencing, framing stuff and flooring, and much of it makes excellent siding, shingles, etc.

When large timber is cut, the remaining young trees grow with accelerated rapidity, and as soon as prairie fires are checked timber springs up on the open prairies, and in our rich soil soon becomes available for domestic uses. Besides, as is shown elsewhere, it is a very easy matter to grow a thrifty young forest. In these ways the growth of native timber in the older settled prairie regions of Illinois and Missouri have exceeded the consumption, so that there is actually more timber in many localities than there was fifty years ago.

PRAIRIE GRASS.

Some writers have erroneously treated of "prairie grass" as a distinct variety of grass, whereas all grasses growing upon the prairie are classed under this general name. There are many distinct varieties of these wild grasses, which it would be tedious and profitless to mention by name.

Excepting those varieties which pass under the general name of buffalo grass, the prairie grasses of Kansas are similar to those of other prairie states. They cover the entire surface of the earth, and stand from one foot to six feet in hight. Tall coarse grasses grow on the bottom lands, and the hay made from them sells in towns for a dollar or two per ton less than "upland hay," which is made from the shorter and finer varieties grown on higher lands. A constant change takes place in the varieties of prairie grass—certain kinds disappearing upon the settlement of the country, while other varieties take their place. The wide-leaved blue-stem or blue-joint—a very valuable variety—occupies most of Eastern Kansas, and is rapidly extending Westward. The nutritious pea vine and wild rye grow abundantly among the grasses in many places, and make a hay which is equal, if not superior, to the best of tame hay.

Upland prairie grass, when properly cut, cured and stacked, makes a hay but little inferior to timothy. There are good farmers who feed both kinds and have little preference for either, but their prairie hay as well as tame grass hay is carefully prepared and stacked.

Wild grass like tame grass ought always to be cut for hay as soon as it is "in bloom," that is, when the pollen can be rattled from the head like a fine dust. By allowing grass to stand any considerable length of time after this period, the sugar, starch and other elements which give it value for food, are converted into woody fibre, as any one can see who notices how hard and stiff the grass gradually becomes. Many persons neglect hay cutting until the grass is not only hard and unpalatable to stock, but permit frost to come and find them haying. It is not surprising that such farmers think prairie hay of little value. Hay should be cured and stacked as soon as possible after cutting. By sprinkling a little salt upon it, the stock will eat it more freely, and as many think with better thrift; and if the hay is a little damp when stacked, salt will keep it from spoiling.

Hay is generally stacked in ricks about ten feet wide, twelve or fifteen feet high, and as long as convenient. Stacks or ricks of hay (or grain) ought to be kept the highest in the middle from the commencement of the rick; carry the sides straight up for two-thirds the hight of the stack; when complete, twist large hay ropes and pass them across the top of the rick, fastening a heavy weight to the ends, or tie two rails or poles together, and throw across the top. Hay is put up in this manner with mowing machines and horse rakes, for two dollars to three dollars per ton, and by selecting a good locality, and stacking on the ground where cut, it can be put up for one dollar and a half per ton. Our prairies yield from one to three tons per acre, varying with the soil and the season.

From early spring to midsummer, the prairies are gaily decked with flowers of various form and hue, presenting through this season a fascinating pano-

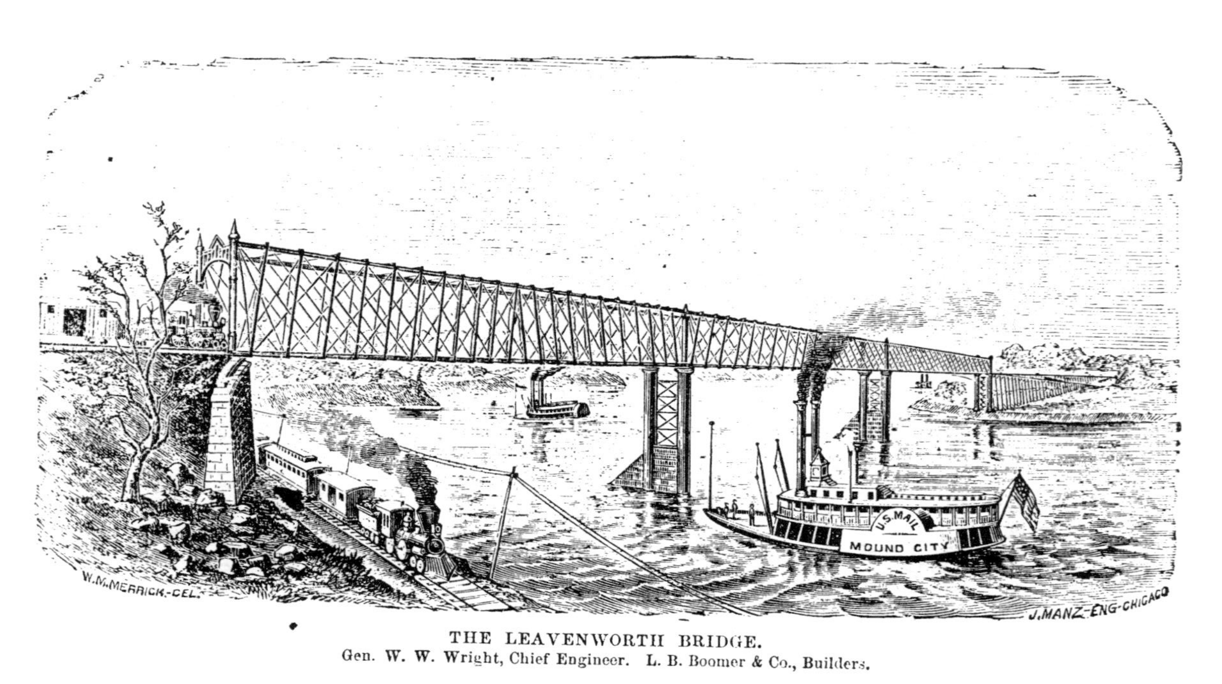

THE LEAVENWORTH BRIDGE.
Gen. W. W. Wright, Chief Engineer. L. B. Boomer & Co., Builders.

rama of ever changing color, and affording boquets which rival the delicate tints of costly exotics.

THE MUD.

"How many days in the year," asks one, "is the mud deep and sticky in Kansas?". I answer that on the average, during three hundred days of the year, you can put your span of horses to your buggy and drive at a smart trot over our common natural prairie roads. At times the mud is deep and sticky, but this is a feature *inseparable* from a good soil, and owing to the excellent natural drainage of Kansas, the mud dries very soon after the frost goes out of the ground, or after a rain.

Excepting other portions of this peculiar trans-Missouri region, there is no other good agricultural country so favored in this regard. The mud is not as troublesome here as in Ohio, Indiana and Illinois.

No people from any locality, which is a good farming region, need fear the mud of Kansas, and those who wish to live in towns will find sidewalks ready made, or if not made, the price of lots will be so low that they can afford to endure the discomfort of thick boots occasionally, to be benefited by the inevitable rise in such property as they purchase.

THE ROADS.

The entire State of Kansas has the best natural roadways of any State in the Union, excepting Nebraska, which in this regard is like Kansas. (Indeed, if Nebraska had our timber and stone and coal and climate and soil, she would be as good a State as Kansas is.) With either a carriage or a loaded team, you can drive over the entire State regardless of roads, by selecting good natural crossings at the streams. There are no swamps as in Michigan, Ohio, or Indiana; no sloughs as in Illinois or Iowa; no bogs or half-filled ponds as in Minnesota.

No labor whatever is expended on the prairie roads. The first settlers ride over the country, selecting such routes as suit their convenience, and making a trail which soon becomes a well beaten track. The double track made by teams is soon worn below the level, leaving a ridge in the middle which is inconvenient for a single horse in a buggy. This is eventually worn down, and a wide smooth road-bed is formed whereon in dry weather the horses' feet clatter, as if upon the macadamized roadways of Central Park, in New York. Very few drive less than two horses in this country, because feed is so cheap that the keeping of one or two horses, more or less, is a small matter.

Men who have floundered through the interminable sloughs of other Western States, can appreciate the satisfaction one feels at driving into a ravine or bed of a run, and passing over upon solid rock or a gravel bed. The only difficulty in crossing streams here is at the steep banks of the larger streams, or from high water. Short stretches of bad roads are occasionally to be found on river bottoms. As before remarked, the roads upon the rolling prairies, or the second bottoms, need little repairing, making it a small matter to secure splendid public highways at all seasons of the year. For bridging the streams, rock and timber are usually at hand upon the river bank.

Those who manage the public highways often make the same mistake here that is made elsewhere, by attempting to round or "pike" up with dirt, or fill in with stone at bad places, without *first* cutting ditches to carry off the water. Who ever saw a railroad that was not thoroughly drained by open ditches upon each side? Professional road makers understand that the basis of all good roads is drainage. All must have noticed that our roads even in the lowest places, are firm and smooth when the ground is *dry*. This ought to teach that such drainage as shall make it impossible for water to stand a single hour upon the road, is the first thing to be secured; without this, all other labor is vain, and in nine cases out of ten, this is *all that is needed* in our deep soil. Whatever is thereafter done, will be permanent and enduring. At a small cost, therefore, there will everywhere be solid roads in Kansas.

Limestone rock broken in pieces, none of which contain more than eight cubic inches, two inches each way, is placed upon our city streets at prices ranging from seven to ten cents per cubic foot. The layer is made from six inches to a foot thick, and this is called "macadamizing the streets." If the road bed is well drained and rounded a very little, this is probably the most economical and enduring pavement we can use. The city of Lawrence, however, is testing wooden pavement by putting it down on her principal street.

WIND AND WINDMILLS.

The most disagreeable feature of prairie life—and what life has not some disagreeable features—is the wind. I call this a feature of prairie life, because there is more wind on prairies than there is in the timber. So far as my observation extends, there is no more wind in Kansas than in Illinois, Iowa or Minnesota, and it is reasonable to believe that there is less, because the country is not in general so flat as in the greater portion of those States. There is compensation to be found, if we seek it, in all the ills of life, and the general reputation of the prairie regions for healthfulness, is, without doubt, to be largely ascribed to the motion of the atmosphere.

It is rarely entirely calm throughout any day in the year, a gentle breeze prevailing from the south during the warmest days or nights of summer. A close "muggy" atmosphere is unknown here.—A night when you strip off and sit down to gasp and pant for a breath of air; such a night is never experienced in Kansas. There are days when the wind blows and the dust flies in a very disagreeable manner, but I have seen as unpleasant days in this regard in New York or Boston, although there are more of them here. But people readily accustom themselves to almost any condition of the weather, when they are healthy and prosperous. Western people "reckon the wind is a good thing," and some regard it as a blessing.

Of wind-mills there is not much to be said, because few farmers are obliged to pump water for stock, and the exhaustless and universally diffused supply of coal, will make steam a cheap motive power. Add to the latter consideration the fact that water power is abundant over a considerable area of the State, and it will be seen that there is not a great demand for wind-mills. There is at Lawrence a wind grist mill of the old fashioned kind, such as were built a hundred years ago. It has been in constant use five years, and is a paying investment.

Professor F. H. Snow, of the State University, furnishes me with the following transcript from his records concerning the wind for the year 1870:

"From the 1095 observations, it appears that the wind was from the south, 325 times; north, 185 times; northwest, 182 times; east, 106 times; west, 77 times; southwest, 71 times; northeast, 56 times; southeast, 56 times; calm, 37 times."

The average duration of the winds from the different quarters, as deduced by Assistant-Surgeon, G. W. Sternberg, U. S. A., from the recorded observations for nine years, at Fort Riley, Kansas, is in the following proportion:

N.	NE.	E.	SE.	S.	SW.	W.	NW.
19.	11.	7.	9.	23.	10.	12.	7.

GEOLOGY.

No thorough Geological survey of the State of Kansas has yet been undertaken, but preliminary examinations and reports were made prior to 1866, by Professors G. C. Swallow and B. F. Mudge, State Geologists, assisted by Major F. Hawn. Prof. C. D. Wilber, late Superintendent Illinois Scientific Survey, also made a more recent examination of a portion of the State, in the interest of certain railroad and mining companies, of which survey an instructive report was published. These reports are so nearly out of print, as to be inaccessable to the public, and I have therefore taken some pains to collate therefrom such matter as will be most likely to interest and instruct my readers.

In no other prairie State is the study of Geology to interesting as in Kansas, because in none other is there such a variety of formations. In general terms the eastern one-fourth of the State belongs to that Geological system called Carboniferous, in which are found all the bituminous coal measures of the State. The greater part of this area is known as Upper Carboniferous, the Lower Carboniferous only coming to the surface in the southeastern corner of the State. This formatiou is composed of many different layers or strata of limestone, sandstone, coal, marls, shales, fire-clay, slate, selenite, etc., varying in thickness, and occurring irregularly. It has been asserted by all prior geologists, that there is a slight dip to the west, in the strata of this State, but this is disputed by Professor Wilber. Professor Swallow divides the carboniferous system into the following series: Upper Coal series, three hundred and ninety-one feet in thickness; Chocolate Limestone series, seventy-nine feet; Cave Rock series, seventy-five feet; Stanton Limestone series, seventy-four feet; Spring Rock series, eighty-eight feet; Well Rock series, two hundred and thirty-eight feet; Marais des Cygnes Coal series, three hundred and three feet; Pawnee Limestone series, one hundred and twelve feet; Fort Scott Coal series, one hundred and forty-two feet; Fort Scott Marble series, twenty-two feet; Lower Coal series, three hundred and fifty-three feet; to which is to be added the Lower Carboniferous, one hundred and twenty feet, making a round total of two thousand feet.

We have spoken of the gradual increase in altitude, as one goes westward in Kansas, and a study of the figures at the railroad stations on the accompanying map, furnishes an instructive lesson as to the undulations of the country. But from this it will be seen that the greatest elevations within one hundred and twenty miles of the eastern State line, which is about as far west as the carboniferous system extends, is only about four hundred feet above the lowest; as, for instance, Parker, in Morris county, above Wyandotte at the mouth of the Kansas River. It is evident therefore that many of the series enumerated above, can only be local in extent. If each one mentioned, projected westward, under those which lie higher, then it would, in all cases be safe to sink shafts for coal, for by going deep enough, it could certainly be found. The coal series are as likely to be wanting, as any other of the strata, and no experiments should be made in sinking shafts, unless the most careful borings have shown the presence of coal. Fortunately the outcroppings of coal are so abundant, that such experiments are hardly necessary, as will be shown farther along.

In the carboniferous system, Professor Swallow

counted forty-four distinct strata of limestone, varying from one foot to thirty feet in thickness, and making, in the aggregate, about three hundred and sixty feet of limestone. He also counted twenty-four strata of sandstone, measuring in the aggregate, two hundred feet. The sandstone is chiefly found in the lower coal measures, and in heavy beds, from five to fifty feet thick. The coal beds counted by Professor Swallow, number twenty-two, many of which are too thin to be of any value, but he says "ten of them range in thickness from one to seven feet." I think, however, that no coal beds have been worked in Kansas, which exceed four feet in thickness.

CONGREGATIONAL CHURCH, LAWRENCE.

The next higher system, which exhibits itself west of the foregoing, is called by Prof. Swallow Upper and Lower Permian. He gives their respective thickness as one hundred and forty-one and five hundred and sixty-three feet, making a total depth of seven hundred and four feet. In this system he counted thirty-five different strata of limestone, making a total thickness of about two hundred feet of this rock. The limestones of this system are chiefly known as magnesian limestone. This system also contains beds of gypsum. The boundaries of the Permian system are not defined by the geoloologists, but upon the Kansas River it commences in the neighborhood of Manhattan and extends across the State, from north to south, in an irregular belt perhaps fifty miles wide from east to west.

Next higher, and to the westward, Prof. Swallow places the Triassic system. The total thickness of the strata in this formation is given as three hundred and thirty-eight feet, and it is composed of limestone, sandstone, thin coal veins, gypsum, selenite, and magnesian marls and shales.

To the westward of the foregoing is the cretaceous formation, extending to the foot hills of the Rocky Mountains, which has been more extensively examined by Prof. B. F. Mudge, of the State Agricultural College, Manhattan, than by any other geologist. By the kindness of Prof. Mudge I am permitted to present the following memoranda, transmitted to me by by him, January 7, 1871. It is a valuable contribution to science, because it contains the most recent geological items published in relation to Western Kansas.

"The first geological formation west of the Carboniferous, is the Permean, which crosses the State through Davis and Riley counties, in a northeasterly and southwesterly direction. The fossils correspond in a great degree, with those of the Permean of Europe, but the Carboniferous fossils unite with the Permean in many of the contiguous strata, so that no distinct line of demarcation between the two can be seen. West of this is a red sandstone tract, which corresponds to the Triassic, (or new red sandstone of old authors), but the fossils are so few that the boundaries, like the preceding, cannot be clearly defined. The Cretaceous formation is still farther west, crossing the State in a northeasterly and southwesterly direction, near the mouths of the Saline and Solomon Rivers, and thence covering the whole westerly portion of the State. This is one of the richest deposits of the United States, in its fossils, and possesses great geological interest. It not only abounds in well preserved fossils, similar to those of other parts of the United States, as well as of Europe, but contains many species new to science

"In illustration of this, the fact may be stated that the writer, at one locality, twenty miles west of Salina, obtained fifteen species of marine shells, new to science, and in a brief excursion near Fort Wallace, and on the Solomon, he procured three new species of reptiles and five of fishes, many of large size.

"The predominant fossils of the eastern portion of this formation, are dicolyledonous leaves, of which about fifty species have been found, a dozen of which are new to science. Among these is the cinnamon, now growing only in torrid climes. More westerly are quantities of the remains of sharks and other fish, equaling in size the largest now known, also saurians and other amphibians of large size and peculiar forms.

"The soil of all these formations is rich. Even the sandstone region has so much of lime and organic substance in the loam, that the farms are equal to the best in the State. The Saline, Solomon and Republican valleys are well timbered (for a prairie country), the soil rich, deep and well drained.

"Fifteen miles west of Fort Harker, at Wilson Creek, is a deposit of lignite coal forty-two inches in thickness, underlying an extensive portion of the country. It is also found in a corresponding situation in the valleys of the Solomon, Saline and Republican Rivers, but though affording a present supply of fuel, it is inferior to the bituminous coal found on the line of the railroads in the southeastern part of the State. The lignite from Wilson Creek was at one time on many of the locomotives of the Kansas Pacific Railway.

"The most valuable mineral in this part of the State is salt, which is found in numerous springs and extensive salt marshes in sufficient quantities to supply half the population of the United States.

"Stone for building material is abundant in all the geological formations. In the Cretaceous, the lime beds are frequently from twenty to sixty feet in thickness, soft, easily wrought and making excellent quick lime. The buildings at Fort Wallace and some at Fort Hayes are made from it. Those at Fort Harker are constructed of a brown sandstone. Some of the limestone strata run into a white chalk, which is fully equal to that imported from England. Gypsum is more or less abundant, sometimes in strata from ten to fifteen feet in thickness, and in future will be found by our farmers to be one of the most valuable natural deposits of our State."

Professor Mudge gives above sufficient evidences of what all geologists assert to be true: that this entire region was submerged in water during the past ages. At this period a portion of the rocky formations, enumerated above, were ground to powder, and intermixed in such a manner as to give to our soil its various and valuable chemical properties, which have been so fully described in preceding pages.

STONE QUARRIES.

Frequent allusion has already been made to the important part which rock deposits play in the frame work of Kansas scenery, and in the economy of Kansas life. The importance of the subject in its pecuniary aspects merits still further mention.

The rock of Kansas chiefly consists, as is shown in the foregoing, of limestone, sandstone and gypsum. At least 90 per cent. is limestone of various texture and color. There is no better limestone in the United States than is to be found in Kansas. Columns dressed to eight inch face, fourteen inches deep, and fourteen feet high, are used in two story brick fronts at Topeka.

Professor J. A. Bent, of Wheaton College, Illinois, expresses the following opinion which is founded upon extensive travel and observation: "No state in

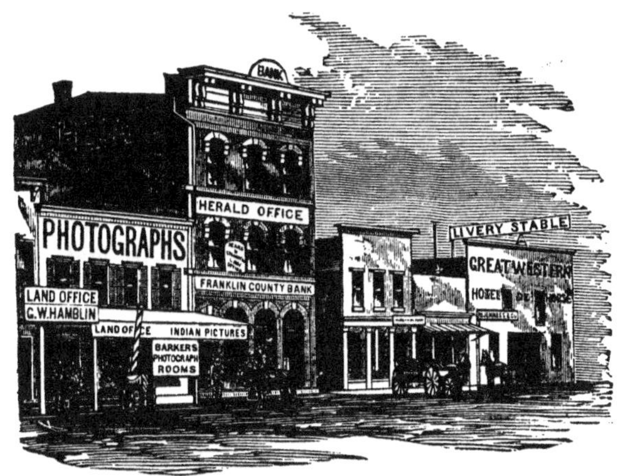

CORNER MAIN AND SECOND STREETS, OTTAWA.

the Union is so generally and so well supplied with rock as Kansas, and at the same time so free from rock which comes in the way of cultivating the soil."

The reason why these two advantages are here combined in so extraordinary a degree, is found in the fact that the strata of rock are nearly all horizontal, while the entire State slopes very considerable to the east. The strata are thereby caused to appear one above another, like broken and irregular terraces, or steps all the way westward. Then consider that excepting some of the river bottoms, there are no flat surfaces in the State, but that the entire face of the country is swept by valleys, and rolls, and gentle bluffs, and it is easy to see why the rock is found on almost every farm, so situated at its projecting edges as to be convenient, but not troublesome. Above the rock are several feet of earth and soil, and below it, upon the sloping sides of the bluff or roll, is to be found a soil which is especially deep, quick and fertile.

Horace Greeley writes from Kansas to the New York *Tribune*, October 9, 1870, as follows: "Whenever a declevity, however moderate, is seen, there choice limestone for fencing, or building, or burning, may be rapidly taken out with the pick or bar. Most of it is in flat, square, (or oblong) blocks of ten to sixty pounds, whereof the poorest may be laid up with facility into excellent wall, leaving the better available for building. This limestone has yielded, and is still yielding, near the surface, to decay, enriching the soil, while increasing the facility with which the uncorroded portions are broken into convenient blocks for use."

With this rock, wells, cisterns and cellars are walled, and foundations laid for wooden or brick buildings, while cheap and substantial buildings are erected of stone. Many hundred miles of stone wall have been built at a cost of $1.50 to $2.50 per rod. Frequently the rock is quarried on the fence line, and the wall laid by the side of the ditch thus made. Judge James Hanway, of Lane, writes me: "I have a stone wall which three hands quarried, hauled and put up at the rate of four rods per day, using two yoke of oxen, and a low wagon, and hauling a few rods. A skillful man can lay up five rods in a day, while others would be industrious at two rods."

The following account lately appeared in the *Topeka Daily Commonwealth*, of a new quarry of flag-stone opened at Osage City, on the Atchison, Topeka & Santa Fe Railroad, thirty-five miles from Topeka: "The visitor sees, laid one over another in beautiful regularity, layer after layer of blue limestone, from one to four inches thick, in slabs from three to eight feet wide and from ten to thirty feet in length. These flag-stones are as smooth and even as a board, and are so situated that they may be taken up, one after another, with wonderful rapidity. The toughness of this stone may be estimated when I say that I saw a slab twenty-four feet in length, three feet wide and only three inches and a quarter in thickness, and weighing 2,800 pounds, suspended by a chain in the middle of it without breaking! It is very hard and durable, and can be put down in sidewalks for much less than our cut stone walks, and will be equal if not superior to the very best of them. The thinner grade of flagging will make good walks for front yards, gardens, etc., and can be put down almost as cheap as board walks. The quarry is known to extend a mile along the edge of a ravine. The side track from the railroad to the ledge will soon be completed."

This rock has the appearance of slate, but an acid test indicates the presence of lime. I have examined the stone and seen it placed in sidewalks, and it promises to be very valuable. I measured one slab which was brought to Topeka. Its dimensions were 7½ feet wide, 28 feet long and three inches thick. Stone of the same quality was found near Vineland, in Douglas county, several years ago, and used to pave sidewalks in Lawrence. One layer less than two inches thick, was used upon a sidewalk which has stood constant usage for about six years with little injury. This ledge did not prove to be extensive.

Occasionally a traveler, following the principal roads which uniformly seek the high divides to avoid streams, will pass over a rocky piece of ground which looks uninviting. But no man need purchase such land, (although it is valuable for pasturage,) when there is a plenty to be had for nothing, or at a nominal cost, as beautiful and as fertile as any the sun shines upon, and which has upon it rock sufficient for use.

Magnesian limestone and gypsum, which together cover an area including most of western Kansas, can be cut with hatchet or saw like wood, into blocks of any desired size, which soon harden upon exposure to the air. The former stone has been extensively shipped from Junction City to the Missouri River, where are large factories, at which it is sawed and turned into various shapes for architectural purposes. It is reckoned by scientific men as among the most durable kinds of rock in the world. The State House at Topeka, is built of it. The abutments to the Leavenworth bridge are also magnesian limestone.

Until recently it has been supposed that magnesian limestone was not to be found far east of Manhattan, but I find it exists in all parts of the State in isolated quarries, and geologists say there are more than twenty varieties. There is a fine ledge near Quenemo, in Osage county, others near Pomona, Franklin county, others in Johnson and the eastern portion of Miami counties. In Labette county it is abundant, and probably will be found in nearly every county in the State. In township seven, range sixteen, Jackson county, this is the prevailing stone, while in the remainder of the county it is not known to exist.

The sandstone as well as limestone, is firm in texture and is largely used for building purposes. It should be understood that stone needs seasoning as well as lumber, before it is used for good work. When quarried it contains a considerable quantity of water, and upon drying may expose seams not at first observable. If cut and used for fronts while still damp, and cold weather comes on immediately, it is liable to be cracked by the expansion of the water it contains. Fine buildings have thus been disfigured in Kansas through the ignorance, or more likely the neglect, of builders who did not like to delay their work. Stone is frequently thus condemned, when in reality it only needed seasoning.

MARBLE.

This variety of limestone is found in many places in Kansas, ordinarily of various shades of buff, brown and black. No white marble has been discovered.

Marbles have been found at Fort Scott, near Lawrence, also in Doniphan county, at Leavenworth and other localities, which take a fine polish. The Fort Scott marble is black, "full of yellowish veins." The Leavenworth marble was found in sinking the coal shaft hereafter described. It is four hundred feet below the surface; its thickness is sixteen feet three inches, and it is described as "solid, fine in grain, of a drab color, very handsomely mottled, and the hardest merchantable marble in the United States."

Experts who have examined Kansas marbles say that the quality is such that a large demand may be supplied for mantle pieces, tops to bureaus, washstands, etc., but the question of export depends altogether upon the fashion as to colors. In other words, the stone is suitable, if the color is acceptable.

FREESTONE OR SANDSTONE.

Enough has already been said concerning the excellent quarries of this rock to be found in almost every county, excepting as to its adaptation to the making of grindstones.

Many persons have selected fragments which they

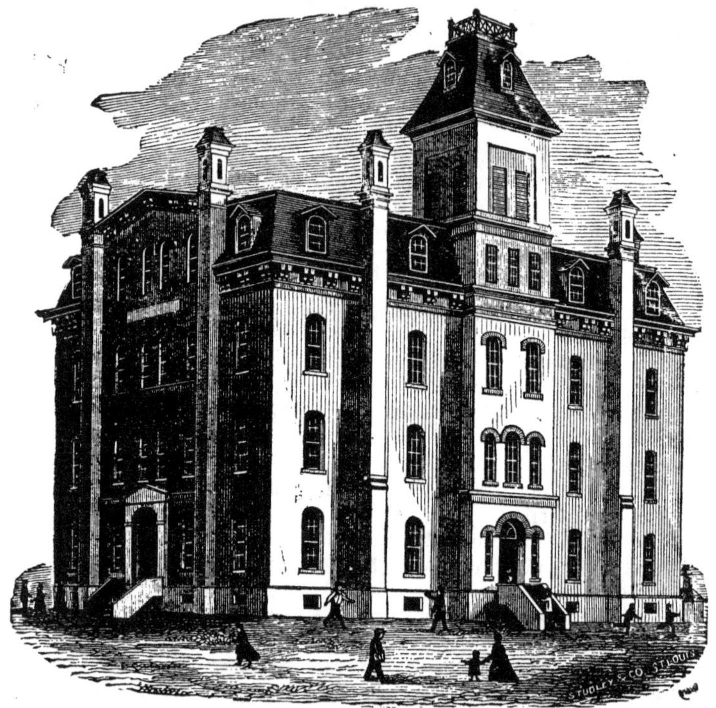

MORRIS PUBLIC SCHOOL, LEAVENWORTH.

used for sharpening edge tools, but as yet, however, I do not know that quarries have been opened which furnish stone of precisely the right grain for this purpose. But no two quarries are alike in their characteristics, and there is reason for believing that among the thousands of various texture and degrees of hardness, a good variety will yet be found for grindstones. All of these articles now used in the West are brought from Ohio.

GYPSUM.

This exceedingly valuable rock is not found, to any considerable extent in the carboniferous formation which we have described, but it prevails to a greater or less degree over the western three-fourths of the State—that is, over an area of about sixty thousand square miles. The most easterly beds reported by the geological survey, are in Marshall, and perhaps Nemaha county, in Northern Kansas, whence it crosses the State to the southern line. It is found in beds of all thicknesses up to fifty feet, and in the western half of the State it occurs in crystalized semi-transparent sheets, resembling mica (or isinglass) in texture, and alum in color.

It will be seen by a glance at the map, that five of the Railroads now running in Kansas, cross the gypsum deposits, thus making it easily available to all portions of the State.

The uses to which this article is applied are various and important. It is used as a cement, and in taking casts by artists, dentists, and others; in making busts and ornamental designs for the ornament of inner walls, as well as in giving to the walls themselves an elegant and durable "hard finish." But it is most extensively used as a fertilizer, whence it is called "land plaster." Vast quantities of this article are imported to the Eastern States from Nova Scotia. It is also sold from beds in Virginia, New York and Michigan, but I think is not found west of the latter State. Desiring to publish accurate information as to the proper method of preparing gypsum for various uses, I applied for this purpose to the State University at Lawrence, and received the following letter:

"STATE UNIVERSITY OF KANSAS,
LAWRENCE, January 18, 1871.

Mr. C. C. Hutchinson :

DEAR SIR: Your lettor of inquiry in regard to the effect of heat on the fertilizing properties of gypsum is received.

"Heating gypsum would injure it as a fertilizer. If heated below 300 degrees Fahrenheit, till the water of crystalization is driven off, it would harden on coming in contact with the moist soil; if subjected to a high heat it would be decomposed.

"As a fertilizer gypsum is most valuable in a finely ground state. I hope in your forthcoming work, you will strongly press its claims upon Kansas farmers, for it would be especially valuable on our rich prairie soil.

"To make plaster of paris, ground gypsum should be subjected to a heat of about 250 degrees Fahrenheit, till watery vapor ceases to rise, but the heat should not exceed 300 degrees Fahrenheit, for if heated above that point it will not harden on adding water.

Respectfully yours,
Wm. H. SAUNDERS, M. D.,
Professor of Chemistry."

It is usually applied to land at the rate of one to five bushels per acre. The practice most in favor is to sow it broad-cast over young grain or grass, especially clover, or to apply it by the small handful upon and around vegetables and Indian corn, when young. I have seen good planters in Virginia put a "pinch" in each dwarfed or stunted tobacco plant, in order to bring it forward. The best immediate effects seem to follow its application during damp weather, or just before a shower. Gypsum is largely used by good farmers who have rich lands and who want to keep them rich. Its use in Kansas, applied directly to growing plants, would doubtless be highly beneficial. Its almost universal presence in Kansas soil accounts in part for the extraordinary yield of our land.

In reply to a correspondent who inquired as to the relative value of lime and gypsum as fertilizers, *Moore's Rural New Yorker* recently published the following: "On heavy clay soils, the action of lime is to disintegrate and loosen; on sandy soils it supplies a lack; it sweetens some soils; it decomposes organic matter in all soils. Plaster, applied as a top dressing to land, furnishes plants with sulphur, absorbs and retains for the use of plants the ammonia of the atmosphere, and is a useful application on limestone soils, or on soils that have been dressed with lime. It exercises an entirely distinct agency from that of lime in promoting vegetable growth."

As an article of commerce our gypsum beds are to be of great value. It is every year coming into more general use by farmers, and we have enough to supply the entire Mississippi Valley. The quality of much that is found in this State is said by experts to be equal to the best in the world, it being uniform in grain and pure white in color.

COAL.

The geological formation called carboniferous, (coal-bearing,) occupies the entire eastern portion of the State, having a general width from east to west of about one hundred and twenty miles. Its western limit crosses the Kansas River through Davis and Riley counties, in a northeasterly and southwesterly direction, and its area is about seventeen thousand square miles. There are outcroppings of bituminous coal throughout the entire extent of this vast surface, an area more than twice the size of the State of Massachusetts. Professor Swallow, the State Geologist, counted "twenty two distinct and separate beds of coal. Many of these are thin, and of but little value, but ten of them range in thickness from one to seven feet of coal, suitable for domestic and manufacturing purposes." The thickest outcropping veins are displayed in the southeastern portion of the State, and it is supposed that these continue westward under the other veins which lie higher, and which appear at the surface further west and northwest.

No considerable experiments have been made in boring, or by test wells or shafts, excepting at Leavenworth City, where, at the depth of seven hundred and ten feet, an excellent quality was found, the bed varying from twenty-two to twenty-eight inches in thickness, averaging twenty-five inches. This mine has an excellent steam engine and good facilities for delivering coal. It is proposed to sink the shaft to a greater depth, as it is believed that a vein three feet in thickness can be reached at a depth of a thousand feet from the surface. The miners receive nine to nine and a half cents per bushel, and the coal has been sold by the car load for eighteen cents per bushel, but is now reduced to fifteen cents per bushel for manufacturing purposes. One of the upper coal veins, much inferior in quality to the shaft coal mentioned, was formerly worked a few miles distant from Leavenworth, and other veins have been worked in several localities in northern Kansas.

The coals of the upper strata, which are most worked, are in Osage and Franklin counties. The western portion of the latter county, and perhaps the entire surface of the former, with portions of adjoining counties, are occupied by veins showing themselves in many places, and everywhere within a few feet of the surface. The citizens usually work the mines by drifting into the banks, but mining companies also work by putting down shafts or wells. There is one company in Franklin county, and four or five in Osage county, that deliver coal on the railroads. The mines in these two counties show about twenty-two to twenty five inches of solid coal. It is sold throughout the counties at the mines for fifteen to twenty cents per bushel of eighty pounds.

I quote from a letter dated Topeka, January 27, 1871, received from W. H. Fisk, Superintendent of one of the Companies working in Osage county, as follows:

"We have two shafts at Osage City, some fifty feet in depth, and a mine at Carbondale entered by a slope or drift, the main entry being some eight hundred feet long. Our present force and facilities will enable us to take out twenty car loads per day, six thousand bushels. We have contracts with the Kansas Pacific, and Atchison Topeka & Santa Fe Railway Companies, to supply them with coal. Our Osage coal is pronounced by good judges to be equal to any in the State. The dimensions of the Osage shafts are 5x13 feet, 50 feet in depth."

Mining is prosecuted extensively by organized companies in Bourbon county, near Fort Scott, and in Crawford, Cherokee, Neosho, and Labette counties. Extensive mines are opened near Chetopa in the latter county; one company ship from twenty-five to forty car loads per day from Fort Scott, employing about two hundred and fifty men. The veins that are worked in this region range from two to four feet in thickness, and are but a few feet below the surface. Coal is found in workable veins in every county throughout the coal formation, but approved methods of exploring and opening these. veins have been employed in but few instances. Very little, indeed, is known, as yet, of the resources of the State in this regard, and discoveries are constantly being made. Six years ago, it was supposed that coal could be found in but three or four places in the entire extent of Franklin and Osage counties. Now it is known to be almost universally diffused in workable veins. The same result will follow thorough explorations in other counties.

The coal of which we have been speaking is bituminous coal, and of a superior quality. There is considerable luster to its broken edges, and it does not crumble to dust by handling and shipping, as does much of the coal in other Western States. It contains but little sulphur. It is used npon all our railroads, both for locomotives and in machine shops. It is also extensively used for domestic purposes, and universally by our blacksmiths. It is retailed in our towns and cities for twenty-five to thirty cents per bushel; but it should be remembered that it was not in the market in salable quantities until the construction of railroads, which cut some of the better veins, and this has only been accomplished within eighteen months of this writing. When properly developed—and there is in its development ample field for capital and enterprise—coal will be delivered at less rates, but with great profit to mining companies. All the coals of this State, it should be mentioned, lie like the rocks, in a position nearly horizontal.

Concerning its quality we introduce the testimony of Professor C. D. Wilber, late Superintendent of Illinois Scientific Survey: "These coals are excellent for all purposes; making iron either in furnaces or rolling mills; making steam whether for factories, mills or locomotives; in gas works or for domestic use. They are singularly free from sulphur, and burn with the clear white flame of Pittsburgh coal."

In western Kansas, beyond the carboniferous formation, there is a species of coal which is spoken of by Professor Mudge in his preceding letter. Major Hawn, of Leavenworth City, who was associated with the Geological Survey of the State, and who has made extensive explorations of Western Kansas, in connection with the lineal surveys of Government, writes me as follows, under date of January 9, 1871 :

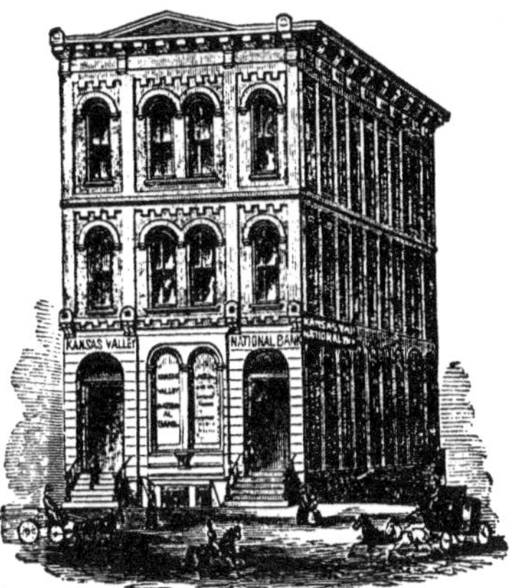

KANSAS VALLEY NATIONAL BANK, TOPEKA.

"There is a species of coal in the western portion of Kansas classified as 'lignite.' This is a distinction without an apparent difference to the ordinary observer, between the best specimens of it and the common bituminous varieties. It is a lighter coal, containing more gas and less carbon. Generally, the proportion of fixed carbon is so small that it is not suitable for smithies, but answers well for heating purposes. From recent discoveries, it seems to have a wide distribution, and will play an important part in the settlement of that region."

Little is really known about the mineral deposits of Western Kansas, as the State Geological Surveys have not extended so far; but there is evidence that among its abundant sources of wealth, we must reckon the coal deposits as not the least valuable. The lignites have been little examined, and yet they are to-day held in higher esteem than were the coals of Eastern Kansas a dozen years ago. The veins of lignite coal now worked in Colorado, near Denver, are from six to ten feet in thickness, and the coal, while not so heavy as our bituminous variety, is suitable for all mechanical purposes, and burns with a brighter flame, making a very cheerful open fire. Preparations are making to use it extensively in smelting the gold and silver ores of Colorado, which are now shipped across the Atlantic to Wales for smelting. This coal is chiefly found in perpendicular veins thrown up by volcanic action. Scientific gentlemen, who recently visited these mines, have informed me that they are found in the same geological formation as that which prevails in Western Kansas. They also believe that the same veins continue, at an unknown depth, eastward, and that the lignites discovered in Western Kansas, are their broken and irregular out-croppings. They think that further explorations will undoubtedly reveal a vast supply of this coal in Kansas. There is not space here to present concurrent testimony upon this point; but all, whether pioneers or manufacturers, may rest assured that Kansas is abundantly supplied with coal of excellent quality.

A vast amount of coal lies under the surface, even of a small farm. Mining engineers allow one million tons for every foot in thickness of bituminous coal covering one square mile. This gives five hundred thousand tons under a farm of one hundred and sixty acres, in a vein only two feet thick. Estimating that a ton of coal is equal to one and one-half cords, and some say two cords, of good hard wood, it appears that most of the farms of a quarter section, (one-half mile square) have under their surface coal equivalent to about one million cords of wood. "Let us suppose all Kansas to be covered by a forest, affording one hundred cords of wood to the acre. This would be considered an ample supply of fuel. Yet a six foot vein of coal under *sixteen townships*, or five hundred and seventy-six square miles, (the ordinary size of *one county*,) will afford more fuel than the entire State if covered with such forests."—Professor Mudge.

But all geologists assert that there is not only six feet under one county, but two to six feet under every county in all the carboniferous region of seventeen thousand square miles. This will do very well for a country that has been said to be destitute of fuel.

SALT.

The statement is made by Professor Mudge that "the most valuable mineral in this (western) part of the State is salt, which is found in numerous springs and extensive salt marshes, in sufficient quantities to supply half the population of the United States.

There seems to be no reason why any limit should be placed to the capacity of Kansas for supplying salt, as the following exhibit will show. And first we copy from the "First Annual Report on the Geology of Kansas," by B. F. Mudge, A. M., 1864:

"The buffalo licks or tramps, so common in almost every county of the State, in most cases owe their origin to the presence of salt brine, even when it does not appear in the shape of springs at the surface. The valleys of the Verdigris and Fall Rivers have salt springs which supply a part of the loca demand, though no exertions have been made to develop the supply, the water from open springs or wells only being used, which is much diluted by the surface streams."

Here follows an enumeration of springs and wells in Eastern Kansas from which salt has been made in small quantities, but which I think have all been abandoned as unprofitable. They are but the surface indications of the vast reservoir farther west.

We continue to quote from the report. "On the boundary of the State, a very large deposit of crystalized salt exists south of the great bend of the Arkansas River, in which it lies in beds from six to twenty-eight inches in depth. In one instance, two Government wagons were filled in a few minutes, without being moved. The salt is so compact as to require a hatchet to cut it. These deposits are undoubtedly caused by the drying up of salt ponds or salt branches of the Cimmarron River. But this is situated so far from the settled portions of the State, or any regular route of transportation, that at present it is of no practical value. A railroad toward that region would make it of vast commercial importance." The Professor thus dismisses these great salt plains, for he had at that time little idea that railroads would so soon reach their rich stores. The Atchison, Topeka and Santa Fe Railroad is speedily to be completed to that region, and other lines are pushing in that direction. The area of these plains is estimated by the best authorities at more than five hundred square miles, entirely covered with an incrustation of pure salt of various degrees of thickness. Very few white people have ever visited this remarkable spot. But many bushels of excellent salt have been brought from there, and the wilder Indian tribes who formerly inhabited Kansas, annually went thither to procure a supply of salt in addition to that furnished them by the Government.

These salt plains lie partly in Kansas and partly in the Indian Territory, and are surrounded by a fine grazing and agricultural region.

Professor Mudge proceeds to describe the salt region of Western Kansas, which he says embraces a tract of country about thirty-five miles wide and eighty miles long, crossing the Republican, Solomon and Saline Valleys. Here are to be found numerous springs, but more frequently, extensive salt marshes. One of these he thus describes at length, as illustrative of the character and appearance of them all.

"Take that in town four, range two, west of the sixth principal meridian, in the Republican Valley, about seventy-five miles northwest of Fort Riley. It is sometimes called the Tuthill marsh. The valley here is wide, gradually rising to the high prairies so common in that part of the State. The marsh covers nearly one thousand acres, more or less impregnated with saline matter. About one-third is entirely void of vegetation, which the brine will not allow to grow. It is perfectly level, and at the time of our first visit was as white as a wintry snow field, with a crust of crystalized salt.

"The incrustation of salt is frequently three-eighths of an inch in thickness. This is scraped up and used, in its natural state, for salting cattle, etc., but for domestic purposes it is dissolved, by being mixed with about twenty gallons of water to a bushel of salt, when the mechanical impurities, sand, etc., readily settle. The salt is again returned to a solid state by evaporation. According to the observations of Mr. J. G. Tuthill, who lives near, and has made borings in over one hundred different places, to a depth of twenty or thirty feet, there is a very uniform supply and strength of brine. The water preserved for analysis was obtained by me from a boring made at random. It was found at four feet from the surface. The density, by the salome-ter, was 24 deg., (6.16 Baume, or specific gravity of 1.0421,) with the thermometer at 60 deg. This should give a bushel of salt for one hundred and thirty gallons of the water, (not counting the impurities,) which is three times the strength of the ocean. It was taken at our second visit, immediately after a heavy rain, which must have diluted the brine.

"The large quantity of salt, within the tract designated is evident from the fact that the waters of the Solomon and Saline are so impregnated as to have a saline taste from points eighty miles above

STREET SCENE, HUMBOLDT.

their entrance into the Smoky Hill river. The waters of the latter, when the stream runs low, also show the presence of the brine. The supply of salt sufficient to meet this daily and hourly amount thus carried down, must be immense."

Here follows a statement of localities, where the Professor found salt marshes, varying in size from a few acres up to three thousand acres, the latter located in townships four and five, of range five west. Throughout the country south of the Arkansas River, there are also extensive and very promising indications of salt.

Having shown that these deposits are found in the true salt bearing geological formations, as developed in this country and in Europe, and having proved that the strength of the brines is entirely satisfactory. Prof. Mudge proceeds as follows:

"The analysis of the *salt* and brine from the Tuthill marsh, made by Prof. C. F. Chandler, of the School of Mines, Columbia College, New York, is as follows:

	Salt.	*Brine* 100 *pts.*	*Brine,* 1 *U. S. gal.*
Chloride of Sodium (salt)	96.689	4.708	2,861.20
Sulphate of Soda	1.959	0.573	348.23
Sulphate of Lime	0.216	0.157	95,41
Chloride of Magnesium	0.300	0 231	140 39
Oxide of Iron		trace	trace.
Sand and Clay	0 050	0.010	0.61
Water	0.786	94 221	57,327.35
	100,000	99.900	60,773.19

Density of brine, 1.0421—6.16 Baume.
Total saline matter in brine, 5.779.
Chloride of Sodium per U. S. gallon of 231 cubic inches 6.53 oz.

"This gives one bushel of solid matter to one hundred and ten gallons, or one bushel of pure salt to one hundred and thirty gallons of brine. The water was taken by me from a boring made at random, within four feet of the surface. The salt, I took from one of fifty *hollow logs*, in which it was being made. The percentage of solid impurities is 2.55, and contains *no chloride of calcium.* No attempt was made to purify the salt, as the parties making it had no previous knowlede of the business. The ordinary market salts of the United States contain from two to six percentage of impurities; a larger portion being nearer the latter than the former standard."

The report of the Onondaga Salt Springs in the State of New York, shows that the "Factory filled refined for table and dairy," contains 1.60 per cent. of solid impurities. The celebrated "Stoved Ashton

Salt," of England, contains about the same amount of impurities, and they are prepared with great care, and are acknowledged to be among the best salts in the world. Thus it is seen that our unrefined salts are nearly equal to the best commercial salts.

Subsequent to the explorations of Professor Mudge, a few gentlemen, residents of Kansas, stimulated by these discoveries—in which indeed they had taken part, by defraying certain expenses incurred therein, organized the Continental Salt Company and obtained eight hundred acres of land in the forks cf the Solomon and Smoky Hill Rivers.

"The first thing done was to sink an artesian well in the ordinary manner, at a point where the brines oozing through the soil at the river bank had formed by solar evaporation an incrustation of salt thereon. Indications were apparent at twenty feet from the surface, which steadily increased in volume and strength to the depth of two hundred feet. The driling was continued to the depth of six hundred feet, but the strength of the brine was not very perceptibly increased below two hundred feet."

This company is yet in its infancy, but they have a number of vats with movable covers, and by solar evaporation have manufactured salt for three years. They have produced several thousand bushels with very satisfactory pecuniary results, as is proven by the increased number of vats used each year, and the erection of dwellings for workmen. This salt, in its unrefined state, as taken from the vats, has been analyzed by Professor Gossman, of Syracuse, New York, with the following result:

Chloride of Sodium (salt)	980.565
Sulphate of Lime	17.220
Sulphate of Soda	3.511
Chloride of Magnesium	2.400
Chloride of Calcium	*Not a trace*

It is to be noticed that "not a trace" of *Chloride of Calcium* was discovered by this analysis, agreeing perfectly in this important particular, with the analysis already given from Professor Chandler, of the Tuthill marsh salt and brine. It is asserted upon good authority that no other brines have yet been discovered in the United States that are entirely free from these "deleterious bitter waters."

Even the celebrated "Petite Ause" deposit of salt in Louisiana, which has been repeatedly claimed as the purest salt in the world, contains Chloride of Calcium, as shown by the following analysis, made by Dr. Rindall in 1863, acting under the direction of the United States Government:

Chloride of Sodium (salt)	98.86
Sulphate of Lime	76
Chloride of Magnesium	25
Chloride of Calcium	13
	100.00

In order to make butter which can be preserved sweet and good any considerable length of time, it has become the universal custom of dairymen to use ground rock salt, manufactured with great care and at considerable cost in the United States. But here in Kansas, in the center of the Union, are found inexhaustible stores of salt, *entirely free from these bitter waters.*

This salt supply is also where it will be in great local demand, both for dairy purposes and for packing beef. There can be no question in the minds of any who read this book that numerous beef-packing establishments will soon be erected where cattle are so easily grown and fattened, and salt so easily manufactured. And those who examine the testimony given by the letter of Rev. J. Sternberg must concede that Kansas promises wonderful results in dairy products also. Add to this the fact that there are no salt works west of Michigan, and it will be seen that here are openings for enterprising capitalists which cannot long remain unoccupied.

People will ask the thoughtless question, "Why have not these salt resources been developed?" One might as well ask why people settled in the forbidding regions east of the Alleghanies, when Illinois and Kansas were all unoccupied. It takes time to develop great resources, and it is an advantage which Kansas offers to the enterprising, that there is something here *to be developed.*

The Saginaw Salt Works produced twenty thousand bushels in 1860, but now they produce three million bushels annually. The demand for salt in each State is nearly one bushel per annum to every inhabitant, and probably more than that in the great beef and pork packing Western States.

IRON.

Iron ores, varying considerably in character, have been found in various portions of the State; but, as yet, nothing has been discovered which gives any promise of competing with the vast supply of iron found in Missouri, at a distance of only about one hundred miles from our eastern border; and, in Colorado, but three hundred miles from our western border. We have the coal for manufacturing, and it is not far to bring iron, either from the east or the west.

But it is not improbable that it will yet be found in paying quantities in unexplored Western Kansas. Professor Swallow says: "The tertiary strata in the western part of the State probably contain extensive beds of this ore." Professor Mudge says: "We have been shown a specimen of brown hematite iron ore from the western part of the State of very superior quality, and containing nearly sixty per cent. of iron.

LEAD.

Lead has been taken out to a small extent in Linn

county, and those familiar with the locality believe that it would be profitable to develop the mines. It is evident from the debris about the excavations that considerable work has been done here many years ago, but there is no clue by which we can determine who were the miners, and there are no evidences of ancient habitations in that vicinity.

Lead ore from Howard county was presented to the Kansas Historical Society by Professor J. D. Parker, in December, 1870, and was analyzed by Professor W. H. Saunders of the State University, with the following result:

Sulphur	13 33
Lead	86.67
	100.00

The analysis will be seen to be satisfactory, but whether the ore exists in paying quantities is undetermined.

Geologists tell us that there is no probability that lead exists in any considerable quantities in Kansas; but it has often been asserted by friendly Indians that they knew of extensive deposits of lead ore. The Ottawas, who lately removed to the Indian Territory from Franklin county, were confident that within a half mile of a certain spring on their reservation, there is lead in abundance. I once had in my possession a very fine specimen of lead ore, which an Indian of the Sac and Fox tribe asserted that he found on their reservation in Osage county, but the location he would not point out. Uneducated Indians believe that the Great Spirit will be angry if they reveal to white men any mineral deposits.

TIN.

Concerning this metal, Professor Mudge holds the following language: "Frequent reports have been in circulation that this, usually rare mineral, is found

NEW EPISCOPAL FEMALE SEMINARY, TOPEKA.

here. Several fine specimens of rich protoxyd of tin have been, on several occasions, produced by the Indians. As their statements concerning them were, in some cases, not true, it still remains an unsettled question whether they originated in the State.

* * * * *

"Until we find some eruptive rocks breaking through the recent strata, we must conclude that it is not native to Kansas. The western portion of the State, however, is so far a geological terra-incognita that it is possible that some local igneous action may have brought tin to the surface."

ALUM.

On page 28 of Professor Mudge's report occurs the following:

"We have noticed the presence of alum in quite a number of places in the State. At Zeandale it is found in small crystals; also, at several points on Mill creek, in Wabaunsee county. In the eastern part of T. 4, R. 10, west, it is found in connection with a seam of lignite coal. It is associated with native sulphur. A similar deposit is seen on Chapman creek, in T. 11, R. 2, east, about twenty miles west of Fort Riley, with the additional associate of salt-petre or nitrate of potash. It is also found in various places on the southern side of the Smoky Hill, from Salina eastward, over a tract of fifteen or twenty miles in extent. It exists in a sufficient quantity to make a commercial commodity, whenever capital and labor shall become more abundant in our State.

"In England, alum is manufactured from alum slate and analagous minerals, in which it becomes necessary to calcine and pulverize the material before the alum can be extracted. But in our deposits the article is so free that the manufacture will be much more easy and economical."

HYDRAULIC CEMENT.

Professor Swallow says: "Limestone suitable for hydraulic cement is abundant."

From Professor Mudge I quote as follows:

"A bed of brown hydraulic limestone was worked, about eight or ten years ago, by the late Dr. F. Barker, at his farm four miles northwest of Lawrence. Not being familiar with the manufacture of the article, he probably did not succeed as well as a person of experience. Still he made a good cement, which was used by various builders at Lawrence, for cisterns and other similar purposes. Many of the cisterns are still in use, with the cement in good condition. They show a durability which compares favorably with the best Kentucky cements now sold in our State. Dr. Barker was intending to pursue the business more systematically and extensively, when his death closed the operations. No one has worked the bed since his decease. His experiment, so far as it was tried, was perfectly satisfactory, and the stratum has all the qualities of a good hydraulic cement. This bed of hydraulic limestone extends across the country over Leavenworth and Atchison counties, and also southwesterly, nearly, if not quite, to the southerly bounds of the State, and probably it will be found to retain good cement properties in the whole of that extensive area."

It is probably the same bed which has but recently been opened in Cowley county, near the Arkansas River, which I am informed produces an excellent article of cement.

PETROLEUM.

This oil flows to the surface through the fractures

in sandstone rock in many places. The Indians from earliest times, have collected it from springs and used it for medicinal purposes. Whether it exists in sufficient quantities to furnish an article of commerce, remains unsettled.

Considerable expenditures have been made in borings in Miami county, and oil in quantities was obtained, but the final results were unsatisfactory.

Professor Mudge says:

"It is found at so many different places, that it is reasonable to suppose that a large body may exist below. The nature of the clay shales which compose a large portion of the deposits for seven or eight hundred feet below the surface, would not readily allow it to come up, if it were there. Should it be found in paying quantities it is probable that it will be below the coal measures. No one should invest in the business more than he could afford to lose without embarrassment. The question cannot be considered as settled without numerous borings to a depth of eight hundred or one thousand feet."

PAINTS.

Professor Swallow says: "There are several beds of purple shales in the coal measures which appear to have all the properties of a good outside paint. One of these beds has been used at Parkville and other places, and found beautiful, durable, and fire proof when used in thick coats. The bed thus proved is over ten feet thick, and crops out in the bluff of the Missouri all the way from White Cloud to Wyandotte, and up the Kansas to Lawrence. It also appears southeast to Mound City. Other beds which appear equally valuable crop out on the Big Blue, the Neosho, the Cottonwood and the Verdigris."

At Fort Scott, twenty-five miles south of Mound City, a vein or bed of paint was discovered after the above was written. This is a few feet below the surface, and is extensively used in that locality. It is also coming to be an article of export to other places, and gives good satisfaction. There is no room for doubt that in Kansas, awaiting development, there is material for making a fire proof and water proof paint for roofs, as well as for walls and fences.

Learning of a deposit of paint at Osage City on the Atchison, Topeka and Santa Fe Railroad, I addressed a letter of inquiry to one of the principal citizens of the place, Mr. John F. Dodds, and received the following reply, dated March 1st, 1871 :

"The mineral paint at our place is ochre. The vein or bed is about three fourths of a mile in width, one mile or more in length, and twelve feet six inches thick. It lies from five to eight feet below the surface, and upon a strata of solid limestone rock, varying in thickness from two to three feet. The pigment has been analyzed by Dr. W. H. Saunders, of Lawrence, and by Dr. Murray, of Dayton, Ohio, with the following results, viz:

Ochre	98
Alum	1
Lime	1
	100

"I send you the following figures, taken from accurate measurement of the strata underneath our town:

Section of 34 *feet* 8 *inches below the surface.*

Soil and earth	5	feet		
Ochre	12	"	6	inches
Limestone	2	"	6	"
Clay and Shale	3	"		
Limestone	3	"		
Slate and Shale	3	"		
Coal	1	"	8	"
Fire Clay	4	"		
Total	34	"	8.	"

CLAY FOR BRICK.

Notwithstanding the abundant supply of excellent stone for building purposes, many people prefer to build of brick. There is a plentiful supply of clay for brick making, and it is often so intermixed with sand as to be ready for tempering and molding. With clay and timber convenient to the house site, a farmer may, with the aid of an experienced brick maker, and two or three cheap hands, burn a kiln of brick at a small cost for the construction of his buildings. When sold at kilns, the prices range from eight dollars to ten dollars per thousand, in the season for the business, but the supply is always exhausted before the demand ceases in the fall, and prices become somewhat higher.

LIME BURNING.

From what has been said of the configuration of the country, and of the location of stone quarries, it will readily be seen that it is little trouble to make quick lime. Any of the limestone rock makes lime, but the strongest quality obtained from common limestone, is made from the darker layers. All the varieties of magnesian limestone, make strong and white lime.

Having selected a good quarry, and one need not go far to find it, an excavation of the desired size is made in the side of the hill, all quarries being upon the edge of a declivity. This opening is walled up from the bottom, and an open arch five or six feet high is left on the lower side, where the fuel is put in and the lime taken out when burned. The top of the kiln is drawn partly together to cause a draft. Rock are then laid up roughly on the bottom in the form of an arch, to contain fuel, and upon this rough arch the stones for lime are thrown from the top, until the kiln is full. Either wood or coal is used for fuel, and a brisk fire is kept up three or four days, after which the lime is ready for use. When coal is used it is mixed with the stone, instead of being placed under it, as is the case with wood. The lime thus burned is somewhat injured chemically, owing to the presence of more or less sulphur in the coal. To obviate this, a patent coal kiln is used, wherein water can be applied in such manner as to counteract the effects of the sulphur. If left in the kiln the top and entrance should be covered to keep out water. Lime long exposed to the air re-absorbs carbonic acid, which was thrown off by burning, and becomes limestone again, in a finely pulverized state.

In slacking lime, add to it at once enough water to cover it, and stir it constantly until it is slacked, when it should be of the cousistency of cream. If only a little water is added at a time it injures the quality of the lime.

Fresh lime is largely used by many eastern farmers, and especially in the famous and fertile Shenandoah Valley of Virginia, as a top dressing for the soil, five to fifteen bushels per acre being applied about every ten years. That valley is in a limestone formation. There is little doubt that much of our Kansas soil would be benefited by the application of lime. For whatever purposes needed, whether mechanical or agricultural, it is abundant in Kansas. It sells at the kiln for about twenty cents per bushel and with a good profit to the burner.

WESTERN KANSAS AND THE BUFFALO GRASS.

The western third of Kansas now demands our particular attention—the portion so lately included in that mythical region, "The Great American Desert." I am firmly persuaded that no portion of the

United States east of the Rocky Mountains deserves this title, for the simple reason that there is no desert. Wherever buffalo, antelope, and deer graze and fatten, there domestic cattle may also graze and fatten, and it is known that these animals have from

BAPTIST CHURCH, LEAVENWORTH.

time immemorial, ranged in countless numbers in all the region called the plains. Certainly it is a misnomer to speak of any country as a desert, that will, by a few months grazing, so fatten cattle that they actually compete in Eastern markets with stall-fed cattle. This may be done in all that country alluded to. It is true that there is a great difference in the amount of feed produced per acre in different localities, but even the poorest of all this vast area produces scattering tufts of buffalo grass.

The treeless expanse called "The Plains," sweeps along the base of the Rocky Mountains, two or three hundred miles in width at its southern extremity, and gradually widening as it extends fifteen hundred miles northward into British America. On most of this vast area, the grass is not simply scattering, but is a continuous mat of fine herbage, three to six inches high.

The best grass growing in Texas is called mesquit, and produces two or three times as much feed per acre as the buffalo grass. Near and among the Rocky Mountains, is gramma grass, and also a variety called bunch grass. On a portion of the plains is a grass called small, or bastard mesquit. All these grasses have a curled leaf. The name, buffalo grass, is given to all grasses of this kind in Kansas. Some think the true buffalo grass to be a distinct variety from the small mesquit, and others claim that they are identical. The buffalo grass spreads on the ground somewhat in the manner of a strawberry vine, and its leaf curls close to the ground, so that it looks more like a bed of bleached moss than it does like common grass. Its seed grows on one side of a delicate stem. This grass is extremely sweet, and the more so the nearer its roots.

It is true that there are considerable alkali tracts on the plains, (but not in Kansas, according to the best information which I can obtain,) where grazing is not practicable, by reason of bad water, but not for lack of a fertile soil, because, by irrigation, alkali lands, as in Utah, become extremely productive. Most varieties of these grasses are in a growing condition from early spring until autumn, when, during the beautiful weather of that season, they cure upon the stalk. Thus they retain their nutritious qualities through the dry winters, which invariably bless the herdsman and his herd in these regions. Other varieties are green in Western Kansas during the winter months, as the attentive reader can learn from the letter of Rev. L. Sternberg, of Fort Harker.

Add to this sufficient evidence, the indisputable fact that cattle in vast herds, not of hundreds simply, but of thousands in number, are to-day grazing upon buffalo grass, and that not alone in Kansas, but also in Colorado, Nebraska and Wyoming.

Travelers who pass through Kansas upon the Kansas Pacific Railway, enter upon the Buffalo grass region after riding about two hundred miles through the fat meadows, the luxuriant corn fields, and the vigorous wild grasses of Eastern Kansas, and as they come in sight of the brown and shriveled buffalo grass, it seems indeed contemptible. It is very true that vast herds of buffalo are seen, extending for miles in either direction, sometimes huddled in distant masses which resemble low islands in the sea, or, at other times, are so numerous and so persistent in keeping to their course, that the engineer is obliged to stop his train and give them the track, until they cross it in their line of march. The traveler also sees the dressed carcasses of buffalo and antelope at every station, which are as fat as stall-fed beef; and yet many people return from the trip and talk about the "Buffalo Grass Desert." Who would suppose that buffalo would return to a "desert" for feed year after year? nay, that they would stay there the year around, as thousands annually do stay in the valleys of the Republican, Solomon, Smoky Hill and Arkansas rivers, and their tributaries? Many an eastern farmer would gladly turn the flocks and herds on to this desert, which crop the low grass in his high priced pastures, or during six months of winter, eat the hay he has so laboriously garnered.

I think the higher and drier portions of Western Kansas is in some respects superior as a winter stock range. The less rain falls upon the grass, the richer it will be. This is not a theoretical opinion. Stock that ranged on grass during the hard winter of 1860-'61, which succeeded the famous "dry season," came out in the spring in better order than usual. The grass was short, but very nutritious—having cured on the ground. The time is not distant when the western portion of the State, one hundred by two hundred miles in extent, will be selected as the choice pasture land of the continent. Its altitude of twenty-five hundred to thirty-five hundred feet above the ocean level, makes the climate all that could be be desired. It is plentifully watered for stock purposes, by springs and running streams, whose water is palatable to the herds and flocks, and upon the banks are small timber growths, and high bluffs for shelter. There are also stone quarries, from which houses may be cheaply constructed for the herdsmen.

I think it true that everywhere in Kansas, a little hay ought to be put up as a safeguard against light snows, accompanied by wind, which may render grazing difficult for a few days at a time. Such snows occur every two or three years, in all the region we have been considering; but are much less severe in Kansas than farther north. Whenever they occur, great herders expect to lose more or less stock. It is one of the chances they take, and the aggregate results for a series of years prove that with all the risks, the business is still very profitable. But in every part of Kansas there is grass in abundance to make hay. The wide bottoms afford from one to three tons per acre, even at the western limits of the State, and on ground as smooth as a floor, it is little trouble to put up hay with machinery. Perhaps half the year it would stand untouched, while stock fattened on the buffalo grass. But it is better to provide against contingencies, and if not used, it will keep over in good condition, if well stacked. The estimated amount that ought to be put up per head in the buffalo grass region, is from four hundred to six hundred pounds. Among scores of experienced stock men, with whom I compared notes upon this subject, none set it higher than the latter figures.

John S. Chisum, one of the most noted stock dealers and breeders of Texas, a man who handles cattle by the ten thousand head, said: "For Kansas, from four to five hundred pounds." Major H. Shanklin, of Lawrence, who has wintered cattle in the Arkansas Valley several seasons, said: "Five hundred pounds, and it may rot down unfed every other year." Rev. L. Sternberg, who lives at Fort Harker, on the Kansas Pacific Railway, said: "Five or six hundred pounds, and probably not half that amount will be fed out." Nor is this precaution desirable for Kansas alone. In Colorado, prudent persons provide a little hay for their stock, and think that it pays them a profit to do so, and with the rearing of improved breeds this will be an acknowledged necessity. Large herders with thousands of cattle, do not consider the loss of a few score head of cheap Texas stock as a matter of importance. But when each bullock comes to be worth fifty or seventy-five dollars, the case will be different.

The foregoing was written in December, 1870. It is now April, 1871, and we have passed through a very severe winter, snow having lain on the ground longer than ever before known. During this winter many thousand head of cattle have fed on buffalo grass and winter grasses, without any hay or grain whatever. The result has been surprising to all.

Among Texas cattle, or stock bred from them, (and there is little other stock in the buffalo grass region,) there has been less loss than in the more eastern or southern portion of the State, where they were fed on hay or hay and corn. The cattle thus wintered will soon fatten upon the fresh grass. It is natural for this stock to get its own living on the range, and they do not do well on corn the first year they are brought from Texas. Next to their native range

WIRE SUSPENSION BRIDGE, OTTAWA.

a field of standing corn stalks, after the ears have been plucked, seems the best suited to their wants. Sheep have also done well in Western Kansas this winter, on grass alone. I am convinced that herders, with several hundred or thousands of cattle, will do better to seek some of the many *canyons*, or sheltering bluffs, or timber patches, to be found in the buffalo grass region, with plenty of water, and graze stock all the season, than to cut hay for them.

The loss in the former case will not equal the additional expense in the latter case. Small stock raisers and farmers will undoubtedly do well to put up a little hay.

In short, Western Kansas and its buffalo grass offers the *best advantages in this State, or in any State for stock raising*. I do not advise people to rush into that region—that is, to the remote high prairies where nothing grows but buffalo grass—who are destitute of means, but with a little capital to invest in stock, a living is certain and easy. There is certainly no need for any to suffer for meat in that region, for buffalo meat is toothsome and nutritious, and to be had for the killing, while the peculiar waxy fat furnishes to the hardy frontiersman a sweet and healthful substitute for bread.

The amount of feed on a given space of buffalo grass, is also much greater than most people suppose. Even Horace Greeley, who was the first man of prominence in the east, to recognize the value of the trans-Missouri country, speaks of grazing one bullock to each quarter section, (160 acres.) But the most intelligent of experienced observers, reckon from three to five acres of buffalo grass as furnishing as much feed as one acre of our best prairie grasses, such as are found in eastern Kansas and in Illinois.

In confirmation of what has been said, I take pleasure in presenting the following letters, relating respectively to the northern, central and southern portions of Western Kansas. All are written by gentlemen well known in their respective localities. The first is from a farmer, Mr. A. B. Warner, in northwestern Kansas:

"REPUBLIC COUNTY, KANSAS,
November 28, 1870.

Mr. C. C. Hutchinson:

DEAR SIR: I send you a few facts concerning the northern part of the State, or at least that portion of it which has come under my personal observation. The portion I shall refer to, is chiefly watered by the Republican River and its tributaries. These streams have many beautiful mill sites, and we think here it would be hard to find a portion of prairie country more highly favored in respect to water, notwithstanding it is in 'drouthy Kansas.'

"About eighty miles west of this county, a tributary takes in to the Republican, called Prairie Dog, and a beautiful stream it is, having quite a belt of timber along its banks. Its bottoms are wide and fertile, and all who see it are in no wise sparing of their praise. There is yet little or no settlement along the stream, and none on the adjacent prairies, but there is strong talk of a settlement there in the spring. White Rock is another tributary of the Republican and enters it about ten miles from where the last named stream crosses the western line of Kansas from Nebraska and in range five west. On its lovely bank, on lands the most beautiful eyes ever rested upon, we have taken up our abodes. Its line towards the head is a trifle south of west, and it is about sixty miles long. It has quite an abundance of timber, though not quite so much as Prairie Dog, and besides the stream is not so large. The waters of the latter run the year round, while those of White Rock, in very dry weather, will sometimes cease to run, though at all times it contains a sufficiency of pure water for stock. Its bottoms are very fertile, as well as the adjoining prairies. The former are all taken for thirty miles from its mouth, but of the latter there are thousands and tens of thousands of acres of as rich and beautiful prairie lands as ever graced a western State. The old inhabitants say they can get a living here easier than in any other place they ever saw.

Yours respectfully,

A. B. WARNER."

The next letter is from Rev. Dr. L. Sternberg, a Lutheran clergyman of high standing, who went to Western Kansas for his health, and to open farms with his sons. He formerly resided in New York, and afterward in Ohio and Northern Illinois, and is consequently familiar with the best dairy regions in the United States. I call especial attention to the testimony he adduces as to the character of this region for

Dairying.

"FORT HARKER, December 10, 1870.

Mr. C. C. Hutchinson:

DEAR SIR: You desire to know if the Plains are well adapted to butter and cheese making, and also my method. In replying to the first inquiry, it may be proper to say that I am not prepared to speak of the Plains generally. Portions of them may be barren and destitute of water and of natural shelter for stock. My remarks are intended to apply more especially to Ellsworth county, the eastern limit in this part of the State of the buffalo grass region. Whether a country is well adapted for stock and dairy purposes, depends upon its grasses, water and climate.

"We have both winter and summer grasses. Our winter grasses are such as keep green, and grow somewhat during the winter, especially in sheltered places in ravines and near the banks of streams. They come forward very early in the spring so as to afford good pasturage, in this region generally about the middle of March. The principal variety ripens about the first of June, and resembles what we used to call the early June grass in New York. When green, it is sweet and tender, and cattle eat it with avidity.

"Our summer grasses may be divided into two classes, consisting of such as are only fit for grazing, and such as are also suitable to be cut for hay. The term buffalo grass, includes the gramma grass, or the curled mesquit, both of them remarkably nutritious, even when ripened and dry, and affording almost as good pasturage in winter as in summer, but too short to be cut for hay. The blue joint is our principal grass for hay. It is the latest of our grasses in coming forward in the spring, only appearing about the time when our winter grasses are beginning to ripen. We have at present little more of this grass than is required for hay; but I am sorry to say that it is slowly but surely supplanting the buffalo grass. The milk produced from these grasses is remarkably rich, and our cows have access to no plants giving their milk an unpleasant flavor, except that late in the fall they sometimes eat a species of wild sage, giving it a bitter taste.

"Good water is a prime necessity for a stock and dairy country. It should be running water. Stagnant water affects the quality of the milk injuriously. Water drawn by hand involves too much labor, and is too uncertain a reliance. Our river water, and that flowing from our numerous springs, is most excellent for stock.

"Our climate is of a medium character. We are subject to occasional storms, when cattle need some natural or artificial shelter, and it may be some hay. Usually, however, they graze upon the open prairie, in winter as in summer. Thus far I have not been required to feed my cattle more than about a dozen times during the winter, and they reach the spring in fine order, unless they should be pulled down somewhat by some special cause, such as coming in too early. In summer our climate is not warmer than in more northern latitudes. However warm it may be during the day, our nights are invariably cool and refreshing. The heats of summer, therefore, interfere but little with butter and cheese making, to those who have a suitable place for the purpose, and I know of no reason why we may not compete succesfully both as to quality and quantity with the dairymen of any part of our country.

"In the manufacture of butter, I am careful as to the condition of my cream, not leaving it to stand too long. I use the dash churn. I am careful to work out all the buttermilk, and yet not destroy the grain of the butter. This requires both experience and skill. The salt which should be of the purest kind, and about an ounce to the pound of butter, should be thoroughly incorporated with the butter, and dissolve in it. If the cream be too warm in churning, the butter will be of an inferior quality, and will readily soften in warm weather. The proper temperature is from fifty-six to sixty degrees. The cooler the cream, the longer the butter is in coming, but the better the butter.

Yours truly,

L. STERNBERG."

At the last annual February meeting of the Farmers' Institute, held at the State Agricultural College, in Manhattan, Rev. Dr. Sternberg was present with his friend and neighbor of Ellsworth county, Mr. Long, who is engaged in the cheese business. Mr. Long said:

"Kansas is looked upon as a great beef-producing State, and we can certainly make as good cheese here as in Ohio, and can do it with less expense. Our cows cost less, and they net more. In Ohio it costs twenty-five dollars a year to keep a cow, in Kansas less than one-half that. Cheese in Ohio brings twelve and a half cents per pound; mine brings eighteen and a half. Good cheese *can* be made in Kansas. Dairy farming is destined to become one of the most interesting and profitable branches of industry in Kansas."

Some one then asked, "How much cheese can you make from one gallon of milk?" Mr. Long answered, "In Ohio, one pound from one gallon, or *ten pounds* of milk; here, one pound from *eight and two-thirds pounds* of milk. This is the quantity from the common cow; from the Alderney, we can make more."

Dr. Reynolds asked, "Do cows give as much milk here as there?" Mr. Long thought they did, full as much. "*The buffalo grass produced as much, and richer milk, than the tame grass.*"

OTTAWA UNIVERSITY.

Dr. Sternberg said, "our season being longer we can have *two months more for butter and cheese making.*"

Mr. Long was asked about exporting his cheese, but he has no need; he finds a ready market for all his in the State. Also about rennets. He sends to Utica, New York, and gets them at thirty cents, when they will cost fifty cents if bought here.

The next letter is from Mr. Ernst Hohneck, a surveyor who has resided in Western Kansas about fourteen years, and is entirely familiar with the country he talks about. This letter throws light upon the "desert" question. There has been great inquiry for that desert for several years, and of late it has come to be believed that the whole account of "a desert" was a stupendous humbug of ancient geographers, but there has long been talk in scientific quarters about the "sand hills of western Kansas," which certainly must have had some foundation in fact. I have occasionally met a man who had seen them, but could get no precise information as to their location until the following letter came to hand. After describing various counties in that region, and showing that all are possessed of good water and good soil, with considerable quantities of timber, and coal opened of fair quality for fuel, he proceeds:

"Rice county, south of Ellsworth, through which runs the Arkansas River and several tributaries, is, with the exception of timber, which is rather scarce, a most beautiful county, and contains, I believe, a greater per centage of tillable land, than any other county in the State I know of. The southeast part is already somewhat settled, and a colony from Ohio is expected to settle on Plum Creek next spring. Cow Creek is also in this county. Around Fort Zarah, in Barton county, near the mouth of that fine stream where the Big Walnut empties into the Arkansas, the nucleus of quite a settlement is now forming, and about two hundred families are to settle along the River and Walnut next spring. The advance of a German colony, about ten families, settled eight miles above Zarah last spring, and raised quite a crop of corn, with pumpkins, melons, etc., without end. I have not a doubt but that the bottoms of the Arkansas River, will turn out to be prodigious corn land.

"Walnut Creek Valley runs in a westerly direction for over a hundred miles, with abundance of timber and water, and as fine bottoms as a man wants to see. The only drawback to the settlement of that part of our beautiful State, may be Indian difficulties.

"In conclusion, let me give you the result of my observations during a residence of fifteen years in the State, the greater part of which I spent in the western part.

"The story of the American Desert, as far as it relates to that portion of Kansas that lays north of the Arkansas River, is a myth, and never had any foundation. That "belt of land," beyond which, according to early histories of Kansas, the Desert commenced, exists only in imagination. True, there is a range of sandhills, from one to two miles wide, on the west side of the Little Arkansas, as far north as the mouth of Jarvis Creek, emptying into Cow Creek, and also another narrow range of sandhills on the west side of Cow Creek, from the Plum Butes, on the old Santa Fe Road, extending, with intermissions, about ten miles north. But the land west of these hills is just as good as east of it.

"I suppose the idea of this desert originated in this way: During that season when the buffalo roam north in immense numbers, they eat the whole country so closely that it looks to the casual observer entirely bare, and devoid of vegetation. Buffalo and even horses, will find sustenance on this very ground, it being the nature of the buffalo grass to be continually growing, and the part next to the ground, almost in it, being the most nutritous part, and very sweet; horses, which are used to the plains, will graze on this very ground, when loose, in preference to places, where the grass has not been pastured. Another peculiarity of the buffalo grass is, that it only grows in packed ground, and dies out as soon as the buffalo quits the country, and the action of the rains and frosts loosens the soil. After the buffalo have left a portion of the country for good, in a few years single stools of blue stem grass will appear, which increase in size from year to year, until the whole country, which grew once the short buffalo grass, is covered with blue stem, and then has all the appearance of an agricultural country. I have watched this transformation ever since 1855, and it is a fact and no theory. Thousands of tons of prairie hay can be cut now, where ten years ago nothing but buffalo grass grew. Whoever opens a farm in a buffalo grass region, needs to plow his land *deep*, from *six to eight inches at least*, so as to prepare it at once for crops. And all this great region in the western part of the State, will be thus transformed shortly, and will be found to be the granary of the west."

Upon receipt of this valuable letter I wrote to the author requesting him to explain why he confined his remarks to the region north of the Arkansas River, in showing that the country was generally good, and that a few square miles of sand hills had been magnified into a boundless "desert." In reply the following letter came to hand:

"When I spoke rather negatively of the country south of Arkansas river, I had in my mind a pear shaped tract of land, with its stem end near Fort Dodge, and the opposite about south of the mouth of Cow creek, which empties into the Arkansas in Rice county, with a width at its broadest part (south of Pawnee Rock, seventeen miles west of Zarah) of about sixty miles, which consists of a series of sand-hills, naked sandy flats, and bunch grass prairie. This part is entirely destitue of timber, but in most parts well watered, and having considerable salt water branches running through it.

"The Arkansas river is also, with the exception of a strip of about fourteen miles running east from Fort Zarah, destitute of timber from below the mouth of Cow creek to the west line of the State,

LIBERTY
HALL.

and beyond to near Fort Lyon. The Atchison, Topeka & Santa Fe Railroad has been surveyed and located to Fort Dodge, which will open these wide and fertile bottoms to settlement. The sandy district, however, spoken of above, will be a great grazing country, as the grass on it is very nutritious, and the configuration of the country affording a great deal of shelter to stock in the winter. South of this district lays a beautiful country, along the tributaries of the little Red river, or Red Fork of the Arkansas. Mulberry, Turkey, Medicine Lodge, Bluff creek, etc., are among these creeks. The soil is here red in all its shades, and every little thaw or rain, will color the streams red.

"Two years ago this winter, I found the bottoms covered with the tallest blue stem grass. A great deal of winter grass, which we generally call June grass, grows also here. The country is also timbered with Cottonwood, Cedar in great quantity on the bluffs, Mulberry, Elm, Walnut, Oak, Hackberry, and on the South Fork, with China tree. I found bodies of timber containing from forty to eighty acres. Rock is very scarce here; the deepest *canyon*, as well as the highest bluffs, are devoid of it. In my opinion, it will not be very long before this country will be the great winter quarters of the stock men of Western Kansas. As for shelter, there is nothing that will surpass it in these parts.

"Since my last, I learned that about fifty claims are taken on Walnut creek, and the Arkansas, in the vicinity of Fort Zarah. So the Star of Empire is moving westward at a lively rate. It is some satisfaction to contemplate, that in fifteen years civilization has conquered two hundred and fifty miles of wilderness.

Yours truly,

ERNST HOHNECK."

Here is the new geography at last. Here is the "G. A. D." reduced in its extent to a small area, and then, still worse for the fictions of the past, even this sand hill district *"will be a great grazing country, as the grass on it is very nutritious, and the configuration of the country affords a great deal of shelter to stock in the winter."*

At last we have "corralled" the "Great American Desert," and we find it to be a well watered, pear shaped pasture field, good for summer and especially excellent for winter grazing.

Others whom I have lately seen, who have been through this region, assure me that it greatly abounds in wild fruits—berries of different kinds, and several varieties of large and luscious plums and grapes. The sand hills north of the Arkansas, described by Mr. Hohneck, also produce an abundance of wild fruit and small scrub oaks.

And yet it is easy to see how this fiction went abroad. All the sand hills spoken of by Mr. Hohneck, lie in the path of the old Santa Fe wagon road over which ten years ago two or three million dollars worth of goods were annually carried in wagons, and over which a stage coach ran. This road has been traveled for many years. Thirty years ago, teams from Chihuahua, in Mexico, hauled goods to that place, by this route, from St. Louis. Of course there was truth enough in the sandy part of the story, to account for the errors of the miserable geographers. It is also true that as we near the base of the Rocky Mountains we enter upon a country covered with what seems to be a bed of sand and coarse gravel. At what point one leaves the soil of Western Kansas and enters the sandy regions of Colorado, I am unable to say, having only passed over the country in the night, by railroad. It is probable, however, that the transition is a gradual one, the finer portions of the sand and soil from the mountain bases having been washed down toward the Missouri River. Even this sand of Colorado, however, is covered with our never-failing buffalo grass, and in the poorest localities, where this is partially crowded out by the Cactus, heavy crops are always grown by irrigation. Mr. Hohneck further explains the barren appearance of the plains by showing how the buffalo eats the grass down close to the ground. The sweetness of the lower stalk of this grass is apparent to the taste of one who chews it. The little wild prairie dogs live chiefly on the lower stalks and roots of the buffalo grass, and when they have pulled it all in one locality, they move their village to fresher fields. It is believed by frontiersmen that wherever prairie dogs establish their habitations, water may be found at a moderate depth by digging. The theory is reasonable, and is probably not less true than the infallible test on more eastern prairies, by which a crawfish hole may always be followed to never failing water.

In the first letter of Mr. Hohneck, an important suggestion is made about plowing these lands *deep*, the deeper the better. It is not simply that the rains may be caught and retained in a deep bed of soil, and that rootlets may find nutriment deep in the moist earth, when they would dry out in a shallow soil, but the action of the atmosphere, and of frost, is desirable to bring this hard earth into a proper condition for producing crops. Not that the earth is difficult to plow, or stiff and heavy like a clay soil, but it has been beaten by the storms of centuries, and trodden under foot by millions of buffalo, until it is so compact that air cannot enter it, and rain can hardly penetrate its surface.

Among the most important objects accomplished by the plowing of any soil, is the exposure of its particles to the air, in order that certain chemical changes may take place, which induce the growth

5*

of vegetation. Especially do these soils of Western Kansas need to be plowed deep, that they may have the benefit of this ameliorating process. Here the STEAM PLOW is eventually to win its triumphs. On those broad fields, free from sloughs and miry places, there are possibilities open to inventors and large farmers in this direction, which are forbidden by the small lots, or stony land, or heavy clay soil, or deep mud, of eastern farms, or of other prairie States.

THE CATTLE BUSINESS.

The *New York Tribune*, of January 6, 1871, says: "The belt of beef supply is receding year by year. In 1866 only 44 head of Texas cattle reached this market. * * The chief supplies of beef already come from regions west of the Wabash, and south of the Ohio. If this is true of 1870, what may be expected in 1875, or even 1873? * * Evidently it is of no avail for the farmer east of the Wabash to contend with those vast plains, covered with the most nutritious grasses. The herdsman there can produce a three-year-old steer that will dress 550 pounds, as cheaply as the former can fatten a spring pig."

It is easy to see why the cattle business cannot so readily be overdone as most other kinds of business. By the employment of sufficient capital and labor, manufacturers may in a few months, flood the market with goods and ruin the business. The necessities or fashions of the day may also change, and fail the manufacturer. The farmers of the country are only limited in the amount of grain they raise, by the labor they choose to employ in seed time and harvest, and for this reason, in connection with the uncertainties of the weather, grain raisers in all parts of the world are liable to extreme fluctuations in the price of their products.

But it is evident that the supply of beef cattle is limited by the natural increase, and it is also evident that it will not soon become unfashionable to eat beef. Therefore it is that everywhere the cattle business is among the most secure and certain of all occupations. But it needs no argument to show that a region abounding in such grasses, as we have described, with a plentiful supply of stock water, in a healthy climate, and in a region traversed by

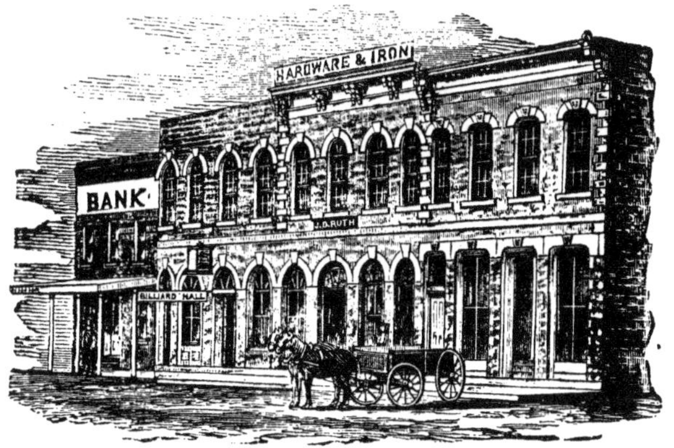

BLOCK IN HUMBOLDT.

railroads, furnishing competition in freights, *must distance all competitors in its attractions for stock raisers or dealers.*

The business in Kansas is already immense. There were during the year 1870, about 200,000 head of cattle shipped out of Kansas, of which number about 150,000 consisted of Texas cattle, part of which were direct from Texas, while the remainder had been herded a few months in this State. Estimating 150,000 Texas cattle all around, at $30 per head, including those wintered here, and we have a sum of $4,500,000. The native stock averaged $50 per head, making for 50,000 head $2,500,000, or a gross total of $7,000,000, which is probably as close an approximation as can be made of the business.

Texas cattle are descended from the Spanish cattle brought to America by the conquerors of Mexico, and the characteristics of the original stock have been hightened by their treatment and the climate in which they have been raised. No attempt is ever made to improve the stock by selecting breeders, and about the only attention a herd receives, is to brand the calves when young. They range at pleasure, summer and winter, in immense herds, and are only driven together by the swiftest horsemen or caught with the lasso. None, or very few, of the cows are reserved for milk, and no calves killed, and the increase of the herds is therefore much more rapid than in those countries where a large share of calves go to the butcher, or are killed before they are old enough for veal.

People sometimes talk of "Cherokee" cattle, and "Wichita mountain" cattle, and either confound them with Texas cattle, or class them as a distinct breed. They are cattle descended from the Texas stock, but have been crossed with northern stock, which before the war was driven extensively into the Indian Territory—called from its principal tribe, the "Cherokee country." These crosses show all grades of stock, and at once show how easy it is to improve the original long horned, long legged, gaunt, race-horse breed of Texas cattle. It is becoming a very popular practice in Kansas, particularly on the western and southern frontier, to purchase a herd of one or two year old Texas heifers, paying therefor from five to eight dollars per head, and cross them with the best bull the breeder can purchase. With a thorough bred or full blood short horn sire, the first cross is decidedly better than the common American stock. I will not stop to figure out the profits resulting from this business, with the advantages here presented.

The original Texas stock improves in this country —they broaden out and take on more flesh. This is undoubtedly owing to the climate, which is much more vigorous and bracing than their native plains. Yet, notwithstanding all that I have said, and much more of the same favorable sort, is true, there is a strong prejudice against Texas cattle, but *uniformly*, so far as I have observed, men who have dealt in this stock to any extent, and *all* who have bred from it, are favorably inclined toward it. At the same time nearly all are agreed that if a man have the means to buy all the cows he wishes to commence the business with, it is better to buy the best stock he can get, and then improve it as rapidly as possible.

Last fall, I met in Colorado John S. Chisum, of Fort Concho, Texas. Mr. Chisum is one of those companionable frontiersmen who has the best instincts of a gentleman, and yet prefers to broil his slice of beef on a stick before a camp fire, and wrap himself in a blanket on the open prairie with his saddle for a pillow, and all out doors for a bed room, rather than board at the Fifth Avenue Hotel. Now Chisum told me all about the "Texas cattle fever," and this is the story:

In their native condition the cattle range to please themselves. They get up and lie down; graze early and late; go to a salt lick for salt, or drink fresh water at pleasure, or if their appetite inclines, can browse on buds and bushes. By this life, they keep healthy and hearty and under such circumstances *never* have Texas fever, Spanish fever or any other fever or contageous disease. But in an evil hour for them, the owner decides to drive them north. A corrall or rail pen is built of great strength, but only large enough to hold the herd that is to be driven. Boys and men, mounted on swift horses, and armed with terrible whips, which in their hands crack like pistols, collect the trembling beasts, and holding them on a close range by day, pen them in the yard every night. From one to three months is occupied by this process, according to the size of the drove, or the means at the command of the drover. The owner of the drove is probably with it very little, or if with it he is probably indifferent as to its necessities. The result is, that during the time of preparing to move the drove north, it is confined on a limited range, watered at irregular times, entirely deprived of salt, at night confined in the close pen, which often is deep with mud, and generally the poor creatures are kept in a constant state of excitement and privation, totally unlike their former free and easy life.

By the time they are started on their journey they are falling off in flesh, and the drover hurries them forward with rapid marches, to get into market before they become too poor to sell. They go in droves of from 1,000 to 10,000 head, and upon the average one man in the saddle is required to each hundred head of cattle. On the "cattle trail," as the lines of travel are called, they have short feeding times, and close herding, and get no salt unless they cross a salt lick, (spots of earth where salt water oozes out and is evaporated, leaving salt upon the surface, to which all herbivorous animals resort, whether wild or tame, and with their tongues *lick* up the salt.) They often pass over considerable distances without water, and traveling in hot weather, and amid the dust raised by themselves, they become extremely thirsty, and upon approaching the narrow ford at which a stream is crossed, they rush in headlong haste to reach the water. At narrow streams the crowding of those in the rear sends the foremost out without a full drink, and the reckless, hasty drivers add to the general hurry and excitement.

The consequence of all this is, that the drove becomes feverish and diseased. Mr. Chisum says he can tell whether a drove is healthy or not, the moment he goes among them, not only by their general appearance, but especially by a peculiar smell emitted by those which have the Texas fever. He says he never had this disease in any drove he handled, because he took proper care of them, and the disease was never communicated by one of his droves to any other cattle, and he has taken many Texas cattle among northern cattle during the worst season of the year.

It is a peculiarity of this disease, that the cattle among which it originates do not die, but only those northern cattle with which they come in contact. It is also true that Texas cattle, after being wintered in this or any other northern region, are as liable to die with the Texas fever, if afterward exposed to it, as our finest northern stock. Cattle die with this disease, which have not been among the diseased Texas cattle, but only ranged upon ground and drank from water lately frequented by a diseased Texas drove. Cold weather destroys the influence of the disease and it is not communicated after heavy frosts come, and therefore the laws of Kansas do not permit Texas cattle to be driven into this State during the period between the first day of March and the first day of December of each year, and at no time are they permitted to be driven east of the 6th principal meridian, but they may be shipped through the State on railroads at any time.

Texas cattle are largely bought in the fall and kept through the winter, and until they fatten on the grasses of the succeeding summer when they are in fine condition for beef. Those who have only seen this stock immediately after its arrival from Texas, by the mode of driving that our friend Chisum describes, really know nothing about its quality. The remark of a blind man to whom a friend was boasting of a fine horse, is also applicable to these cattle: "Is your horse fat?" "Yes." "Then of course he looks well."

I quote from volume seven, Transactions of Illinois State Agricultural Society:

"Butchers tell us that Texas cattle are better for packing than ordinary western cattle, the meat being finer grained, richer, and more tender than the rough, coarse stock hitherto shipped from the west. As a matter of profit they are considerably ahead of native cattle. The hides are worth from fifteen to twenty per cent more, and the yield of tallow is far larger."

Some of the fattest cattle ever killed in this State were corn fed Texas steers, but they were brought here when young, and had wintered here two or three seasons, and become accustomed to our climate and grasses, and to eating corn.

Mr. Andrew Wilson, of Topeka, is one of our most successful dealers in Texas cattle, and he has kindly furnished me with many items about the business. He buys four and five year old steers in the fall, at about $22.50 per head, averaging 900 pounds. In winter he has kept about 300 head together, and in summer, 1000 to 2000 head. Summer and winter he provides one man and horse for every hundred head. It is very important to salt *freely* and let the stock have constant access to water. Heretofore he has wintered in Eastern Kansas, on prairie hay and corn stalks in the field, (the latter being the best) and a few bushels of corn per head. Hereafter he intends to graze his Texas cattle the year round in Western Kansas. Last winter he kept 3000 head and sold in September for

$4.25 per hundred, gross weight, the average being 1312 pounds (excepting 350 cows). Another party kept 1000 head, bought from the same Texas herd, and sold at the time Mr. Wilson did, and only received $40 per head, a difference on 1000 head of $15,760. This loss was caused solely by short feeding and lack of care. Last summer, Mr. Wilson's Texas cattle gained about 406 pounds per head on grass. He usually sells to buyers who come into the country. For fattening exclusively on grass, he prefers Texas cattle, but to feed on corn, he prefers native stock. Here are his figures:

1000 head good Texas steers at $20	$20,000
Interest upon same one year, at 10 per cent	2,000
Winter care in Eastern Kansas, with salt, feeding, etc,, at $10	10,000
Summer care salt, etc., at $3	3,000
Interest for six months on amount paid for care and feed, $13,000, at 10 per cent. per annum	650
Add 3 per cent for losses of cattle	600
	$36,250
Average weight 1300 pounds, at 4 cents gross, equal $52 per head.	
Sales of 970 head, at $52	50,440
Deduct total cost and interest	36,250
	$14,190

The above estimate puts all expenses at the highest figures. If the selling price falls below the above, of course the buying price for the fresh stock will decrease proportionally. In grazing through the season on buffalo grass, he estimates the entire cost for the year not to exceed six dollars per head, and while the losses will sometimes be greater, the profit will be much more than by keeping the cattle on hay and corn.

If a stock raiser have the capital he advises to buy good native heifers, but from his own observation he is satisfied that the first cross of Texas stock with Short Horn, makes a stock fully equal to our common cattle, and Texas heifers, which have their first calves in this country, and are subject to ordinary herding, become gentle and easily handled.

6

Mr. Wilson is a native of Ohio, and has lived in Sangamon county, Illinois. He considers, as do all who are familiar with it, that Kansas is the best stock State yet opened. Its unsurpassed wild grasses, and abundant streams, with gravelly or rocky bottoms, place it far ahead of the best portions of Illinois for grazing purposes. He has some of the finest stock in the State, among which is the

PUBLIC SCHOOL, POMONA.

Short Horn bull of which a life-like cut is given elsewhere.

Western farmers talk of *stall-feeding* cattle, when corn in the ear is thrown to them. They are also fed hay or permitted to run in standing cornstalks, from which the corn has been picked. Frequently the cornstalks are cut and put before them, ears and all. In either case it is desirable that there be two fields or yards, and fattening hogs are each day put in the yard occupied by the cattle, the day previously. Upon the farm of Lieut.-Governor Elder in Franklin county, I found the husked corn placed in troughs, conveniently elevated on legs, and th hogs running with the cattle. He thinks, after several years careful experiment, that he saves twenty-five bushels to each steer by husking his corn, instead of feeding in the shock. He fattens annually about 200 head, feeding them all they will eat for six months, which is about eighty bushels of corn each. Hay or corn fodder is also given. Corn is placed in the troughs twice a day, and all feeding is done with the strictest regularity. Feeding twenty to forty bushels to a steer, he deems, as do all experienced feeders, almost a waste, as they are not made good beef, and will not do any better on grass the next summer than cattle which have had but two or three bushels given them the last month of feeding time.

Four-year-old native steers in the fall are worth 3½ to 4 cents gross, weighing 1,300 to 1,400 pounds. They gain by six months feeding about 250 pounds, and sell for 6½ to 7 cents gross, in the spring when grass-fed cattle are not in the market. An equal number of hogs are put with the cattle, to take their waste and leavings, and the *net* profit on each hog is ten dollars. By this method his corn *nets* him above interest on capital invested, from 80 cents to $1.00 per bushel. The only shelter his fat cattle have from the wind, is a gentle bluff, upon the south side of which is his feeding ground.

I give below the annual average prices of beef cattle for six years, at the cattle market, Chicago, Illinois, taken from the report of the United States Commissioner of Agriculture, Hon. Horace Capron. The prices are per hundred pounds gross weight. It should be noted that the great range of prices for each year, results chiefly from the difference in quality of cattle. It is always bad management to send poor cattle to market:

Prices of beef cattle in Chicago, Illinois, per hundred, gross weight.

1864	$2.56 to $5.72	1867	$3.52 to 8.02
1865	2.94 to 8.46	1868	3.41 to 8.10
1866	3.53 to 7.72	1869	3.79 to 7.66

Average price for six years, $3.24 to $7.61. The average expense of shipment per head, from the Missouri River to Chicago, is about five dollars.

Arrangements have been perfected by which it is expected to send fresh beef and buffalo to New York and other eastern cities from Kansas, during this summer, in Rankin's Patent Refrigerator cars, an invention of one of our citizens, Mr. T. L. Rankin, of Lyndon, Osage county. Experimental trips were made last year with eminent success. The car is nearly air tight, and contains ice, and beef in quarters can be sent in perfect order, at less rates than when shipped alive, as thirty head can be carried, while but eighteen live bullocks usually go in a car. Meat was carried 100 hours in one of these cars, from July 25 to August 1st, 1870, at a temperature of 50 to 55 degrees. The walls are composed of fifteen separate and tight partitions, made of wood and paper, with spaces between.

The *Hearth and Home*, of New York City, for February 4, 1871, contains an illustrated article upon this subject, showing that our exhaustless meat supply is to be carried to the door of our eastern friends.

A new class of stock cars are also put on to railroads this year for the first time, called Steel's palace stock cars. In these cars, cattle are watered and fed while in transit, and the time to New York or any other distant point is less than half that required under the old system of transporting live stock.

The foundations are being laid for giving Kansas

a reputation, as to the quality of its stock, equaled only by the profit with which it is reared.

Many very fine breeding animals have been brought to this State at great expense to their owners. Among those who have considerable herds of thorough-bred and full blood Short Horn cattle, are Judge N. L. Chaffe & Sons, Manhattan; Andrew Wilson, Topeka; John Inlow, Olathe; I. N. Insley, Oskaloosa; Wm. S. Pickrell, Ottawa; Mr. Moler, of Anderson county. Among those with thorough-bred or full blood Jersey cattle, are, I. S. Kalloch, Lawrence; E. A. Smith, Lawrence; Rev. Winfield Scott, Leavenworth, and others. Hon. S. C. Pomeroy, United States Senator, also has upon his farm at Muscotah, some thorough-bred Holstein cattle, which are famous for combining the qualities of good milkers, docility, size, and a readiness to take on fat.

All those gentlemen mentioned above, and many others, have fine herds of swine, including fine stock of all the best breeds; Berkshire, Essex, Poland China, Suffolks, Chester White, etc. Alfred Gray, Secretary of Kansas State Agricultural Society, has upon his farm at Wyandotte, probably the finest lot of Berkshires in the west. He has visited all the breeders of note in the United States and the Canadas, and has purchased the best animals he could find. He has made this business a speciality for several years, with eminent success.

THE SHEEP BUSINESS.

Perhaps there is no branch of ordinary husbandry at which one should serve a longer apprenticeship before entering upon it for himself, than the raising of sheep. Sheep must have care and attention to thrive anywhere, and it is not advisable for men, or for boys as has often been the case in Kansas,

S. W. CORNER SECOND AND DELAWARE STREETS, LEAVENWORTH.

who are utterly ignorant of the business to commence it with a large flock.

The cattle business is so easily learned, gives so little trouble, and is so safe and profitable, that nearly all who have any inclination to the stock business, seek herds of cattle rather than flocks of sheep, but there are many million head of sheep in Ohio and States west of it, that must in some way be handled by their owners, who are greatly dispirited by the low price of wool. Such flocks should be driven to Kansas. There are also multitudes who own poor or profitless farms in those States, who understand the sheep business, and could easily and profitably convert their farms into sheep and bring their sheep here to be converted into cash, not by selling, but by keeping. For the benefit of these, and other interested people, let us glance at the sheep business in Kansas.

The pasturage is boundless and it is good. If left to themselves sheep will keep the grass down in certain places by close feeding. The short fresh herbage is more sweet and nutritious, and the ground is also drier under their feet than would be tall grass, from which the dews and rains do not so quickly dry out. This is also an advantage in cases of foot rot. From this disease many flocks of sheep have been cured by bringing them to Kansas. The climate is more congenial to sheep as well as man, than the damp atmosphere of regions east of the Mississippi, and our comparative freedom from mud is another great advantage over the older western States. By herding sheep on a moderately close, rather than a wide range, never driving or hurrying them, and giving them a plenty of water and salt, they are kept during the summer at a trifling cost, and in good condition.

It is the almost universal opinion among men of experience, that sheep do not do as well if fed exclusively on prairie hay. It is said that it has a constipating effect upon them, which it does not upon other stock, and that to correct this, a small feed of corn should be given every day through the winter, giving them hay and corn as soon as the frost strikes the grass. By commencing to feed corn early, a very little with prairie hay will keep them in excellent order. An amount equal to about a half bushel per head for the winter, is considered sufficient with *good* hay. If sheep are fed upon corn fodder, as is frequently and profitably the case, this is deemed sufficient. Many feed sheaf oats instead of corn, and think them even better. But for large profits in wintering sheep in Eastern Kansas, one should have blue grass pastures or winter rye for grazing. With access to either, there are not upon the average, two weeks in the entire winter, but that sheep will keep fat without other feed. All sheep do better to be protected from the occasional winter rains, and I think it wrong to ask people to bring their flocks here without informing them that they will be well repaid in money as well as in comfort of mind, by providing rough shelter for their ewes.

But the best place in Kansas for keeping large flocks of sheep, yes the best place in the United States, all things considered, is the buffalo grass region of Western Kansas. The altitude and dryness of the atmosphere and consequent freedom from disease in these regions, the comparative exemption from winter rains, the boundless range upon the short, sweet and nutritious grasses which afford feed of about equal value the year round, the abundant supply of pure and palatable water, the overhanging bluffs and ledges, and skirts of timber and various conveniences for making a shelter for the weak and helpless, the excellent grass for hay, of which a few pounds per head should be put up as a contingent provision against storms, the convenience by railroads for marketing mutton or wool, and finally the fact that *all these advantages* are offered absolutely *without cost*, these inducements ought to bring millions of sheep to Kansas this year. Sheep do not need grain when they have access to buffalo grass. Many flocks are herded in New Mexico and Colorado without feed, excepting grass, and without shelter except timber or bluffs, and the business is extremely profitable if taken in hand by those who understand and like it.

In that region two or three shepherds often start off with their flock of 2,000 head, taking a team, perhaps of oxen, and a wagon laden with provisions, a tent, and conveniences for camping. They permit the flock to range pretty much at pleasure, following with the team at the rate of one to five miles per day, and camping when night overtakes them. Having several trained shepherd dogs, who keep on the outskirts of the flock, it is not much trouble, by taking turns on guard, to keep the little prairie wolves, or coyotes, at a distance. At times finding good pasturage, water and shade, they may remain a week at one encampment. They keep goats or a cow or two for milk, while the flock supplies them with fat and juicy meat.

This romantic, easy-going and vagabond sort of life, is followed from shearing time until cold weather, by which time they will have returned to the vicinity of their homes. Here they find the grass which has been growing all summer, ready cured for winter use, and their flocks can stay on the "home range" for several months. There are many puny boys and men, dragging out a pampered and miserable existance in the east, to whom a summer's campaign of this sort on the high, rolling, healthy pasture fields of Western Kansas, would give a new lease of life. Health for the feeble and good pay for all, awaits those who enter the sheep business in those regions.

I speak with the utmost confidence, when saying that Western Kansas offers extraordinary advan-

UNIVERSALIST CHURCH, LAWRENCE.

tages for raising wool or mutton. I speak with feeling when I call to mind the fact that there are thousands of wool-growers in the east who are upon the verge of ruin from the low price of wool, coupled with the high price of land. They are almost ready to give away their flocks, but by bringing them here they can, even at present prices, not only save themselves, but enrich themselves at the business. Mr. Jesse Connell, a wealthy farmer near Leavenworth City, who has lived upon the border for thirty years, informed me some years ago, that with wool at twenty-five cents per pound at Leavenworth, he could double his money every year on sheep, by taking them where there was free pasturage, and by giving them personal supervision.

This subject is so important and is fraught with so much of good to those wool-growers who will heed what is proven, that I solicited a letter upon the subject from Dr. Bocking, of Alma, Wabaunsee county, who has had extensive experience in many parts of the world, including South America and Australia. His reply is given as follows:

"Kansas by its climate, soil, water, and short winters, is eminently a wool growing country, and was selected for a home by me four years ago. My experience on sheep in Europe and in the Branda Oriental del Uruguay of South America, during four years, (from 1857 to 1861,) gave me a taste for wool-raising, having had under my superintendency on Mrs. Wendelstadt's farm, on the Rio Negro, as many as 72,000 head.

"To commence with the trade, one has to decide himself beforehand, if he wants to raise for the butcher or for the improvement of wool, both being a business altogether apart, and much depending on the circumstances given. To go sure, and I intend to walk that path, raising for the carcass is for the present state of our communications the most advisable, and may afterwards, when a good foundation is laid, easily be turned to the other. If a man with large means intends to raise for wool merely, or principally, I leave it open to him to select Negrettes or Combwools, as both will pay with necessary care; and although I belong to the old merino school, I am last to deny the qualities of a Cotswold.

"The stock to commence with, is our native stock anyhow, and this sheep can be had amply in Michigan, some parts of Iowa, northern Illinois, and the very best in Ohio. Keep out of Missouri flocks, or elsewhere, where there is principally a timber pasture. Not more than a thousand head should be herded in one flock, except where there are wethers enough already to be herded separately with the rams to the middle of November, when the latter may be put among the ewes for a fortnight.

"For a shepherd not everybody is fit, the more the man loves his kind of stock, and the more easy tempered he is, the better it will be for the owner. An old man will generally do better than young ones, and rather abstain from the aid of dogs if you are not convinced of the phlegm of your herdsman and the thorough training of your collies. Fat flocks can not be attained with a lad exhausting his pony and his sheep with needless disturbance. About the summer care, much need not be told. Turn the flock out after dew, that they have ample time yet to fill before eleven, then let them lay down to ruminate, and past the midday heat herd them slowly homeward, not forgetting the water, because contrary to the general opinion, your sheep are great drinkers. But starting from the siesta, (range,) let the herdsman look after sleepy lambs that they get the necessary awakening. When the flies become very troublesome, I find it better to stay all night on some lofty spot, rather than to shut them up in the corrall. In winter, as sheds are mostly nothing but "pia desideria," let your flock enjoy the most protected spot of timber accessible to you. Do not grow impatient when you see the ewes' wool hanging loose around their sides early in spring, it is not yet clipping time. The lambs should not come before the middle of April, and they should all be there at the first of May. That the owner morning and evening be always at the spot to inspect the tail of his flock is a matter of course; of foot-rot and divers complaints, he will not find much, and a little pine tar in an eggshell will generally perform the cure, but itch in rainy seasons he will find to beware of. Of herbs poisonous to sheep, there is not a single one known to me in Kansas.

"Now about the dollars and cents. To keep less than five hundred will not pay, and many a good farmer of my acquaintance has become sheep-sick by a little flock that annoyed him by its intrusions and daily damages in summer in the fields, and in winter on the haystacks and in the orchard. The sheep are to be *herded* and kept under a careful eye all the time. You cannot turn them out at large like horses and cattle. But with eight hundred ewes (as a minimum) and thirty-two rams, the business will pay. With eight hundred, the wool, (four pound a piece, and at an average price of twenty-two cents per pound, at the nearest railroad depot) will pay the expenses, (herdsman, hay, shelter, salt, loss, etc.,) and the lambs will be your profit, but with a thousand your books will show other results, and the more if you ship your fleece directly east. My experimental flock gave me 75 per cent twin lambs, of good constitution, and as we need not, in Kansas, kill the buck lambs for want of milk in the mothers' udders, which is the case on the Rio de la Platte and in Australia, by the first of September your young ones will hardly be discernible from the old ones. Your expended capital of $3.00 will bring you 80 cents interest in wool, which is equal to the running expenses and customary losses, and you have besides a sure offspring that will double your principal capital every two years, as sure as death and taxes, if you apply the necessary care, and if *extraordinary* losses do not occur. Is there any other honest business that can beat that? Our water is clear, summer care costs nothing, and hay you can make on Uncle Sam's realms as much as you please for a dozen years to come.

"Now good bye. For the different breeds and the general management, lots of books are open, and Orange, Judd & Co., in New York, will be happy to sell them to you. All I want to add are my first words: Kansas is a wool-growing country, if there is any, and open to enterprise and energy for everybody, who takes naturally an interest in animals and raises them as nature teaches."

From T. C. Hill, Esq., of Americus, Lyon county, I received the following figures, which show one of his transactions in the sheep business, in buying a lot of poor run down sheep:

Dr.		*Cr.*	
600 sheep at $1.25	$750	200 to butcher at $3.00	$600
Attendance 6 months at $40	240	Fleeces of 350, 5 lbs, at 28 cts	490
Herding 4 months	125	200 lambs at $1.50	300
Feed of pony and dog	25	350 old sheep at $2.50	875
600 bushels corn	300	50 pelts	30
Rough fodder	100		
Salt a bbl., per month	25	Total	$2,295
Interest	60	Deduct expenses	$1,625
Total	$1,625	Net profit	$670
		If one attended his own flock, add care as above	$365
			$1,035

The remainder of this flock after above sales, Mr. Hill let out for three years, he to receive two pounds of wool per head each year, and the original number to be returned in good order, or failing in the latter particular, he received $2.50 per head for each missing sheep. He says, after an experience of twelve years in Kansas, that one *good* man—he employs no other—will care for 2,000 head in the summer, (being mounted,) and 1,000 head in winter.

He feeds *no* prairie hay after the middle of January. If sheep cannot have corn stalks, sheaf oats, winter rye or blue grass, give them corn and allow them to range the prairies in the middle of the day for rough feed.

MULE BREEDING.

From Mr. J. Reynolds, of Longton, Howard county, member of the House of Representatives from that county, I obtained the following: It will require two men to care for 100 mares and one jack. Colts should come in April. The average loss of mares by death, until they are fourteen years old, will not exceed two per cent. Loss among mules next to nothing. In the fall the mules are separated from the mares, and an old white mare put among them with a bell on, who at once becomes their leader. It is believed that the older and more worthless she may be the more attached do the mules become. The mules of all ages are kept together and it costs no more to handle them than so many cattle, while they will thrive on coarser food and under greater exposure. The mares need a little grain in the winter. It is a very low estimate to say that 80 mules can be sold from 100 mares each year. Good mares for this purpose can be bought for $100 each. A first rate jack should be bought, and he will cost from $500 to $1000. The mules are quick sale at the breeder's farm, and are worth from $75 to $100 each at two years of age, and $300 per span, unbroken, when three years old. I shall give my readers an opportunity to figure out the profits of the business, which they can do from data already furnished. I believe that if a man understands this business and likes it, there is more money in it for a term of ten years than in any other branch of stock business.

Mr. Reynolds brought from Wisconsin about 25

fine horses, among which are two thorough bred brood mares, by Lexington, one by imported West Australian, one by Cheatham, also brood mares, colts and filleys, by Creighton, Escape, Patchen, Daniel Boon, Leopold, Bald Chief, Swygart, Green's Bashaw, etc. He also brought Escape, by imported King of Simirie, dam thorough bred. Also a trotting stallicn, Leopold, since purchased by I. S. Kalloch, of Lawrence.

TAME GRASSES.

The question, "can you raise tame grasses?" has been asked in every new settlement from the Atlantic seaboard to Kansas. Thirty or forty years ago it is said to have been a matter of doubt in Ohio, and when I first came to Illinois from Vermont, seventeen years ago, it was discussed pro and con, and half the settlers were convinced, without experiment, that timothy and clover would not succeed on the prairies.

The same question is now discussed in some portions of Kansas and among some people, but any man who will travel through the older settled counties of Eastern Kansas, will be convinced that the question no longer admits of discussion. About Fort Leavenworth timothy and clover has produced a good crop of hay for many years. In Wyandotte county are blue grass pastures, which have been fed twenty-five years and are constantly improving. The northeastern portion of Johnson county is nearly all thick set with blue grass. Rev. Mr. Johnson, the old missionary among the Shawnee Indians, used to carry blue grass seed in his pocket, and scattered it whenever he saw a spot of broken prairie sod, where fresh earth was exposed by a gopher, or the rooting of hogs, or the deep track of a horse, etc. From this it has spread all through that vicinity. Wherever in Kansas the old Indian traders, or other travelers from the blue grass regions east of Kansas, were in the habit of camping, there blue grass is now abundant, and is rapidly spreading. I am speaking of Kentucky blue grass, *Poa Pretensis.* It grows during the entire season excepting in mid-summer, and it is therefore a feed for all seasons of the year excepting summer, when it is better not to put stock upon it. Mr. Tipton, of Anderson county, successfully seeded a quarter section to this grass ten years ago, by sowing the seed in the fall upon the prairie sod, and then harrowing it thoroughly. It catches easily upon plowed ground, by sowing in the fall or winter. 14 lbs. of common threshed seed, 6 lbs. of clean, or 2 lbs. of *extra clean*—which can hardly be obtained—will seed an acre. Clean seed is evidently better than seed in the chaff for sowing on raw (unplowed) prairie, as it will more readily sink into the soil and take root. Once established in any locality, the seed is carried by stock, or blown by the wind, as well as spreading by its roots, and it will take possession of all Eastern Kansas in a few years. This soil and climate is peculiarly congenial to it, and nowhere else does it appear as promising, except in the famous blue grass regions of Kentucky. It is the most profitable grass in the world, and unless a lawn mower is to be used frequently, it is our best lawn grass.

Orchard grass, *Dactylis Glomerata*, has been sown by several farmers, and furnishes better feed during midsummer than blue grass. It can also be cut for hay, as it grows tall, much like timothy, excepting that its head resembles herds grass or red top. Blue grass does not make hay, it being strictly a grazing grass. Timothy and clover also do well here. Timothy furnishes very good winter pasturage. I know of a field of thirty acres in Franklin county, which has been fed all winter, keeping green and fresh, excepting a few of the most severe days. There can be no doubt that Eastern Kansas is unsurpassed as a tame grass region. About the most profitable use to which land can be put, is to seed it to blue grass. Allow it to grow four to six months and turn upon it during the winter stock that has been grazing on the open prairie. There is yet abundant summer range in Eastern Kansas, and the capacity of this region for producing *tame grass and corn*, has made it famous as a beef producing country. Stock may be raised with great profit in Eastern Kansas, and it is the only part of the State where feeding to corn has yet been practiced. The time is not very distant, however, when Eastern Kansas will all be fenced with Osage Orange hedges, grown at a cost of less than fifty cents per rod, and stock will be raised in Western Kansas and taken to the blue grass meadows and rich corn fields of the eastern part of the State to be finished off for the best market prices.

FRUIT GROWING.

Our limited space forbids any lengthy dissertation upon the general subject of fruit growing. Here, as elsewhere, the nurseryman and orchardist must exercise patience and care, if he would be successful, but the soil and climate certainly are very favorable to the growth of plants, trees and vines, and to the production of fruit. The best evidence I can furnish upon this point is to present cuts showing the exact size of the Great Gold Medal awarded to Kansas, over all other States, at the national exhibition at Philadelphia, Pennsylvania, in 1869, for which I am indebted to Geo. T. Anthony, Editor *Kansas Farmer.*

Kansas is not entirely exempt from the vicissitudes of climate which make fruit growing so precarious in nearly all parts of the United States, and the peach crop is probably no more certain than in Southern Ohio, Indiana and Illinois. The apple and pear orchards are very promising, and small fruits are grown successfully. The capacity of Western Kansas as a fruit region has not been tried, but from the character of the soil, from its altitude of 2,000 feet or more, and from the extraordinary growth of wild fruit there found, I am of the opinion that the sandy hills and slopes described by Mr. Hohneck, in the vicinity of the Arkansas River, will prove very favorable to the production of fine fruits. At my

KANSAS FRUIT MEDAL.

request, Messsrs. Topping, nurserymen and fruit growers at Ottawa, prepared the following brief description of their method and its results in *small fruit culture.*

' It is folly for a new settler to wait years without fruit, for his apple trees to bear, when he can have abundance of delicious fruit the first and second years by a judicious planting of small fruits. Earliest in the season is the rhubarb, or pie plant, yielding considerable for the family the first year. Next the strawberry, most delicious of all fruits, lasting four weeks. Then follows the raspberry. Next in close succession follows the blackberry and then the grape, all of which are in full bearing before the first specimen apple is produced from trees planted at the same time. The experience of fruit growers in Kansas for several years has placed the success and profit of small fruit culture beyond a doubt.

"*Strawberries.*—Our first crop of strawberries illustrates what can be realized in one year without extra care and without manure. We took great care to procure the *pure* Wilson's Albany, as we had known of failures resulting from *impurity* of stock planted.

"*Soil*—Authorities usually recommend sandy loam. Yet we used such as we had, a heavy prairie loam, dark and deep, nearly level. It had been under cultivation three years, and cropped with corn.

"*Cultivation.*—We plowed about 12 inches deep and pulverized well—planted in rows four feet apart and twelve inches apart in rows—used the Moline fine-tooth cultivator, drawing it together as the young plants spread out each side of the row, which finally altogether prevented cultivation about August. Mulching in winter was done with clean straw about 2 inches deep.

"*Results.*—The next spring over 4000 quarts of strawberries were gathered from this bed of seven-eighth of an acre, the sales netting $865, or at the rate of fully $1000 per acre. We made sales at Ottawa and other towns in this State. The entire expense of planting, cultivating and picking was not more than $250.

"*Raspberries*—Are almost as successfully raised. Planted four by six feet they yield a partial crop in one year and almost a full crop the second year. We plant chiefly a variety of black cap which we brought from southern Illinois, which appears to be identical with the so called Mammoth Cluster, and yields large crops annually.

"*Blackberries*—Are completely successful here—no larger crops anywhere. The *true* Kittatinny, the favorite, both in quality, fruitfulness and hardiness.

"*The Grape*—The grape for the million here as elsewhere is the Concord—but other varieties appear almost equally successful. Planted 8 by 8 feet they commence bearing the second year, and thus far no failures of crop have occurred and no diseases have appeared to damage the fruit.

"All kinds of fruit here are remarkably free from any stings of insects. Apples and peaches as well as grapes and small fruits are perfect in development.

"We have chiefly used the Robinson trench plow, manufactured in Ottawa by the Robinson plow company, in preparing prairie sod for fruit planting. We plowed in late fall and early winter, and by spring the soil was in best condition. The forward share of this plow cuts the sod about 3 inches deep, which is laid at the bottom of the furrow and the next share cuts the subsoil about 4 inches below, and this is thrown over the sod, burying it so deeply that it is smothered. Four heavy horses will break about 1½ acres per day with this plow.

"The best season for breaking raw prairie is in May, when a crop of corn can be raised at once; but one great advantage of this plow is that it can be done with good results in the fall, when ordinary breaking would be worse than useless."

Mr. Wm. L. G. Soule, a nurseryman near Lawrence, writes me as follows:

"The largest and most thrifty orchard I have seen in Kansas is near Vinland, on a light sandy ridge, the land having received no manure, and cultivated with some kind of crops between the trees every year since they were planted.

"The following varieties of apples have done well in Douglas county, and I think in all other parts of the State:

"Early Harvest, Red June, Red Astrachan, and Early Strawberry for summer; Maiden Blush, Fameuse, (or Snow,) Fall Wine, Rambo, Duchess of Oldenburg and Lowell for autumn; and for winter the Wine Sap, Janet, Large Striped Pearmain, Rome Beauty, Missouri Pippin, Kansas Keeper, Baldwin, Rhode Island Greening, Jonathan, Milan, Mother, Willow Twig, Golden Russett, Fallawater, Swaar, White Winter Pearmain, Tallman Sweet, and Sweet Romanite.

"As an ornamental tree the improved varieties of crab apple have no equal among fruit trees, while the beauty and large size of the fruit, added to its superiority for domestic use, and its early fruiting, render it one of the most desirable trees the farmer or fruit grower can plant. I have seen a specimen of the Soulard grown in Kansas nearly three inches in its largest diameters. The Hyslop and Transcendent are both beautiful, fine flavored fruit, while the Pyramid cannot be excelled as an ornamental tree. The Queen's Choice, Blushing Maid, Sweet Crab, and several others have very attractive qualities.

"The peach has been planted very extensively, and some fine crops have been raised, though mostly on seedling trees. It requires elevated land with a northern exposure for the protection of its buds in the spring, otherwise the fruit buds expand before the frosts are over and the crop is destroyed. In some parts of the State the pear has been successfully cultivated for a number of years, but in some sections the blight has done considerable damage to the trees, but so far there has been but little injury done trees south of the Kansas River.

"In 1869, having but just commenced raising small fruits, I marketed about 1900 quarts of strawberries, about 900 quarts of blackberries, and between 300 and 400 of raspberries from an acre, while in 1870, an unusually dry and unprofitable season, I picked about 500 quarts of strawberries, 200 of blackberries, and not more than fifty of raspberries. In 1869 the price of strawberries was 23 cents; cost of picking, $57; cultivating, $5.00; boxes, $19.00; man and team to market 12½ days, $37.50; profits, $318.50; sold enough plants from small fruit to pay for cultivating. But grapes gave more than two-thirds as

KANSAS FRUIT MEDAL.

large a yield in 1870 as in 1869. The apple and peach crops were cut short in 1870, by severe frosts after the trees were in bloom, making the yield scarcely one-tenth of what it was the previous year. But this need be no discouragement, for in no State do they succeed in getting full crops every year. And judging from present prospects, 1871 will be even more fruitful than 1869. So taking all things into consideration the prospect for fruit growing becomes more flattering every year, and as railroads open up new markets both south and west, the difficulty will be in furnishing fruit enough to meet the increased demand."

Profits of a Vineyard.

Mr. W. E. Barnes settled in 1856 upon unimproved prairie 10 miles south of Lawrence, at Vineland station. He was a young man, not worth enough to pay for his land and unacquainted with the nursery business. In 1857 he set a few grape vines brought in a carpet bag from Massachusetts by W. L. G. Soule. He now has a large amount of bearing fruit of all kinds, from which he reaps such profits that he refused $20,000 for his farm and nursery of 160 acres in 1869. His buildings are not costly and the offer was made because of the actual value in his fruit orchards and vineyards. Probably twice that amount would not buy his place. The following estimates from Mr. Barnes are therefore not theoretical but are based upon actual experience.

"In accordance with your request I send the following estimates for 10 acres of vineyard for five years, the land to be located convenient to a railroad station;

FIRST YEAR.

Ten acres unimproved prairie at $20	$200 00
Breaking sod in May at 3 50	35 00
Planting corn at 1 00	10 00
Fencing with wire at 75c per rod	120 00
Total	$365 00
Deduct value of corn crop $50 00 to $100 say	50 00
	$315 00
Add interest at 10 per cent	31 50
	$346 50

SECOND YEAR.

		DR.
Amount brought forward		$346 50
Subsoiling (trench plowing) 12 inches at $6 00 per acre	60 00	
Harrowing once 1 00 per acre	10 00	
9000 vines at 3 cents	270 00	
Planting, 5 00 per acre	50 00	
Cultivating	50 00	
Fall pruning, cutting vines back to two eyes	10 00	
		450 00
		796 50
Interest		79 65
Total		$876 15

THIRD YEAR.

Amount brought forward		$876 15
3500 oak posts at 15 cents	525 00	
2500 pounds No. 9 wire at 7½ cents	1875 00	
150 pounds staples	16 00	
Putting up trellis	100 00	
Cultivating and tying vines	80 00	
Fall pruning	50 00	
		$2,646 00
		$3,522 15
Interest		352 21
Total		$3,874 36

FOURTH YEAR.

Amount brought forward		3,874 36
Cultivation	70 00	
Training vines and gathering fruit	300 00	370 00
		$4,244 36
Deduct 3,600 pounds grapes at 7 cents		2,520 00
		1,724 36
Add interest		172 43
Total		1,896 79

FIFTH YEAR.

Amount brought forward		$1,896 79
Cultivation	$100 00	
Training and gathering fruit	600 00	700 00
		$2,596 79
Add interest		259 67
		$2,856 46
Value of 72,000 pounds grapes at 7c	$5,040 00	
Deduct total cost to date	2,856 46	
Net profit in five years	$2,183 54	

"To this must be added the value of ten acres of vineyard in first rate order, and requiring but a trifling outlay for trellis during the ensuing five years.

"The above calculation is made with reference to the Concord and would not apply to the Delaware, Iona and some others, but with the former variety, where the requirements indicated above are complied with, it may be relied upon, except so far as price is concerned. Very few grapes have been sold for less than nine cents per pound heretofore—instead of seven cents, as above estimated—but it is evident that the price must soon be much lower. While the product of many Kansas vineyards has fallen below the above estimates, it will be found that there has not been expended upon the same vineyards more than one-third to one-half the amount above indicated, in the way of cultivation, erection of trellis, etc.

"By using the trench plow, or following a breaker with a stirring plow, to throw the soil on top of the inverted sod, in the winter of the first year, as much might be accomplished in one year as is indicated above in the first two years.

Respectfully yours, W. E. BARNES."

FARMING.

The table of farm products given on page nineteen, is the most reliable and thorough exposition of the results of Kansas farming that can be made. She stands, by that table, ahead of nearly every other State, excepting for one year, and then she fell but little behind, excepting as to corn. (For the benefit of any English reader into whose hands this book may fall, I will state that the word "corn" is used in this book, as it is universally used in this country, to represent "maize.")

In Eastern Kansas, spring wheat is little sown, as it does not do well, while winter wheat yields bountifully. West of Emporia, Council Grove and Marysville, spring wheat is a profitable crop. Some in Western Kansas are unsuccessful with winter wheat, because they put it in too shallow, only covering it with a harrow, and the light soil is blown away from the stem and roots during winter, and it "winter kills." Wheat, and indeed all seeds, should be put in quite deep in that soil, and a frequent use of the roller would be highly beneficial. I think the rule applies generally in Kansas that seeds should be planted deeper than in Illinois. It has for many years been the universal practice in Western Missouri, to plow oats under in March, about three or four inches deep, and those Kansas farmers who follow that practice always raise good crops of oats.

In 1857 having occassion to write a series of newspaper articles on Kansas Farming for the Lawrence *Republican*, edited by T. Dwight Thacher, I kept three standing rules or mottos, as follows: *Plow deep. Plant early. Use the roller.* Of course the matters of fine tilth, subduing the weeds, stirring the ground, etc., are not to be neglected, but I then believed and now am fully persuaded that the three cardinal principles above laid down are *especially* applicable to Kansas. *All* farmers who have practiced those principles have raised good crops continually.

Colonel A. S. Johnson, of Shawneetown, Johnson county, Kansas, a native of the State, and whose father sowed the good blue grass seed already mentioned, broke, in 1862, 105 acres with a double Michigan, plow, upper plow cutting two to three inches deep, lower plow cutting five inches; commenced with the first grass in the spring, and plowed until too dry; put it all in wheat, sown broad cast, from 1st to 10th of September, and harrowed in thoroughly, two bushels per acre; harvested in June, the next year, by measurement, 35 bushels per acre, and

NEOSHO FALLS, WOODSON COUNTY.

measured the ground. It made a trifle over 60 pounds per bushel. Next year he broke 107 acres, 22 acres in corn, harrowed and cultivated as old ground, made an average of 45 bushels of corn per acre; in September, 1st to 10th, sowed in wheat, corn land and all, and harvested 35 bushels per acre. He could not tell the difference between corn land and the other.

Col. Johnson has a large farm, much of which has been in constant cultivatiion for 30 years and still produces good crops. It is his practice once in three years to double his teams and plow about a foot deep with a trench plow, or to use a subsoil plow. For this purpose another Kansas Johnson has invented a subsoiler, which can be attached to any plow in a few minutes. It is called Johnson's Patent Kansas Subsoiler. Mr. C. A. Wright, of Lawrence has the control of the patent for the United States. The implement is made of iron, curved like a hook. A steel shovel, like a cultivator tooth, and with sharp edges to cut roots, occupies about six inches of the end or point of the subsoiler. The implement curves behind and below the plow, and stirs the soil without throwing it out, to the depth of four to ten inches below the bottom of the furrow. It hangs centrally in the line of draft, and adds but the draft of one horse to the team. Its cost is but six dollars and it is unquestionably destined to work a revolution in methods of cultivation. Whenever used it has added largely to the yield of all crops.

Breaking Prairie costs about four dollars per acre to hire it done. By this process the grass sod of the prairie is turned over to the depth of two and a half to four inches, with a plow which is kept sharp to cut the tough roots of grass and flowering plants. A pair of heavy horses will break an acre a day for an average of two months with a light plow *kept sharp.* Three horses or mules, worked abreast, makes an excellent breaking team. But the cheapest breaking team is about four yoke of young oxen, attached to a large plow which is so arranged with wheels as to steady itself. One good man can manage this outfit after the first week, and the cattle, if properly handled, will gain in flesh by feeding upon prairie grass. The share or cutting part of a breaking plow is heated and hammered out thin by a blacksmith once or twice a week, and it is kept sharp in the field by the frequent use of a large flat file. Ordinary breaking as above described, may be commenced as soon as the grass is high enough to furnish good feed, and may be continued into or through the month of June. If done at any other season of the year the sod does not rot well. If a lower furrow is turned on top of the inverted sod, as already described, prairie may be broken any time of the year, and the ground planted and treated like old plowed ground. This saves one years time, except for winter wheat, and land thus broken produces better crops. Corn may be planted early in the season upon freshly broken sod by cutting through the sod with an axe or spade, dropping into the opening the seed corn, and then stepping upon it. Winter wheat is sown in September of the same year the ground is broken. Winter wheat should be sown before, rather than after the middle of September, usually the first week.

HEDGES AND FOREST TREES.

By the law of this State any person planting one acre or more of any forest tree, excepting black locust, or one half mile or more of forest trees set in row on a public highway not more than a rod apart, shall receive two dollars per acre, or two dollars per half mile, each year for a term of twenty-five years; *provided*, that the trees shall be cultivated and growing three years before the bounty begins. [*General Statutes p.* 1094.]

The following essay was prepared for this book by Mr. S. T. Kelsey, of Pomona, Franklin county, it being the substance of an essay read by him before the Kansas State Horticultural Society at its Annual Meeting, December 15, 1868. Its clear and concise directions are founded upon the experience of twenty years in the business, six years of which period have been spent in Kansas:

Set a row of stakes six to eight feet to one side of the line intended for the hedge, to guide the plowman. As each stake is passed, set it over the same distance to the other side of the hedge line, which will guide you in striking the back furrow. Finish out the land by leaving a dead furrow on the hedge line. It is generally cheaper and better for the farmer to buy his plants of the grower who makes that a specialty, than to attempt to grow them himself. Plant any time during the month of April or first of May, after the soil is rotted and when the ground is in good order. Don't plant when it is too wet, Prepare the ground by plowing deep, throwing the furrows to the center, after which harrow down smooth. Now stretch a cord the size of a clothes line, track it by walking along on the cord, throw it to one side and it leaves a mark to plant by. Plant with steel spade, with blade thirteen inches long and three wide. Use none but good, strong plants. Cut them so that the roots shall be eight inches long and the tops six. Press the spade in on the mark of the line the full length of the blade, push it a little forward, and a boy with a handful of plants slips one down in the opening, two inches deeper than it stood in the nursery. Pull up the spade, and thrusting it into the soil two inches from the opening, press the earth firmly about the root, and the work is done. A good man and boy will in this way plant a half mile of hedge per day. Set the plants one foot apart in the row. Cultivate well the full width of the plowing. In the fall throw a furrow to the hedge on each side, and level down in the spring. As soon as the plants are started the second spring, replace all the dead ones with extra strong plants. I would do no cutting till the third, fourth or fifth year, then plash by cutting each plant half off at the ground, and bending it down into the row, so that it shall rest on the one last cut. The young shoots will then grow up from the roots and along the stem, making, with the old plants, an impassable barrier to all farm stock. After the hedge is plashed, it should be cut back annually to about four and a half feet high, in a pyramidal form, so that a cross section would appear like a capital "A," with base equal to hight. If a wind break is required, the plants may be set six to eight inches apart, cultivated well, and allowed to grow up as they will. It makes a good fence to turn all large stock, but to my eye is an unsightly object. The Osage Orange seems to be at home in our soil and climate. It grows rapidly, and endures our dryest summers and our coldest winters. The gophers are easily destroyed by trapping or poisoning, and I know of no other enemy or disease that injures it seriously. With a little forethought and effort, I am confident that in less than fifteen years, with the Osage Orange hedges, we can and will have the best fenced State in the Union, at one-third the cost of fencing with wood, in countries where timber is most abundant. Having the fence question disposed of, the lines located and the hedge rows broken, the next move I would make on a prairie farm, would be to prepare for planting a forest and orchard, and the first ground broken on the place after the hedge rows, should be for that purpose. On a quarter section I would plant at least twenty acres of forest, and I think forty acres would be still better. It may be planted in a body, or in belts to form wind breaks. It should be so as to protect the orchard, farm buildings, stock, crops, etc., from storms, so far as can well be. Having decided where the forest is to be grown, break the ground early in the season, so it may become well rotted. The kind of trees to be planted now requires our attention, and should be decided upon in time to collect a supply of seeds, cuttings and plants, which should be ready on the ground when planting time comes. I am experimenting with most of the different kinds of trees that have been recommended for forest culture, and thus far I find but three that I can recommend for extensive planting. A tree to be desirable and valuable for extensive forest planting. must be easily and cheaply obtained, and easily grown from seeds or cuttings. It must be a tolerably fast grower, and should produce timber of more than ordinary value for fuel, building or manufacturing purposes. It should be a tree that attains a good old age, and increases in value as it grows in years. It is important also, that it should form one straight stem without any pruning, I have found no tree that comes up to my ideal, and am obliged to accept the nearest approach to it.

All things considered, the Black Walnut is probably the most valuable tree that we can plant. Gather the nuts, which are abundant in Kansas, soon after they drop in the fall, spread them and cover with two or three inches of moist earth, or, still better, with saw dust, to keep them moist through the winter, and plant two inches deep, early in the spring. Nearly every one will grow, and in fair soil, with good cultivation, will make an average growth of about two feet per year, producing firewood in five and six years. In ten years they will make good fence posts, or railroad ties and will begin to bear nuts. In fifteen years they will make a stately forest, producing annually large crops of nuts, as well as furnishing timber. Such a forest, judiciously managed, will increase in value for a century, returning annually, without expense to the owner, better profits than any farm crops with which I am acquainted. The Cottonwood I give the second place on the list. It is readily grown from cuttings made from shoots of the last year's growth, which may be cut any time from the fall of the leaf till needed for planting. I usually cut during winter and pack them away in moist saw dust, or bury them in the earth till planting time. Make them about one foot long, and plant with a narrow spade, as recommended for planting Osage Orange hedge, leaving one or two inches of the top of the cutting above ground. Be sure that the earth is firmly pressed about each cutting. Where small plants, one year old, can be obtained, they may be planted instead of cuttings. The Cottonwood grows very rapidly when young, making five to six feet in hight annually for several years. In four years it makes a very good wind break and shelter for stock, and if fuel is scarce it will supply the fires with wood. It usually grows with a clean, straight stem. I am of opinion that by alternating the Cottonwood with the Black Walnut, and judiciously thinning out as they grow, the Walnut may make a taller straighter growth than if grown by itself, and be of more value.

The third and last tree that I would place on this list—and I put this on with some hesitation—is the Silver Maple, commonly known as Soft Maple. It is grown from seed, gathered as it ripens from the first to the fifteenth of May, sowed immediately in drills, and covered with one inch of good, mellow soil. The plants come above ground in six to ten days, and by fall they will be one to two and a half feet high. Next spring they should be planted in forest. Plant two inches deeper than they stood before, and press the earth firmly about the roots. Nearly every one will live and make an annual growth, on average soil, with good cultivation, of about three feet. At ten years from planting, they will make twenty-five to thirty feet in hight, and ten to twelve inches in diameter. It is a very beautiful tree while young, and the wood is more valuable for fuel than Cottonwood, or any other available fast growing tree with which I am acquainted. It is also valuable for the manufacture of some kinds of furniture, and the sap makes sugar which is almost, if not quite, equal in quality to that made from the sugar maple. It has the fault of often forking, so as to make two or more stems, and except in favorable situations, I think it is not likely to make large, straight trees. It also has the fault of being too easily split down by wind and sleet.

The forest should be planted as early in spring as the ground can be put in good order. Lay off and stake the rows twelve feet apart. The whole ground may now be plowed, or a strip four feet wide may be plowed for each row, leaving the rest to be plowed afterwards. Plow deep in the line of each row and harrow it down. Now stretch a line, track it, and plant to the mark, putting the plants about eighteen inches apart in the row. Plant the Walnuts with a hoe, like potatoes, the cuttings with a narrow spade, as before directed, and the young plants with a common spade, by throwing out a spit of earth where the plant is to stand; then one person, with plants in hand, puts one in place, another with spade fills in the earth, and the first presses it about the roots with his feet. I have often planted alone pulling some earth to the plant with my foot, and when through the row go back and level with the spade. Now plant two rows of corn or other hoed crop, in each space between the rows of trees, and keep the ground mellow and free from weeds by cultivation. Plant thus between the rows each year, and cultivate well until the trees shade the ground too much for profitable cultivation and seed with red clover If a hedge was planted around the forest as it should have been when the forest was planted, it will now be a fence, and hogs or young cattle may be turned in to pasture on the clover. As soon as the trees are large enough to be out of the way of large cattle, they also may be turned in sparingly; but it is not advisable to attempt too much pasturing in the forest, as it will injure and finally ruin, even a well grown natural forest. Besides, the growth of the timber, and the value of the wood that may be taken annually therefrom, will be ample to satisfy any reasonable man.

There are many other forest trees that are valuable for various purposes, and to those who want a greater variety than I have recommended, who have means that they are willing to lay out in extra expense, or who want to grow the trees for a special object, I would suggest the following: Honey Locust, White Ash, Box Elder, Kentucky Coffee, White, Red, and Water Elm, Butternut, Chestnut. Hickory, Cypress, European and American Larch, Linden, Silver Leaf Poplar, Mulberry, Catalpa, Ailanthus, White and Yellow Willow, and Hackberry, and lastly the Evergreens—the beauty and glory of the landscape, unfading, unchanging "types of the immortal," relieving more than anything else, the monotony of winter, and with their dense foliage checking and modifying the searching prairie winds. These should receive the attention of every prairie farmer, and should be planted liberally about every prairie home as soon as possible after the more pressing wants are supplied. Evergreens grow slowly for the first few years. Most varieties require two or three years to become thoroughly acclimated and are too expensive for general forest planting; but from the experience that I have had with them, and the evidence of success that I have seen with others, I am satisfied that when once established and growing on our prairie soil, they succeed as well in Kansas as farther north and east, and that good. small sized, well rooted trees may be transplanted with very little danger of failure. Too many have bought Evergreens from parties east, who advertise that they have immense quantities which they will sell for one-half (or less) the usual price charged by nurserymen. They are little, spindling things, with scarcely any roots at all, and unused to the sun, even in their northern homes. It will be found much cheaper and more satisfactory in nearly every case to go to the nearest reliable nursery for Evergreens, paying a reasonable price therefor, or if such trees cannot be obtained at the home nursery, send to some other reliable nurseryman and order them, remembering always that it is much safer, cheaper and better to get small trees, not over two feet high, and if possible, get such as have been often transplanted. The best time to transplant Evergreens is in the spring, usually from the first to the middle of April, though I should plant earlier if ground was in good order. In handling the *roots should not be exposed to the sun or air one minute longer than is absolutely necessary.* The surface moisture even, should not be dried off. For general cultivation for ornament and wind breaks, I would recommend the Norway Spruce, White Austrian and Scotch Pines, Balsam Fir, Red Cedar, and American Arbor Vitæ. For amateur cultivators I would add the American White and Black Spruce, English, Irish and Swedish Juniper, Golden and Siberian Arbor Vitæ, Lowsen's Cypress, American Holly and Hemlock. I would also suggest that experiments should be made with native Evergreens from south and west, and we may find something more valuable for our Kansas prairies than anything we now have in cultivation. A few dollars judiciously expended, and a little care in planting and tending, will in a few years give the surroundings of any prairie farm house or any Kansas home a goodly supply of well grown specimens of these most beautiful of nature's gifts.

S. T. KELSEY.

Concerning this practical and highly valuable essay, it is proper to say that most of tree cultivators in other States, think it much better to plant the trees closer together, say in rows three or four feet apart, giving as a reason the fact that by close planting, forest trees make taller and smoother trunks, as the branches tend upward for light and air, instead of expanding laterally. Mr. Kelsey does not lose sight of this fact, but his theory is that a half a loaf is better than no bread at all. Most settlers in a new country are not able to devote land solely to the growth of forest trees, and experience in all the Western States demonstrates that of those who are able, very few can be persuaded to do it. Mr. Kelsey concedes that a better and more valuable forest can be grown by thick planting, and for those who can afford it, he advises it. But it is a question of dollars and cents and his method has the striking advantage that it is *cheap*.

One of the best evergreens for Kansas is the Red Cedar, which is a native of all the region west of the Missouri River, from Texas to the British Possessions. It is quite easily transplanted, and is, when young, a rapid grower. It is natural to dry, rocky and barren spots, and it is therefore not difficult to make it grow upon the open prairie.

Box Elder is another native of Western Kansas, which may be grown from the seeds that can be collected in the fall. It grows rapidly and in beautiful form until about ten or fifteen years old, after which it is inclined to be scraggy. Mr. R. S. Elliott, Industrial Agent of the K. P. Railway, says it can be grown from cuttings, and it is well known that its sap makes a fair quality of sugar.

Osage Orange is almost a native of Kansas, as it grows wild in the Indian Territory not far from our southern border. It matures its seeds here, which

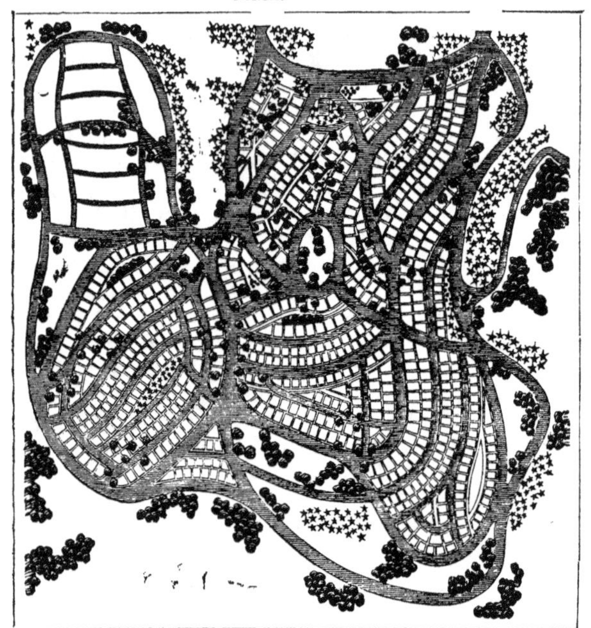

PLAN OF HIGHLAND CEMETERY, JUNCTION CITY.

are held in a ball much like a small orange, whence its name. In its wild state it attains the height of forty to sixty feet. This is a very valuable tree for general cultivation. It grows rapidly, its wood is hard and durable, and it makes an excellent wind break. In this regard it stands next to evergreens from its multitude of small limbs. A belt a rod or two in width, almost entirely breaks the force of the wind. Mr. Kelsey has said enough about hedge rows, but I urge the planting of this tree for wind breaks. Plants a year old can be had for $1.50 to $2.25 per thousand, according to quality and quantity. Or it may be plantd for forests where it is to grow. A pound of the seed will make from 3000 to 4000 plants or trees. This tree would soon furnish excellent railroad ties." Concerning wind breaks, a good shelter is afforded on the prairies even by a clump of hazle bushes, with a few scrub oaks intermixed, and not a tree over ten feet high. The low but impenetrable thicket afforded by Osage Orange, is a perfect wind break for a stock yard or for tender fruits, etc.

Efforts have been made, and I regret to add, by my friend Mr. Elliott, before mentioned, to induce the planting of Black Locust in Kansas, in the vain hope that the borers will not kill it. (This tree must not be confounded with the Honey or Thorny Locust, a short, stout tree, with long thorns, and with a sweet substance in its seed pods, whence its name. The Honey Locust is a native of Kansas, and is perfectly hardy but a slow grower.) This tree is so easily grown from cheap seed and looks so handsome and promising for a few years, that there is a great temptation to plant it. But it has been tried over and over again in Kansas and it universally fails, first or last, just as it fails in all prairie countries, after it is about a dozen years old, by its limbs being cut at the trunk by a borer; no bounty is paid for it it under our State law. Prof. Chas. V. Riley, State Entomologist of Missouri, being quoted as saying that it was not injured by borers when planted in groves, I wrote him, saying that I believed the tree should be utterly discarded, and received the following letter:

"Never give a man's opinion from the curtailed

reports of what he says. I am often reported as saying the most outrageous things.

"If I were to give my opinion in three words, I should state that with regard to the Black Locust, you are correct. There are, however, qualifying conditions and circumstances. The borer is not so bad on high limestone lands—may be in a measure prevented by the proper use of soap and the killing of the beetles during September. The central trees in large groves are less subject to attack than those on the outside, and where fuel or posts are needed the young trees will generally take the place of the old ones as fast as they are killed or cut down. I have my reasons for believing that the tree should not under certain conditions be discarded from your Kansas list; but why urge the Black Locust, when there are other and better trees? Whatever reporters make me say, I have never done so."

Hastily, yours truly,
C. V. RILEY.

The Chestnut is a valuable and beautiful tree and a grove will well pay for the trouble of cultivation simply by fattening swine on the nuts, to say nothing of the timber. This tree, wherever I have noticed it in a natural forest, grows upon a light or sandy soil, or at least upon well drained land. It is yet uncertain how it will do on the deep, rich soil of the prairies, or on the drier western plains.

It is believed by many of those whose experience gives weight to their opinions, that the European Larch is the best tree for general planting. As it is propagated only from seeds, and requires very skillful treatment when young, it is an expensive tree to plants in quantities. Robert Douglas, of Illinois, who has done very much to bring this tree before the public, says: "It is undoubtedly the most valuable timber tree for extensive planting;

combining the durability of the Red Cedar with rapidity of growth, extreme hardiness, freedom from disease and adaptability to almost every soil." He writes me however that it ought to be planted on *dry* soil, and so say all the cultivators. A. J. Downing says: "It is remarkably heavy, strong, and durable, excelling in those qualities the best English oaks." Posts of Larch and Oak were placed in the river Thames, where by the rise and fall of the tide they were alternatly wet and dry. "The oak posts decayed and were twice removed while the Larch remained altogether unchanged." Loudon says vine props of Larch are used in Switzerland and are transmitted from generation to generation an unknown term of years, without showing any signs of decay. Douglas says: "In Great Britain the Larch has become so popular for railroad ties that the forests of Scotland are taxed to their utmost to supply the demand."

He has trees fifteen years planted which are 45 inches in circumference, nine years from seed 27 inches, and five years from seed 9 inches in circumference at the collar. Various plantations of this tree twelve year old show it 30 feet and upwards in hight and 10 to 12 inches in diameter. Robert Douglas & Son of Waukegan, Illinois, offer these trees two years old, 6 to 18 inches high at $2 per hundred, $10 per thousand, $90 per 10,000, and $800 per 100,000. He offers the seed at 25 cents per ounce or $2 50 per pound.

There grows in Wisconsin, Minnesota, and the adjoining portions of Illinois and Iowa, a tree called Poplar, which resembles Aspen, or Quaking Asp. Groves of it sprout up in the same manner as Cottonwood, standing thick on the ground and rising 20 or or 30 feet with no considerable limbs and almost uniform in size, from the ground up. I have seen this tree cut when three to five years old, and peeled or riven through the heart frcm end to end, and nailed to posts for fence. I saw such poles in Glencoe, Minnesota, used for fencing the village lots, which were twelve years old and *perfectly* sound. The tree is grown from cuttings like Cottonwood and is equally rapid in growth, while it is better for fuel and very valuable for timber as the above indicates. Strange to say, there are few localities even where it grows naturally, where the people know that it is durable when the bark is off. When riven and fastened to posts the bark soon drops off. I wrote to several gentlement of practical experience in tree business, but could get no satisfactory information until the followiug letter came to hand from Mr. George Pinney, of Sturgeon Bay, Wisconsin.

"I think there is no doubt but that the tree you describe is what we call White Poplar. The name White Poplar is one of our conventionalities. The botanical name is *Populus Grandidentata.* We have named it White Poplar because of the white down with which the young leaves are covered in spring, giving it the appearance of being laden with white blossoms. It sometimes grows quite large. I have seen them here two feet in diameter, 60 to 70 feet high. It differs widely from Aspen. The leaves are fully twice as large and much more scanty, it makes a growth of two or three times that of the Aspen, and its branches and buds are coarser. I have known of well rooted trees in favorable localities, making a growth of six to ten feet in hight, increasing the diameter of the stem from one to two inches in a single season. When growing thick in good, strong soil, it mounts upward with beautiful straight trunks, with amazing rapidity, and uniform in size 12 to 25 feet. As the trees grow old and large the bark becomes fluted and serriated, similar to the White Wood or Poplar of the east, really the *Liriodendron Tulipifera.* The bark is very thick and stiff, and the laticiferous tissue very abundant, which makes the bark separate with great facility in the spring during the development of the latex. The boys use it in preference to anything else for making whistles. The timber when dried thoroughly with the bark off, is very peculiar in many particulars. It is very light, very stiff and springy, extremely difficult to chop with an axe, more so than seasoned maple or oak, but very easy to saw or shave, and seems to be almost impermeable to water, hence very durable against decay or wear, when not permitted to come in contact with the ground, but when cut and left with the bark on it will become dozy in fifty or sixty days, during the growing season, and worthless in three months. It is very easy to transplant."

I have not Mr. Pinney's prices, but this tree must

be sold cheap as it is so easily propagated. It is not certain that it will thrive in this climate, but it is reasonable to believe that it will, and I recommend it, not to take the place of more valuable but costly trees, but to supplant the Cottonwood, of which we can only say that it costs next to nothing, and is very much better than no tree.

Mr. D. C. Scofield, a noted tree grower of Illinois, says: "The White Pine is next in value as a timber tree to the Larch, nearly equaling it in growth, and will thrive well in nearly all soils; especially as a forest tree on dry, open prairies.

"The result of my experiments will be seen in the comparative growth of the different varieties of wood, as exhibited in the table below, from average measurement. The age of the trees is twelve years, from seedling plants one and two years old, and six to twelve inches in heighth.

Size of trees in Illinois, fourteen years old.

	Diameter.		Hight.	
European Larch	8 to 12	inches	30	feet
White Ash	3 to 5	"	16	"
Silver (or Soft) Maple	4 to 6	"	25	"
Sugar (or Hard) Maple	2 to 4	"	12	"
Black Walnut	2 to 4	"	14	"
Chestnut (common)	3 to 4	"	16	"
American Larch (Tamarack)	4 to 6	"	25	"
American Elm	3 to 4	"	16	"
Scotch Elm	3 to 4	"	16	"
Birch (European)	4 to 6	"	14	"
White Pine	6 to 10	"	35	"
Norway Spruce	5 to 8	"	20	"
Scotch Pine	4 to 8	"	20	"
Black Austrian Pine	5 to 7	"	16	"
European Silver Fir	2 to 4	"	7	"
American Fir	4 to 6	"	10	"

The growth of Black Walnut as above indicated was very slow. Undoubtedly this may be accounted for by the fact which Mr. Scofield notes above, that they were grown from *seedling plants*. The Black Walnut should always be planted where it is to be

7*

grown. If transplanted its long tap root is necessarily cut in the process, and this stops its growth for a long time. In Kansas, when grown where the nuts are planted, its growth is at least double that indicated in the above table.

In 1866 I contracted with Mr. S. T. Kelsey for the planting of a forest on the grounds of Ottawa University, Franklin county. In 1867 fifteen acres were planted to Black Walnut, and five acres to a variety of deciduous and evergreen trees. In December, 1870, I measured the trees, and they averaged as follows:

Size of trees in Kansas, with the age from seed.

	Diameter.	Hight.
Black Walnut, 3 years old	1 to 2 inches	5 to 8 feet.
Soft Maple, 3 years old	1½ to 3 "	8 to 12 "
Cottonwood, 3 years old	2 to 3½ "	12 to 16 "
European Larch, 5 years old	1 to 3 "	6 to 10 "
Red Cedar, 5 years old	1 to 3 "	4 to 7 "
American Arbor Vitæ, 5 years old	——	3 "
Peach Buds, 1 year old	1 to 1½ "	4 to 7 "
Apricots and Nectarines	——	5 to 8 "

Apples and other fruit proportional size.

The European Larch plants were not healthy, having been saved from a large lot that perished. These, as well as the Cedar and Arbor Vitœ, were planted on ground a little too wet for their natural requirements. The Red Cedar grows slowly after a few years, and never becomes a stately tree. Nearly all other forest trees grow more rapidly after the first three or five years, until they attain full size.

AN ENGLISHMAN'S IMPRESSIONS.

It affords me pleasure to present a letter from the Rev. James Chew of Ottawa, recently pastor of the Congregational Church, Mile End Road, London, England, as it bears with peculiar force upon many of the topics treated in this book. The subjoined correspondence explains itself.

Rev. J. Chew,

DEAR SIR: You have resided in this State a few months and have seen a good deal of the country and of the people who inhabit it. Permit me to ask you this question. From the stand point of an Englishman in America, what do you think of Kansas as a place for a home? I also beg leave to use your letter in the little book I am preparing about Kansas.

Wishing you abundant success in the labors which are so highly esteemed by all who enjoy your ministrations,

I remain, very respectfully yours,

C. C. HUTCHINSON.

OTTAWA, FRANKLIN CO., KANSAS,
December 29, 1870.

Mr. C. C. Hutchinson,

DEAR SIR: It affords me pleasure to give you the impressions of an Englishman on Kansas in compliance with your request. There may be those from the old country who, having been longer in the State, would be more competent judges than I; but during the seven months of my residence in it I have travelled hundreds of miles north, south and west, with my eyes open, and can speak what I do know and testify what I have seen. My friends in England are probably of opinion that my chief impression is one of general disappointment, seeing that I have been diverted from the cherished object for which I crossed the Atlantic and came so far west. Instead of supporting my family by farming and preaching gratis, I am again engaged in the Ministry solely, but this change in my plans has been caused, not by the condition of things I have found here, but by the persuasions of Ministers and the entreaties of others.

I confess to having been somewhat disappointed in some things. Land is higher in price near towns. Hired help is not so good, and more difficult to get; clothes, fuel and furniture are more expensive than had been represented. These are evils however which (except in the matter of land) will gradually cure themselves, or be remedied by the growth of towns, the cultivation of land, the influx of immigrants, the multiplication of railways, the development of commerce, etc. The climate is slightly different from what I expected. The heat was a degree or two intenser in the summer than I was prepared for, although singularly tempered by the cooling breeze that came daily and nightly from the south: a peculiarity to Kansas, which the intense heat was not, for while exceptional here as every one assured me, it prevailed according to the telegrams in all the States and in Europe as well. The recent "snap" of cold weather, said to be the severest for years, pressed the mercury considerably lower than I ever experienced it before, though the clearness and dryness of the atmosphere prevented me being more inconvenienced by it than on many an ordinary chilly day in my native country. In truth I felt it less. The occasional sudden changes of temperature are decidedly objectionable. The fruit also (to mention all my disappointments together) was not so abundant in its season as I had hoped—books having described Kansas as a great fruit producing State, meaning, as now appears, not that it actually bears an enormous yield of fruit, but is capable of doing so eventually. Give it time and the extraordinary soil will produce any quality and quantity of the best fruits, but I had stupidly overlooked the fact that there had hardly been time for numerous fruit groves to be planted, still less for them to attain to a mellow and prolific maturity.

These are all the things I think, which are not quite as good as I anticipated With these exceptions I have been agreeably and exceedingly surprised. The climate, taken the year round, is healthful and most enjoyable—sometimes so delightful that, as a Swede remarked to me the other day, "it could not be better if we had the making of it ourselves." The clear skies, the pure, exhilerating air, the glorious sunsets, the lovely Indian summer, and even the bright, bracing early part of winter, which is not wintry, can be described only in language which strangers would deem exaggerated. The country is not so flat nor the scenery so monotonous, nor the water so scarce, nor the trees so small and few, as I feared, The *Marais des Cygnes*, which curves one of its windings near my house, is a truly beautiful river, fringed on each bank by a forest which would do credit to countries celebrated for their timber. Wild flowers in all but endless variety, I have gathered in the forest as well as on the prairie; notwithstanding that I arrived too late to behold Flora in all the glory with which she decks herself in the spring, when likewise the climate I am informed wears one of its fairest aspects.

The inhabitants are more intelligent and respectable than their distance from the centres of civilization would have led one to suppose. All have an independent bearing, shown at times by some almost disagreeably, arising partly, perhaps, from all of them—even the negroes—being apparently in easy circumstances. I have not met with a rude person, nor a beggar, nor a solitary case of beastly drunkenness. Only seven or eight poor creatures have crossed my path whose unsteady steering showed they were "half-seas over." It is amusing now to recall the concern and apppehension which many, not only on the other side of the ocean, but also in American cities out east betrayed, when they heard that my family and fellow-travellers were going to Kansas! They regarded the outlandish region as a pandemonium of savage Indians and border ruffians. The ruffianism I have not discovered, but good society I have, as educated and refined as in any place I know. The institutions, the roads, railways, laws, periodicals, schools, universities, and alike in size, number and style, the churches are for so young a State a marvel; while the people, so far as I have seen, are temperate, enterprising, Sabbath-observing, law-abiding, freedom-loving and religious. Folks at a distance think of Kansas in connection with her early troubles in the cause of freedom and mistake them. They picture her as "Bloody Kansas," rather than as "Bleeding Kansas," as if she had been a persecutor and not a martyr. Nay, she has a noble, albeit a painful history, of which all haters of slavery may be proud, giving thanks that she bleeds no longer, but like the fabled hero has gathered strength from her reverses, and now grows fast, fair and formidable.

There is a good sprinkling of Englishmen throughout the State. Several colonies of them, notably at Wakefield, near Junction City. Where, indeed, will you not find Britishers? And where can the average Briton not make himself at home? Yet would I not advise my countrymen indiscriminately to come here. There are those who would not do as well as at home. Persons, for example, who have been delicately reared, and have not means to build a house and make themselves a comfortable home at once, would be sorely tried here. Sanguine souls who would look for cent pieces lying like stones on the ground and dollar notes hanging like leaves on the trees, would curse the place. Any who have not the power of adaptation, with some patience and perseverence—who have not learned to "labor and to wait," had better stay where they are. There is no "roughing it" in the sense in which that word is commonly understood in reference to new countries; no scorching winds to bear as in Australia; no dense forests to clear as in Canada; no long winters to endure as in Minnesota; yet are there inconveniences, not to say difficulties, at starting, and whoever cannot put up with them will be wise to seek a paradise where mansions are already prepared for them. Speaking generally, capitalists would do well, either by loaning money, for which they would easily obtain enormous interest on the best security, or by introducing manufactures, for which there is an urgent demand, or by raising grain and stock. The hard-handed sons of toil, used to work and ready to turn their hand to anything, inured to privation and not missing luxuries, cannot fail to gain much more than a bare subsistence. Wages are high and most provisions cheap. Farmers and farm labourers, in particular, should come. How often have I thought of the small farmers and their hinds, whom I formerly knew in Cornwall, Devonshire, Dorsetshire, in the north and other parts of England, who had been slaving for years (and their fathers before them for generations) on lands of which they did not own a single rod, and any of whom, by working not near so hard for, say, seven years, would have a competence, owning their houses, farms and cattle, and having their children educated in the bargain. Artisans, uniting as in co-operative societies, would prosper, provided they did not purchase land without seeing it, or if they sent trustworthy pioneers in advance, who understood their business. Ministers of the Gospel are much needed. If there be any willing to labor with their own hands, that they be chargeable to none; if any have some private resources and would be content with such remuneration as small churches can afford; if any have ample means and would consider it a sufficient reward to aid in laying the foundations of society—to assist in forming the commercial, political, educational and moral character of a people surely destined to be great and influential—there are spheres and calls for them. Marked respect is paid to ministers, as I have experienced and gratefully testify.

I would add, sir, that intending emigrants in Europe require more information respecting Kansas, in which the sunny and shady sides of our young and

PRESBYTERIAN CHURCH, JUNCTION CITY.

flourishing State will be exhibited together. I am pleased to believe that your book will go far towards supplying this want.

I remain, dear sir, yours truly,
JAMES CHEW.

INHABITANTS.

It appears almost ludicrous thus to head a section concerning the people who occupy the central State of the United States of America. It seems to betoken the discovery of an unknown country, and with a feeling of curiosity akin to fear we draw near to study the costume and customs of its strange inhabitants.

Yet a book about Kansas would be incomplete unless it contained something concerning the people who live in Kansas, especially as our friends "within the bounds of civilization" have decidedly erroneous opinions concerning us. Those who take the trouble to examine what is shown in these pages about the institutions of Kansas—its Churches, Schools, Newspapers, Railroads, Cities and Public Buildings must conclude that although distant from the homes of our fathers we have not lapsed into barbarism. In fact we all had fathers and mothers who lived in "the East," or some other place, and it is but a few years since we left those dear old homesteads to make homes for ourselves on these lovely prairies. The light has gone out from many of the places where we once lived and loved, but all the way from the Mississippi to the Atlantic, and even beyond its billows, there are fires burning on hearth stones at which we find a welcome and a chair. Those people at the East who suppose that Kansans are necessarily uncouth and ignorant, will do well to reflect for a moment as to the character of those who have left their own vicinity for distant Western States. They know too well that the best blood and brain of the Eastern, Middle, and Southern States is seeking for servedly successful monthly, the *Educational Journal*, of Emporia, is devoted exclusively to the cause of education, and monthly or quarterly issues are made of religious publications. Another class of papers extensively published in Kansas is devoted exclusively to the real estate business. They are issued by private firms for gratuitous distribution, and contain valuable information.

The first settlers of Kansas were men of brains and men of business, and they were moved to Kansas by an idea. Under whichever banner they ranged, whether of freedom or of slavery, it is unquestionable that they were terribly in earnest. In such a community a weak and inconstant press could find no support. From this, among other causes, it has come about that no other State in the Union has proportionally so many newspapers as Kansas, and nowhere else do country papers present so good an appearance and give such evidence of editorial ability. Many names famous in the eastern newspaper world are familiar to Kansas. Horace White, of the Chicago *Tribune;* James Redpath, of Boston; the lamented Albert D. Richardson, of the New York *Tribune;* John Swinton, of the New York *Times;* Col .Samuel F. Tappan, Richard J. Hinton and Wm Hutchinson, Washington correspondents of eastern papers; J. M. Winchell, formerly of the New York *Times;* Col. Wm. A. Phillips, of the New York *Tribune* and *The Nation*, but still a resident of Kansas—these and many other names of prominence, were once connected with the Kansas press. Not alone in aiding the struggle for freedom during our early history, nor yet entirely in disseminating information as to the soil, climate and productions of Kansas, have the newspapers of Kansas helped the State to achieve its triumphant success. The press of this State has been first and foremost in promoting every

8

effort for developing the best interests of the State. Men of character locating in our border have been welcomed by name, and gratuitous advertisement has been given of the merits of improved machinery or valuable stock. Whenever new and attractive fields of immigration have been opened in remote counties, the press of the older settlements have been first to herald the facts. The best methods of tilling the soil, of harvesting the crops and of caring for the stock are obtained from experienced farmers and published by our sagacious newspapers, and a generous rivalry is maintained between farmers, neighborhoods, towns, and counties by the printed reports of progress among all.

Railroads, those necessary avenues of travel and transit, have been built in Kansas with greater rapidity than in any other state in the Union, but the influence of newspapers in preparing the way for their construction is appreciated by very few. Railroad projects must always take shape by the action of the people living upon the proposed line. They alone can afford to contribute the time and money necessary to perfect an organization, to obtain a survey and engineer's estimates, and to secure franchises of lands and bonds, and local subscriptions, and it is only when these things are done that capitalists can be induced to look at the enterprise. Towards the accomplishment of this tedious, tiresome, thankless task the press of the state has always freely contributed its invaluable aid. Notices of meetings, description of routes, labored editorials, columns of statistics and a startling array of figures, all have been issued gratuitously and in profusion.

Manufactures, schools, churches, villages towns, cities, have all received the support of the Kansas press. In short our newspapers have never failed to hold up to the public, the mirror of to-day and have effort for developing the best interests of the State. Men of character locating in our border have been welcomed by name, and gratuitous advertisement has been given of the merits of improved machinery or valuable stock. Whenever new and attractive fields of immigration have been opened in remote counties, the press of the older settlements have been first to herald the facts. The best methods of tilling the soil, of harvesting the crops and of caring for the stock are obtained from experienced farmers and published by our sagacious newspapers, and a generous rivalry is maintained between farmers, neighborhoods, towns, and counties by the printed reports of progress among all.

Railroads, those necessary avenues of travel and transit, have been built in Kansas with greater rapidity than in any other state in the Union, but the influence of newspapers in preparing the way for their construction is appreciated by very few. Railroad projects must always take shape by the action of the people living upon the proposed line. They alone can afford to contribute the time and money necessary to perfect an organization, to obtain a survey and engineer's estimates, and to secure franchises of lands and bonds, and local subscriptions, and it is only when these things are done that capitalists can be induced to look at the enterprise. Towards the accomplishment of this tedious, tiresome, thankless task the press of the state has always freely contributed its invaluable aid. Notices of meetings, description of routes, labored editorials, columns of statistics and a startling array of figures, all have been issued gratuitously and in profusion.

Manufactures, schools, churches, villages towns, cities, have all received the support of the Kansas press. In short our newspapers have never failed to hold up to the public, the mirror of to-day and have painted without stint of color, the possibilities of to-morrow.

[Extract from an address delivered before the Editors' and Publishers' Association of Kansas, January 17, 1871, by Ward Burlingame, Esq.]

"Why is it that Kansas has a greater number of newspapers than any other equal population in the world? It is not because our people are *peculiarly* a reading people, because in that respect other localities rival us. Nor is it because the newspaper business is productive of large and prompt pecuniary results; for I much doubt whether there is any other branch of business, employing the same labor and capital, the gains of which are so small and precarious. The true explanation of the circumstance is found in the fact that Kansas is in its formative state; everything is growing, nothing completed; the map of a year ago is out of date to day; towns, cities, villages, are springing up on every hand; large bodies of land just vacated by worthless and semi-barbarous tribes, are yielding to the impress of settlement and civilization; agriculture encroaches upon the desert; immigrants from every State and of every nationality are flocking to our borders; railways penetrate unpeopled regions, and from nothing thriving communities are evolved by their mysterious influence.

"In securing these results the press is an active and powerful agent. Hence, new towns, new interests invoke their co-operation. Among the earliest of the pioneers is found the country editor—among the earliest of local institutions the country press. Expanding beyond the necessities of the present, it builds upon the prospects of the future, and thus, blending an individual with a patriotic purpose, it strives with admirable and ever-restless zeal for the realization of those prospects through the development of its section. It is surprising to note that newspapers, and good ones, too, are maintained in localities where we would not deem it possible were the fact not apparent. This state of affairs is itself an eloquent tribute not alone to the energy, perseverance and pluck of newspaper men, but also to the practical good sense and wise forethought of the people who sustain them."

If any persons outside of Kansas do not decide to start for Kansas immediately after reading this book, they are advised to select a paper from the following lists, and send to its address the price of a year's subscription. If they do not find in its columns all the information they desire, they have only to inform the editor who will gladly print such statements as will meet the case.

Citizens of Kansas should give to their local papers a liberal support. The man who does not take one or more papers published in his county, commits a crime against his own neighborhood. Help your papers—subscribe for them and urge others to subscribe—furnish them advertising and give items to the editors concerning all matters which interest you. Anything which interests you will be quite certain to interest the editor and his readers. In short, help your editor and he will help you.

List of Newspapers Published in Kansas.

The following list embraces all the names of papers that I can obtain at the time of going to press. New ones are coming out every week, and it is safe to say that there are one hundred papers issued regularly in Kansas, aside from the real estate papers. I have also collected as full a list of the latter papers as possible, which is quite incomplete however. The real estate papers are issued once a quarter or once a month, and are sent free to all.

The newspapers are sent for $2 per annum, excepting the Kansas Farmer, $1, and the Educational

Journal, $1 50, and the Medical Herald, $3 per annum. Only the last or principal names are given. The list is arranged alphabetically in reference to towns, and this will serve to show at a glance in what county the principal towns are situated, and also the county seats. I am indebted to Mills & Smith, of Iola, and Emmert & McCulloch, of Humboldt, for assistance in preparing this list.

County seats in CAPS. d stands for daily, w for weekly, and m for monthly.

Town.	*County.*	*Name of Paper.*
ATCHISON	Atchison	Champion, d and w
"	"	Patriot, d and w
Altoona	Wilson	Union, w
Arkansas City	Cowley	Traveler, w
Augusta	Butler	Crescent, w
ALMA	Wabaunsee	Union, w
Baxter Springs	Cherokee	Sentinel, w
BURLINGTON	Coffey	Patriot, w
BURLINGAME	Osage	Chronicle, w
BELOIT	Mitchell	Mirror, w
BELLEVILLE	Republic	Telescope, w
Chetopa	Labette	Advance, w
COLUMBUS	Cherokee	Journal, w
"	"	Independent, w
COUNCIL GROVE	Morris	Democrat, w
CONCORDIA	Cloud	Empire w
Clyde	"	Watchman w
COTTONWOOD FALLS	Chase	Leader, w
CLAY CENTRE	Clay	
ELDORADO	Butler	Times, w
EMPORIA	Lyon	News, d and w
"	"	Tribune, w
"	"	Educational Journal, m
Erie	Neosho	Ishmaelite, w
EUREKA	Greenwood	Herald, w
Elk Falls	Howard	Examiner, w
Elk City	Montgomery	Star, w
FORT SCOTT	Bourbon	Monitor, d and w
"	"	Democrat, w
Frankfort	Marshall	New Home, w
Fontana	Miami	Gazette, w
Florence	Marion	Pioneer, w
FREDONIA	Wilson	Journal, w
GARNETT	Anderson	Plain Dealer, w
GIRARD	Crawford	Press, w
HIAWATHA	Brown	Sentinel, w
"	"	Dispatch w
Humboldt	Allen	Union, w
"	"	Statesman, w
HOLTON	Jackson	News, w
IOLA	Allen	Register, w
Irving	Marshall	Recorder, w

Town.	*County.*	*Name of Paper.*
INDEPENDENCE	Montgomery	Tribune, w
"	Montgomery	Republican, w
"	"	Democrat, w
JUNCTION CITY	Davis	Union, w
LAWRENCE	Douglas	J urnal, d and w
"	"	Tribune, d and w
"	"	Democratic Standard, w
"	"	Banner, (German) w
LEAVENWORTH	Leavenworth	Times, d and w
"	"	Bulletin, d and w
"	"	Commercial, d and w
"	"	Call, d
"	"	Farmer, m
"	"	Gardener, m
"	"	Presse, (German) w
"	"	Medical Herald, m
LA CYGNE	Linn	Journal w
LYNDON	Osage	Signal, w
Labette	Labette	Sentinel, w
LOUISVILLE	Pottawatomie	Reporter, w
Longton	Howard	Ledger, w
Lindsay	Ottawa	Pioneer, w
MINNEAPOLIS	"	Independent, w
"	"	Settler, w
MARION CENTRE	Marion	Western Giant, w
MANHATTAN	Riley	Nationalist, w
Medina	Jefferson	New Era, w
Mound City	Linn	Sentinel, w
MARYSVILLE	Marshall	Locomotive, w
NEOSHO FALLS	Woodson	Advertiser, w
Netawaka	Jackson	Herald, w
New Chicago	Neosho	Transcript, w
Neodosha	Wilson	Citizen, w
"	"	Enterprise, w
North Topeka	Shawnee	Times, w
OLATHE	Johnson	Mirror, w
"	"	News Letter, w
Osage Mission	Neosho	Journal, w
OSKALOOSA	Jefferson	Independent, w
"	"	Statesman, w
OSWEGO	Labette	Register, w
OTTAWA	Franklin	Journal, w
"	"	Herald, w
PAOLA	Miami	Republican, w
Pleasanton	Linn	Press, w
Parker	Montgomery	Record, w
Parsons	Labette	Sun, w
SALINA	Saline	Herald, w
"	"	Journal, w
SENACA	Nemaha	Courrier, w
Spring Hill	Johnson	Enterprise, w
TOPEKA	Shawnee	Commonwealth, d and w
"	"	Record, d and w
TROY	Doniphan	Republican, w
Thayer	Neosho	Criterion, w
Wathena	Doniphan	Reporter, w
Wamego	Potawattomie	Valley, w
WASHINGTON	Washington	Republican, w
Waterville	Marshall	Telegraph, w

Town.	*County.*	*Name of Paper.*
White Cloud	Doniphan	Chief, w
WYANDOTTE	Wyandotte	Gazette, w
WICHITA	Sedgwick	Vidette, w
“	“	Tribune, w
WINFIELD	Cowley	Censor, w

REAL ESTATE PAPERS.

Atchison	**Atchison**	**Northern Kansan**
“	“	**Index**
Burlington	**Coffee**	**Free West**
“	“	**Register**
Burlingame	**Osage**	**Journal**
Council Grove	**Morris**	**Advertiser**
Cottonwood Falls	**Chase**	**Register**
Emporia	**Lyon**	**Register**
“	“	**Bulletin**
“	“	**Reporter**
Eskridge	**Waubonsee**	**Land Mark**
Fort Scott	**Bourbon**	**Immigrant**
“	“	**Record**
Garnett	**Anderson**	**Index**
Humboldt	**Allen**	**Reporter**
Holton	**Jackson**	**Bulletin**
Junction City	**Davis**	**Register**
“	“	**Guide**
Lawrence	**Douglas**	**Advocate**
Manhattan	**Riley**	**Homestead**
Olathe	**Johnson**	**Register**
Ottawa	**Franklin**	**Guide**
“	“	**Pioneer**
“	“	**Register**
Pomona	“	**Pomona for a Home**
Pleasanton	**Linn**	**Banner**
St. Marys	**Pottawatomie**	**Advertiser**
Topeka	**Shawnee**	**Advertiser**
“	“	**Star of Empire**
“	“	**Publisher**
Wakefield	**Clay**	**Herald**
Winfield	**Cowley**	**Settlers Guide**

COMMON SCHOOLS.

The common school system of Kansas is modeled after the most approved systems of other states with such amendments as experience elsewhere has shown to be desirable. Sections 16 and 36 in each township in the state are forever set apart for the creation of a fund the interest of which is to be used for the payment of teachers. School lands may be sold upon petition of the residents of the county where they are situated. The proceeds are invested in Kansas State, or United States Bonds and the interest only is applied to the payment of teachers wages, in proportion to the number of persons in each district between five and twenty-one years of age.

The above sections are secured for school purposes out of the Osage Trust Lands, but a few smaller Indian reservations were exempt, as well as small military reservations. Were it not for these reservations there would be devoted to this purpose one-eighteenth part of the whole state (there being 36 sections in each township) which would make about 5000 square miles of 640 acres each, or 3,200,000 acres. The amount cannot be less than 3,000,000 acres. About 200,000 acres of school land were sold during the year 1870 at an average of about $6 20 per acre. The school lands are not put upon the market in any county until they are in demand and by law cannot be sold for less than $3 per acre, and it is fair to estimate their value throughout the state at $4 per acre. This will give a fund of $12,-000,000, sacredly devoted to the cause of education.

The following tables are compiled from the Tenth Annual Report of the Superintendent of Public Instruction.

TABLE showing the Statistics of the Public Schools of 1870 *in every county then organized.*

COUNTIES.	Number of districts organized.	Total number of School Houses.	Total numb'r School Houses erected '70.	Total number of teachers.	Total number of pupils enrolled.	ESTIMATED VALUATION.	
						Build'gs and grounds.	Furniture.
Allen	44	29	5	46	1,392	$27,777 00	$1,804 00
Anderson	41	37	5	63	1,496	28,000 00	2,320 00
Atchison	57	54	9	92	2,351	102,546 00	5 620 00
Bourbon	74	64	12	78	3,487	41,288 15	2,370 00
Brown	56	43	11	81	1,763	37 927 00	3,695 00
Butler	26	12	10	15	561	8,500 00	700 00
Chase	21	18	6	28	564	12 750 00	1,000 00
Clay	36	16	2	27	401	5,867 00	156 75
Crawford	92	75	30	77	1,960	5,168 00	995 00
Cherokee	72	36	......	60	2 200	9,480 00	740 00
Cloud	23	10	5	13	297	350 00	50 00
Coffey	......	35	6	52	1.439	28,850 00	2,785 00
Davis	19	14	1	27	696	14,340 00	915 00
Dickinson	27	12	6	18	347	9,190 00	515 00
Doniphan	65	61	6	101	3,310	45,841 00	5,400 00
Douglas	78	72	11	117	4,622	119,095 00	7,196 00
Ellsworth	7	2	......	3	64	2,200 00	....
Franklin	65	53	11	97	2,543	32,995 00	2,120 00
Greenwood	30	21	8	23	622	6.125 00	118 00
Jackson	52	38	9	60	1,670	35,500 00	1,500 00
Jefferson	79	77	25	98	3 180	68 734 00	2,076 00
Johnson	72	65	7	108	2,932	44,610 00	3,648 00
Labette	60	42	18	43	1,634	22 000 00	3,000 00
Leavenworth	70	69	22	129	6,212	177,757 75	17,200 15
Linn	80	67	12	90	3,303	35,230 00	2 922 00
Lyon	49	43	5	77	2,088	47,900 00	2 043 00
Marion	7	3	......	4	85	2,110 00	....
Marshall	57	43	9	54	1,333	33,115 00	1,590 00
McPherson	7	....	1	2	25	400 00	....
Miami	73	60	13	92	2,470	[illegible]0,854 00	2,860 00
Morris	19	13	2	20	619	17,745 00	1,232 50
Montgomery	7	....	......	....	....	....	....
Nemaha	54	47	9	89	1,686	53,415 00	3.663 00
Neosho	77	31	15	36	1,009	11.410 00	700 00
Osage	57	....	......	77	2,067	64,020 50	2,790 60
Ottawa	18	....	......	13	369	....	....
Potawattomie	56	42	15	72	1,352	28,735 00	2,082 00
Riley	42	27	5	46	1,027	29,136 00	2 100 00
Republic	6	5	2	7	183	635 00	....
Saline	23	13	4	20	414	10,200 00	818 00
Shawnee	57	52	10	85	3,000	125,000 00	4,500 00
Sedgwick	10	....	......	5	62	....	....
Wabaunsee	30	19	3	26	550	8,165 00	498 00
Washington	56	21	8	22	648	11,455 00	1,044 00
Wilson	53	....	8	33	933	5,930 90	323 50
Woodson	34	19	5	32	751	6,485 00	415 00
Wyandotte	32	26	10	48	1,833	61,150 00	5,510 00
Total	2068	1,501	359	2,240	63,218	$1,520,041 40	$100,915 50

TABLE showing the comparative advance of the Public Schools of Kansas for ten years, from 1861 to 1870 inclusive.

YEAR.	No. of Co's report'g.	No. of school districts reporting.	Average time school taught.	NO. TEACHERS EMPL'D			AVER'GE SAL'Y PER MONTH.		Value of school houses.
			Months.	Males.	Females.	Total.	Males.	Females.	
1861...	12	144	....	....	....	....	....	....	....
1862...	28	304	3.2	90	229	....	....	....	$ 10,432 50
1863...	33	506	3.8	161	400	564	....	....	32,970 60
1864...	33	640	3.5	205	527	732	$27 00	$16 10	76,500 71
1865...	35	721	3.4	247	652	899	46 74	34 41	122,822 64
1866...	37	871	4.	405	681	1,086	41 27	28 90	318,897 31
1867...	42	1,056	4.3	541	664	1,205	39 44	26 51	573,690 08
1868...	43	1,232	5.	746	855	1,601	39 56	29 08	813,062 75
1869...	43	1,621	5.	896	1,118	2 014	37 07	28 98	1,031,892 00
1870...	47	1,950	5.2	1,079	1,161	2,200	39 60	31 10	1,520,041 40

The reports show that out of 359 school houses built during 1870, 45 were built of logs. The average per cent. levied in 1870 fcr the erection of buildings and all other purposes, was $0.0347. The total amount received by the school district treasurers from all sources for 1870, was $799,318.51, and the total amount paid out was $712,601.73.

In all towns of any considerable size there are graded schools, and one or more central school buildings, costing from $5,000 to $75,000 and other smaller buildings, as the public needs require. All these schools are open and free, being supported by the State school money, and by direct taxation. There are salaried county superintendents in each county whose duty it is to give direct personal supervision to matters connected with public schools, besides which each city has its superintendent. There are two Normal schools, one at Leavenworth and the other at Emporia. That at the former city was but recently opened. That at Emporia has been in successful operation for six years. The attendance for 1870 was 111 males, 132 females. It is devoted to the work of fitting its pupils to become teachers in our common schools, and is supported by the State. The State Agricultural college at Manhattan is endowed by a land grant of 70,000 acres of land. It also receives State aid and is in a prosperous condition.

The State University at Lawrence is open to all of both sexes without tuition fee. Its endowment is

LINCOLN SCHOOL, TOPEKA.

46,000 acres of well located land, and about $150,000 contributed to it for buildings, etc., chiefly by the city of Lawrence. It has a permanent fund of $10,-000 contributed by Amos Lawrence of Boston, and aparatus costing $15,000. It has nine salaried professors, and fitly crowns the splendid school system of this state, by offering an education of high character free to all. Its students for 1870 were 97 males and 116 females. Its buildings are illustrated and described elsewhere.

Besides the State Institutions of learning already mentioned, there are several well established schools of high grade, under denominational control. Among them is Baker University, at Baldwin City, and Collegiate Institute at Hartford, under the M. E. Church; Washburn College, Topeka, Congregational; Episcopal Female Seminary, Topeka; Lane University, Lecompton, United Brethren; Ottawa University, Baptist; Wetmore Institute, Irving, Presbyterian; Roman Catholic Colleges at Leavenworth, Atchison, St. Mary's, Topeka, Fort Scott, and elsewhere; and various other lesser academies and private schools.

BENEVOLENT AND REFORMATORY INSTITUTIONS.

A large and well ordered State's Prison is located near by Leavenworth. The State Asylum for the Blind is located at Wyandotte; that for the Deaf and Dumb at Olathe; and the Insane Asylum at Osawatomie. These institutions are all under the guardianship of the State authorities and are supplied with convenient buildings and necessary attendants.

THE CHURCHES AND THE CLERGY.

The following article upon the above topic was prepared at my request by Rev. R. Cordley, the well known pastor of the Congregational Church at Lawrence, which position he has filled with great acceptance for fourteen years:

"The early settlers of Kansas included a large proportion of religious men. This might have been expected, as a large share of these settlers came as a matter of conscience, to establish freedom and equal rights on these plains of the west. One of the first things they did after setting up a tent or building a hut to shelter their families, was to provide churches and schools, where these families might worship and be instructed. Religion and learning were among their first thoughts. In Lawrence, for example, in one month after the first company of immigrants arrived, regular religious services were established with a settled minister. Steps were at once taken for building at least two churches. In other places, church organizations, with their pastors, went with the colonies in the style of the Mayflower pilgrims. One of the first things now in a new town, is to build a church, and these churches are generally well sustained, and are doing a good work. There is great liberality in maintaining christian institutions, and no people, in proportion to their means, pay more freely for religious objects than the people of Kansas. Within the last three or four years, some very handsome churches have been built. In Leavenworth the Catholics have a cathedral that cost some $250,000. The Baptists have about completed a very fine church in the same city that has cost some $60,000. At Atchison the Methodists are building a very handsome structure. In Lawrence the Congregationalists have a church that has attracted general attention for its completeness and beauty. Its cost was about $45,000.

"All denominations are represented in Kansas. The Methodists take the lead in membership, the Baptists coming next. The Presbyterians are quite strong. Especially in the south part of the State. The Congregationalists have some strong societies and are quite numerous, especially in the northern part of the State. The Episcopalians are very active, and exhibit a missionary zeal that is commendable. There is generally the kindest feeling between different denominations. All joining in the common work, rather than trying to supplant each other. The churches have generally come to the wise conclusion that they can prosper better in the general prosperity of all, than in mere denominational expansion, which builds one up by pulling another down.

"The Kansas churches generally have an able ministry, more than usually so for a new country. While there are no 'stars' that attract special attention, the ministry generally are cultivated, earnest men, and up to the times. They are 'workmen that need not to be ashamed.'

"The churches are having a healthy growth. They are growing both by immigration and conversion. Special interest is reported in many places, and every season witnesses more or less of the fruits of such special interest. The religious future of Kansas is as bright as that of any new State. There are dangers, but there are also promising signs. The churches are sound, outspoken and aggressive. They work as if they meant to 'occupy the land.'"

TAXES.

By the constitution, the state debt of Kansas cannot exceed one million dollars. No town, county, or state debts were incurred during the war, as Kansas volunteers always kept up the state quota. Taxes are less than most states. The state tax levied by the Legislature for 1871 is six mills on the dollar, which includes one mill for general school fund. The levy for 1870 was seven and three-fourths mills.

The assessment of taxes on real estate is made between the first day of March and the first day of July, and the taxes so assessed are due and payable on the first day of November following. If not paid by the tenth day of January next thereafter, a penalty of ten per cent. is added. If not paid by March 1st following, a fee of twenty-five cents for advertising each tract, except town lots, is added, and ten cents for each town lot. If not paid before the first

Tuesday in May following, the land is sold for the taxes and the foregoing expenses. The whole amount draws interest at the rate of fifty per cent. per annum. If not before redeemed by the owner, the purchaser of the tax title receives a tax deed at the end of three years. The purchase money, with all the subsequent taxes up to the date of deed, interest being computed upon the whole at fifty per cent. per annum, and the cost of making and recording the deed, is the *consideration* of said deed.

In two years after *recording* the deed, the same becomes *absolute*, and suit is barred, excepting where there are minor heirs, and they have until they become of age and one year thereafter in which to redeem, by paying for improvements, which may have been made upon the land by the tax purchaser, together with the taxes and interest as allowed by law.

The Topeka *Record* says, January, 1871: "In a recent decision—*Bowman et al vs. Cockrill*—our Supreme Court has affirmed the validity of tax deeds given on sale of land for non-payment of taxes, and sustains the statute of limitations, which bars an action for the recovery of property so sold and deeded after the expiration of two years from the time the deed shall have been recorded.

"The court also decided in the same case, that the statute does not require that the tax deed shall be in the exact form therein prescribed, but only substantially in that form."

I also quote from the Statutes as follows: "As between the grantor and grantee of any land, where there is no express agreement as to which shall pay the taxes that may be assessed thereon, if such land is conveyed between the first day of March and the first day of November, then the *grantee* shall pay the same; but if conveyed between the first day of November and the first day of March, the *grantor* shall pay them." *General Statutes, p.* 1062, *sec.* 140.

Statistical Table Showing the Growth of Kansas, by Counties.

COUNTIES.	Square miles (640 acres) computed by Wm. B. Covel, Princ'l D fts'n Surv'r Gen'l's office.	TOTAL POPULATION.			Total assessed value of all taxable property, as fixed by the State Board.		Actual value of taxable property.	Total State Levy.
		1860. U. S. Census.	1865. Kansas State Census.	1870. U. S. Census.	1865.	1870.	1871.	1870.
Allen	504	3,082	2,737	7,023	$ 469,412	$ 1,408,948	$ 4,226,844	$ 12,328
Anderson	576	2,393	2,659	5,204	728,733	1,944,065	5,832,195	17,010
Atchison	424	7,729	8,929	15,472	3,031,141	4,503,727	13,511,181	39,407
Bourbon	625	6,101	7,961	15,102	1,531,313	4,525,618	13,576,954	39,599
Brown	576	2,607	2,891	6,400	1,000,045	2,022,287	6,066,861	17,695
Butler	1,519	437	294	3,072	60,415	822,174	2,466,522	7,194
Chase	757	808	870	1,992	233,485	879,885	2,639 655	7,698
Cloud	720	....	....	2,323	....	165,908	497.724	1,451
Cherokee	604	....	....	11 047	....	912,319	2,736,957	7 982
Clay	660	163	238	2,839	....	474,693	1,424,079	4,153
Coffey	576	2,842	3,383	6,201	926,838	1,944,148	5,832,444	17,011
Cowley	804	....	....	1,174	....	....	....	....
Crawford	504	....	596	7,881	....	550,000	1,650,000	4 812
Davis	386	1,163	1,189	5,526	310,543	1,597,024	4,791,072	13,973
Dickinson	846	378	442	3,037	128,294	1,322,378	3,967,134	11,570
Doniphan	391	8,083	9,595	13,971	2,047,930	3,254,426	9,763,278	28.476
Douglas	470	8,637	15,814	20,582	4,678,893	6,851,729	20,555,187	59,952
Ellis	900	....	....	2,041	....	253,468	760,404	2,217
Ellsworth	720	....	....	1,350	....	398,402	1,195,206	3,486
Franklin	576	3,020	3,695	10,259	903,894	3,183,837	9,551,511	27,858
Greenwood	1,155	759	1,188	3.485	76,649	1,554,920	4,664,760	13,605
Howard	1,271	....	....	2,796	....	....	....	....

Jackson	556	1,936	2,962	6,053	961,718	1,569,586	4,708,758	13,733
Jefferson	550	4,459	5,853	12,526	1,481,427	3,234,142	9,702,426	28,298
Jewell	900	....	....	205	....	....	....	....
∞Johnson	472	4 364	6,093	13,725	1,632,694	3,146.749	9,440,247	27.534
*Labette	624	....	....	9 979	....	1,117,215	3,351,645	9 775
Leavenworth	460	12,606	24 256	32 472	6,269.105	10,370,630	31,111,890	90,743
Linn	600	6,336	6,543	12,198	1,007.347	2,906,877	8,720.631	25,[illegible]35
Lyon	858	3 197	†2,248	8,016	1,286,238	3,916,927	11 750,781	34,273
Marion	1,044	74	162	767	45,974	225,465	676.595	1,972
Marshall	908	2,280	2,349	7,228	415,860	1,694 859	5,084,577	14,830
McPherson	1,080	....	....	917	....	226 911	680,7[illegible]	[illegible],985
Miami	576	4,980	6,151	11,729	1,702,051	3,459,997	10,[illegible]79,991	30,274
Mitchell	720	....	....	498	....	....	....	....
Montgomery	624	....	....	7,613	....	163,061	489.183	1,426
Morris	655	770	1,141	2,218	261.902	1,231,002	3,693 006	10,771
Nemaha	720	2,436	2,638	7,296	883.513	2,094,015	6 282,045	18,322
Neosho	576	....	777	10,211	56,749	817 883	2,453.649	7,156
Osage	792	1,113	1,169	7,631	496,251	2,071 142	6.213.426	18.122
Ottawa	720	....	178	1,668	....	720 [illegible]31	2.162 493	6,307
Pottawatomie	851	1,529	2,119	7,888	644,058	2,024,119	6,072.357	17.711
Republic	720	....	....	1,290	....	192.[illegible]45	576,535	1,6[illegible]7
Riley	654	1 124	1,813	5 104	468,140	1,394,762	4,184 286	12,204
Saline	720	....	473	4,206	105 834	1,838,996	5,516 988	16,091
Sedgwick	1,512	....	....	1,09	....	....	....	....
Shawnee	546	3,513	3,458	12.940	1 490 257	4,654,690	13,964 070	40,728
Wabaunsee	804	1,023	1,081	3.373	440,251	884,097	2,652 291	7,735
Washington	900	383	....	3,970	92,819	640,210	1,920,630	5.601
Wilson	576	27	....	694	....	556.971	1,670.913	4,873
Woodson	504	1 488	1,307	3,827	140,836	545 311	1,635,933	4,771
Wyandotte	155	2,609	4,827	10,066	110,328	2,258 849	6,776,547	19,764
Total	....	107,204	140,179	353,478	$ 36,140,827	$ 92,528,099	277,58[illegible],297	$ 809,620

†65th district not returned.

THE CHALLIS FERRY BOAT ATCHISON.

TABLE showing square miles of counties not included in foregoing table.

County	Sq. miles	County	Sq. miles
Barbour	780	Phillips	900
Barton	900	Pawnee	900
Comanche	780	Pratt	900
Clarke	780	Reno	1512
Ford	900	Rush	900
Graham	900	Rooks	900
Hodgeman	900	Russell	900
Harper	1152	Rice	900
Kiowa	900	Smith	900
Lincoln	720	Sumner	1152
Norton	900	Stafford	900
Ness	900	Trego	900
Osborne	900		

It should be borne in mind that there are few counties in which there is not more or less land exempt from taxation owing to the title still vesting in the United States. The Osage Trust land was none of it subject to taxation, although largely settled upon. Montgomery county for instance, showing by the last census 7,613 inhabitants.

It is to be noted especially that Kansas has grown to its present position almost entirely *during the last five years*. A comparison of the census for 1860 with that for 1865, will show that the growth was confined almost exclusively to counties containing considerable towns. Kansas did not gain in population during the war like other western states, nor in wealth like all other northern states. But if we exhibit the growth for ten years from 1860 to 1870, it still shows that Kansas distances all competitors in the march of empire.

TABLE showing the increase of population in all the states and the percentage of increase.

STATE.	Populati'n 1860.	Populati'n 1870.	Per cent of increase.
Alabama	964,201	1,002,000	4
Arkansas	435,450	486,103	12
California	379,994	556,208	47
Connecticut	460,147	537,886	17
Delaware	112,216	125,050	12
District Columbia	75,080	131,889	76
Florida	140,424	189 995	35
Georgia	1,057,286	1,185,000	12
Indiana	1,350,428	1,676,046	24
Illinois	1,711,951	2,527,032	48
Iowa	647,699	1,190,845	77
KANSAS	**107,206**	**362,307**	**238**
Kentucky	1,155,584	1,323,264	15
Louisiana	708,002	728,000	3
Maine	628,279	630,243	0.3
Maryland	687,049	781,055	14
Michigan	749,113	1,184,296	58
Massachusetts	1,231,063	1,449,042	18
Minnesota	172,023	335,000	95
Mississippi	791,305	834,190	6
Missouri	1,182,012	1,690,716	43
Nebraska	28,841	116,888	201
New Jersey	672,035	906,514	34
New York	3,880,735	4,370,846	13
Nevada	6,857	41,836	501
North Carolina	992,622	1,085,500	9
*New Hampshire	326,073	318,300	-2.4
Ohio	2,339,511	2,652,302	14
Oregon	52,465	90,922	73
Pennsylvania	2,906,115	3,517,272	21
Rhode Island	174,620	217,319	25
South Carolina	703,708	735,000	5
Tennessee	1,109,801	1,258,326	14
Texas	604,215	797,500	32
Vermont	315,098	330,585	5
†Virginia	1,596,318	1,657,550	1.5
Wisconsin	775,880	1,055,296	36
Territories	150,229	319,053	112

*New Hampshire shows a decrease of two and four tenths, (2 4-10) per cent in the ten years.

†Virginia includes West Virginia in this calculation, there having been no division in 1860.

The following table exhibits the increased valuation of the taxable property of Kansas from year to year from 1865 to 1870 inclusive and the per cent. of increase:

TABLE showing increased valuation for six years.

Year.	Assessed valuation	Per cent. increase.
1865	$36,140,827 00	46.0
1866	50,439 634 96	104.0
1867	56,276,036 00	127.5
1868	66,949,549 88	179.0
1869	76,393,685 00	217.0
1870	92,528,099 00	275.0

KANSAS SECURITIES.

There is no doubt that this State offers great attractions to capitalists or any who have money to loan. The legal rate of interest by contract is twelve per cent. per annum, and an almost unlimited amount of money can be loaned at this rate, payable annually, on long time, with security upon improved farms, or good city property, at one-third their present value. On shorter time and similar security, or good names, money readily commands 18 to 20 per cent. per annum, the surplus over 12 per cent. being added to the note. Decisions have been made which leave no doubt as to the legality of this proceeding. Mortgages are so drawn as to waive the right of redemption, and to include all expense of foreclosure and collection. It is surprising that people will consent to loan money in the eastern states at five, six or seven per cent. per annum, when such rates are to be obtained here. Besides, *our securities are constantly increasing in value*, and by the time long notes would fall due the property will be worth two or three times its present rate. Our county, city, township and school district bonds are also excellent investments, as they are a lien upon the entire property of communities whose rapid growth is shown by indisputable statistics elsewhere given. If any inquire how people can afford to pay such rates of interest, I think they have only carefully to look this book through, and they will discover several sufficient answers to the question. Among the most desirable of the many attractive investments which offer in this State are railroad bonds. The cost of constructing these roads across our comparatively level country is light, while their long reaches of easy grade and of air line road, greatly lessen the cost of keeping them in repair. Running through fertile regions which are rapidly settling with an enterprising people, these roads must become immensely valuable, while the enormous land grants with which they are endowed give additional security to the bonds. These bonds are offered at such rates that they afford an investment which yields an income at least double that to be obtained in the eastern states on loans. They also offer the further advantage that they can be converted into cash at any time, or may remain as a permanent investment for any desired period.

LIST OF BANKS.

LIST OF BANKS AND BANKERS in the State of Kansas on May 1, 1871. Prepared by the Adams National Bank of Topeka.

Augusta.
Brown Brothers.

Atchison.
First National Bank.
Wm. Hetherington & Co.
Atchison Savings Bank.

Americus.
T. C. Hill.

Burlingame.
P. C. Schuyler & Son.

Burlington.
Jarboe, Garretson & Co.

Baxter Springs.
Van Winkle & Slater.
Cherokee County Bank.

Council Grove.
Council Grove Savings Bank.

Chetopa.
W. B. Ketchum & Co.

Emporia.
Riggs, Dunlap & Co.
Neosho Valley Bank.
Emporia Bank.

Eldorado.
Walnut Valley Bank.

Eureka.
Edwin Tucker.

Fort Scott.
First National Bank.
Farmers and Mechanics Bank.
B. P. McDonald.
Van Fossen & Button.
Phillips & Scovell.

Garnett.
John R. Foster & Co.
Humboldt.
Pratt & Ten Eycke.
Allen County Bank.
Iola.
Iola Bank.
L. L. Northrup.
Junction City.
James Streeter & Co.
Robert S. Miller.
Lawrence.
The National Bank.
Second National Bank.
Simpson Br thers.
Leavenworth.
First National Bank.
Second National Bank.
Newman & Havens.
Scott & Co.
Hines & i aves.
Clark & Co.
German Savings Bank.
Leavenworth Savings Bank.
Manhattan.
E. B. Purcell & Co.
Wm. P. Higinbotham.

Olathe.
First National Bank.
C. E. Waldron & Co.
Ottawa.
First National Bank.
Shepherd & McQuesten.
Paola.
Miami Savings Bank.
V. C. Jarboe.
Salina.
D. W. Powers & Co.
Seneca.
Lappin & Scrafford.
Topeka.
Adams National Bank.
Kansas Valley National Bank.
Topeka Bank.
F. W. Giles & Co
Guilford Dudley.
Wamego.
Mucke & Shortridge.
Waterville.
Marshall County Bank.
Wyandotte.
B Judd.
Peter Connelley.
Kansas State Savings Bank.

SURVEY OF GOVERNMENT LANDS.

The public lands of the United States are surveyed under direction of the Commissioner of the General Land Office, Washington, D. C. The United States is divided into surveying districts, each in charge of a Surveyor General. The Surveyor General for Kansas is Hon. C. W. Babcock, whose office is at Lawrence.

All the public lands in the United States are now surveyed under the same system by which they are divided into tracts six miles square, called *townships*, and each township is subdivided into tracts one mile square, called *sections*. North and south and east and west lines are run by government surveyors, who set stones or stakes to mark the corners of the various divisions.

As all the north and south township and section lines are run upon the true meridian—that is, each line, if extended, would pass through the north and south poles—it follows that all these north and south lines converge, or approach each other towards the north. From this the reader will see that neither the townships nor sections can be precisely square, as the line bounding the north side of each tract must be a trifle shorter than the line bounding the south side of the same tract. Besides this, it is impracticable, if not impossible, for the surveyors to measure the lines with perfect accuracy.

In commencing the surveys of each district, *base lines* and *principal meridians* are established, the former running east and west, the latter north and south.

To counteract the error that would otherwise result from the convergency of lines, as above described, and to avert errors arising from inaccuracies in measurement, other lines are established, running parallel to the *base* lines, called *standard parallels.* In Kansas, and always if the townships are numbered south from any base line, these parallels are 30 miles apart, but in Nebraska, or wherever the townships number north from the base lines, the *parallels* are 24 miles apart. Upon the *parallels* the convergency, or tendency to run togeher of the north and south township and section lines, is corrcted. On the parallels is observable a jog or offset in the north and south lines, part of the stones or stakes marking the corners of the townships and sections *north* of the standard, and part marking the corners and sections *south* of the parallel.

For convenience in surveying, guide meridians are also established, running north and south, 48 miles apart.

From the point where the *base line* and the *principal meridian* cross each other, the *townships* are numbered north and south, and the *ranges* of townships east and west.

Any number or series of contiguous townships situate north and south of each other, or in other words any north and south row of townships, constitute a *range.* The ranges are designated as range No. — east (of the principal meridian,) or as range No. — west (of the principal meridian.) No two townships in any one range are numbered alike. In any one row of townships running *east and west, all* the townships are numbered alike, but are distinguished from each other by designating the number of the range in which any particular township is situated, and whether the range is east or west (of the meridian.)

A glance at the map will show a *base line* on the northern boundary of Kansas, and the sixth principal meridian crossing it between Republic and Washington counties. To describe a township, we say it is, for instance, township No. 17 south, of range No. 5 east, meaning south of the *base line* and east of the *meridian.* If north of the *base* or west of the *meridian*, it would be described accordingly. The township just described is in the southwest corner of Morris county, Kansas.

Upon the western portion of our map is an enlarged township, which is subdivided into sections, there being 36 sections in each township, which are numbered from the northeast corner of each township. In subdividing a township into sections, the surveyors commence at the southwest corner of the southeast section and run a half mile north, and establish a quarter section corner, then a half mile further north and establish a section corner, then due east, as it is supposed this course will strike the northeast section corner of section thirty-six, and which corner was set in running the exterior lines of the township. This last line is called a "random" line, and at a half mile distant a random corner is set, whence the surveyors proceed to the northeast section corner aforesaid. If they do not strike the corner, they measure the 'falling," or distance either north or south of the said corner at which they intersect the township line. They then go back to the northwest corner of section 36, correcting the random quarter corner if it was wrongly established by moving it north or south, as the case may be, one-half the measurement of the aforesaid "*falling*". From the last named section corner they proceed northward a mile and then eastward a mile and return, establishing the section and quarter section corners as before. But any excess or deficiency in measurements is thrown into the *last half mile* before reaching the north line of the township.

They then return to a point one mile west of the point of beginning, that is, to the southwest corner of section 35, and repeat the process by which the first tier of sections was laid off. The random east lines are in each case run due east one mile, to the previously established section corner. The surveys of each township are closed out on the *north* and *west* lines of said township, and if there is any excess or deficiency in the land, that is,—as no township makes 36 sections, each *precisely* a mile square—the excess or deficiency is all thrown into the row of *quarter sections* on the north and west lines of each township. This explains why these quarters are always *fractional*, containing more or less than 160 acres each.

Each section, excepting the fractional sections, is considered to be a mile square, and is always reckoned as containing 640 acres—each half, or quarter, a proportional amount. Forty acres, or a tract eighty rods (quarter of a mile) square is the lowest subdivision made by the government in disposing of its lands, but the corners of 40 acre tracts are not marked by the surveyor. These corners are regarded by law as points intermediate between the half mile or quarter section corners. In *fractional* quarter sections the excess or deficiency is thrown into the west 40s, if on the *west* side of a township, and into the north 40s if on the *north* side of a township.

STAKES OR STONES are set at each *township* corner, at each *section* corner and on section lines, half way between the *sectional* corner stones. The latter are called *quarter stones*, for they mark the corners of the *quarter sections*, but no corners are established in the centre of the sections. The only exception to this rule about *quarter* section stakes or stones is, they are not required to be established on the west boundary of the western tier of sections in a township, nor on the north boundary of the northern tier of sections in a township south of and bordering on a standard parallel or base line. This exception applies *only* to such surveys as are made subsequently to the instructions of the General Land Office of June 1, 1864.

Persons having occasion to establish a quarter corner stone in the centre of a section (which is never set by government surveys) will bear in mind that if the section is bounded on its *north side* by a standard parallel or base line, then there is no quarter section corner on said standard or base for the said section, but only for the section laying *north* of the standard or base, *provided* the survey was made since 1864.

Marking the Corners.

When *posts* are used they are to be squared above the gronnd, and at the corners of the townships and sections they should stand diagonally, or with their *corners* toward the cardinal points of the compass. On each surface of the *post common to four townships*, is to be marked the number of the particular township and its range, which it faces. Thus, if the post be a common boundary of four townships, say one and two, south of the base line of range one west of the meridian; also to townships one and two south of the base line, of range two west of the meridian, it is to be marked thus:

From north to east	R. 1 W. T. 1 S. S. 31	From east to south	1 W. 2 S. 6
From north to west	2 W. 1 S. 36	From west to south	2 W. 2 S. 1

The letters preceding the figures indicate range, township and section. The letters following the figures refer to the points of compass

Township corner *posts*, common to four townships, are also *notched* with *six* notches on each corner.

STONES *common to four townships* are only marked with *six* notches, cut with a pick or chisel on each edge or side towards the cardinal points.

Instructions are given that when *stones* are used (flat stones are prescribed) the edges must be set north and south on north and south lines, and east and west on east and west lines.

POSTS OR STONES at township corners on the *base and standard parallel* lines, and which are common to two townships on the north side thereof, will have *six notches* on each of the west, north and east sides or edges; and where such stones or posts are set for corners to two townships *south* of the *base* or *standard*, *six* notches will be cut on each of the west, south and east sides or edges.

Sectional *posts or stones* on range and township lines must have as many notches on them on two opposite angles or sides thereof as they are miles distant from the township corners respectively. If on range lines (which run north and south) they will be marked on the north and south sides. Township lines run east and west, and the sectional posts or stones thereon are marked on the east and west sides.

POSTS OR STONES set *previously* to 1864 at the corners of sections in the *interior* of townships must indicate, by a number of notches on *each* of their four corners or sides, directed to the cardinal points, the corresponding number of miles that they stand from the *outlines* of the township. The four sides of a *post* at the corner of sections will also indicate the number of the section which each side respectively faces, and on one side it should be marked the number of the township and range in which it is situated.

POSTS OR STONES set *subsequently* to 1864 at the corners of sections in the *interior* of townships, will have as many notches on the *south* and *east* edges, or sides, as they are miles from the south and east boundaries of the township.

A *quarter section* or half mile *post* will have no other marks upon it than "¼ S" to indicate what it stands for.

Stones, when used for quarter section corners, will have "¼" cut on them, on the *west* side of north and south lines, and on the *south* side of east and west lines.

A **tree** may be used instead of a corner post if it stand in the proper place and it is to be marked in the same manner as a post; but if its bark be smooth the marks may be on the bark and the tree notched.

Meander Corner posts or stones are planted at all points where the township or section lines intersect the banks of such rivers, bayous, lakes or islands, as are by law directed to be meandered.

Bearing trees are trees adjacent to corner *posts* or corner *trees*. They are distinguished by a large, smooth blaze, with a notch at its lower end, facing the corner, and in the blaze is marked the number of the range, township and section, but at quarter section corners "¼ S" only, is marked. The letters "B. T." (bearing tree) are also to be marked upon a smaller blaze directly under the larger one.

At all *township* and *section* corners, four bearing trees, if such be found, are marked in this manner, one to stand in each of the adjoining sections. A *quarter section* and *meander corners*, two bearing trees are to be marked, one within each of the adjoining sections.

Mounds. Whenever bearing trees are not found, mounds of earth or stone are to be raised around *posts* on which the corners are to be marked in the manner aforesaid. If the mound is constructed of earth, a spade full or two of earth should be taken from the corner boundary *point*, and in the cavity a marked stone placed, or a portion of charcoal, or a charred stake, driven twelve inches down into the centre point. *Since* 1864 it has been required that posts in mounds be driven twelve inches deep at the precise corner point, and the marked stone, charcoal or charred stake is to be placed twelve inches below the surface on one side of the post.

Township mounds are to be five feet in diameter at their base and two feet in height.

Section, quarter-section and meander corner mounds are to be four and a half feet in diameter at their base and two feet high.

Prior to 1864 quadrangular trenches were required, the sides to be six feet long at township corners, and five feet long at section, quarter-section and meander corners.

If a township or section corner *post* fall in such situation that the nature of the ground is not favorable to the erection of a mound, then in some convenient situation near by, a *witness mound* will be erected and with charcoal, charred stake, or marked stake deposited therein as before described The distance and bearing of this mound from the true corner is to be stated in the field notes.

Pits. The excavation made in digging earth to form the mound is called the *pit*, and *since* 1864 it is required that there be four pits, which, for *township* corners shall be eighteen inches wide, two feet in length, and at least one foot deep, located six feet from the post. At *section* corners the pits will be eighteen inches *square*.

At meander corners the *pit* is to be directly on the line, eight links farther from the water than the mound.

At township or *sectional* corners common to *four* townships, the pits should be on the lines and lengthwise to them.

On base and standard lines, where the corners are common to only *two* townships or sections, three pits only are dug—two in line on either side of the post, and one on the north side of the line for *standard corners*, and one on the south side of the line for *closing corners*.

STANDARD CORNERS, are corners on a base or standard parallel—which corners are common to two townships or sections *north* of the base or standard. Such corners are marked "S. C." in addition to the other marks before described.

CLOSING CORNERS, are corners on a base or standard parallel, which corners are common to two townships or section corners *south* of the base or standard. Such corners are marked "C. C." in addition to the other marks before described. Standard corners, are *east* of the *corresponding* closing corners, for all ranges numbered *east* of any Principal Meridian, and they are *west* of the *corresponding* closing corners, for all ranges numbered *west* of any Principal Meridian. Such corners are nowhere else to be found, and are called *double corners*.

LINES run through timber should be marked by cutting two chops or notches on each side of every tree two or more inches in diameter, which is *on the line*. Other trees standing near the line are to be blazed on two sides diagonally, or quartering towards the line.

A surveyor's CHAIN is four rods or sixty-six feet in length, and is composed of one hundred links, each link being seven inches and ninety-two hundredths of an inch long.

Length of lines—1. Every north and south *section line*, except those terminating in the north boundary of the township, must be *eighty* chains (one mile) long

2. Every east and west section line, except those terminating in the west boundary of the township, are to be within *one hundred links* of the actual distance established on the south boundary line of the township for the width of said tier of sections.

3. The north boundary and south boundary of any one section, except in the extreme western tier, are to be within *one hundred links* of equal length.

4. The meanders within a fractional section, or between any two meander posts, or of a pond or island in the interior of a section, must close within *one chain and fifty links*.

All considerable streams or bodies of water are MEANDERED. The courses and distances of their windings are taken and entered in the field notes, and where the bank intersects a township or section line, stones, stakes or mounds are established (on both banks of a stream) which are called *meander corners*.

VARIATION OF THE NEEDLE. The *true meridian* at any place is a line which if prolonged would pass through both the north and south poles.

The magnetic meridian at any place is a line, extending in the direction in which the compass needle lies when at rest undisturbed by local attractions. This line does not coincide with the *true meridian* anywhere in the United

States, excepting upon a certain line which is constantly, but slowly, moving westward and now runs west of north near Cleveland. Ohio.

The *angle* which the magnetic meridian makes with the true meridian, at any place on the surface of the earth, is called the *variation of the needle* at that place, and is east or west, according as the north end of the needle lies on the east or west side of the true meridian.

The variation of the needle at St. Louis in 1840, was 8° 37′ east, and at the mouth of the Columbia River was 21° 40′ east. The variation is different at different places, and even at the same place it does not remain constant any length of time.

In subdividing a township into sections, the compass is adjusted to a variation which will retrace the *eastern* boundary of that particular township.

IN KANSAS the variation at which the public surveys have been made is from about 10° to 15° east.

The variation of the needle, whenever a line is run, is carefully noted in the field notes.

FIELD NOTES are the records made by the surveyors of their work. The government requires that they shall be "a faithful, distinct and minute record of everything officially done or observed by the surveyor and his assistants, pursuant to instructions in relation to running, measuring and marking lines, establishing boundary corners, etc., and present, as far as possible, a full and complete *topographical description* of the country surveyed, as to every matter of useful information, or likely to gratify public curiosity."

There are separate and distinct books of surveys, as follows:

1. Field notes of the *meridian* and *base lines*, showing the establishment of the township, section or mile, and quarter section or half mile boundary corners thereon, with the crossings of streams, ravines, hills and mountains; character of soil, timber, minerals, etc.

2. Field notes of the *standard parallels*, or correction lines, showing the establishment of the township, section and quarter section corners, besides exhibiting the topography of the country on line as aforesaid.

3. Field notes of the *exterior lines* of townships, showing the establishment of corners on lines, and the topography as aforesaid.

4. Field notes of the *sectional lines* subdividing the townships into sections and quarter sections, with the topography as aforesaid.

The variation of the needle is always given. The exhibition of every mile of surveying is complete in itself. The description of the surface, soil, minerals, timber, undergrowth, etc., on each mile of line, follows the notes of survey of each line.

In Oregon, Washington and New Mexico, it is required that the field notes show the *claims* of those settlers who located prior to the survey.

The *original* field notes are retained in the Surveyor General's office, and transcripts are sent to the General Land Office at Washington, D. C

Township plats are furnished to the district land offices, and accompanying them are *descriptive* notes as to the character and quality of the soil and timber found on and in the vicinity of each surveyed line, and a description of each corner boundary.

As the field notes are confined to the *lines* mentioned, they cannot give a *thorough* description of the country, and the mention made of soil gives only an idea of the *relative* value of the land *along each line.*

Locating missing or misplaced quarter section stones.

From a letter addressed to the editor of *The Land Owner*, Chicago, Illinois, dated November 20, 1870, and signed Joseph S. Wilson, Commissioner of the General Land Office, Washington, D. C., I collate the following:

First identify the sectional corner stones north and south, or east and west, then run and measure a straight line between the two stones thus identified. Next examine the original field notes, (or a copy) and if the present measure corresponds with that recorded in the original field notes, then establish the quarter section corner at forty chains, (160 rods,) otherwise establish it *half way* between the said sectional corners.

To locate the quarter section corner in the centre of the section, (which is left unlocated by government survey) run a line north and south, and a line east and west through the centre of the section, between the quarter section corners on the section lines, and the point of intersection or crossing of these lines is the legal centre corner.

How to obtain surveys in advance of regular surveys.

By an act of Congress approved May 30, 1862, it is provided that when the settlers in any township or townships, not mineral or reserved by government, shall desire a survey to be made of the same under the authority of a Surveyor General of the United States, it may be done under certain conditions. (Sec. 10, p. 410, Vol. 12 U. S. Laws.)

It is prescribed by the Commissioner of the General Land Office that applications for surveys under this law must be made to the Surveyor General in writing, upon receipt of which he will furnish the applicant with an estimate of how much the desired survey will cost. Upon receipt of this estimate the applicant must deposit the required sum with any United States Depository, (certain National Banks in each state and territory) receiving a certificate of deposit therefor, made payable to the Surveyor General, and showing for what purpose the money was deposited. This certificate is to be sent to the Surveyor General, and upon its receipt he will contract with a competent U. S. Deputy Surveyor, and have the survey made and returned in the same manner as other public surveys.

The payment of the amount required for the survey will not give the depositor any priority of claim or right to purchase the land, or in any manner affect the claim or claims of any party or parties thereto, and when surveyed it will be subject to the same general laws and regulations in relation to the disposition thereof, as would have controlled its disposal had the survey been made in the regular and ordinary manner.

ACQUIRING TITLE TO GOVERNMENT LANDS.

Title to public lands can only be obtained through the Register and Receiver of the U. S. District Land Offices, of which there are several in each State and

Territory. They act under direction of the Commissioner of the General Land Office at Washington, D. C.

Surveyed Lands—Public lands are considered to be surveyed when official notice to that effect passes from the surveyors through the Land Office at Washington to the land officers in the district where such land is situated. Prior to this these lands are *unsurveyed lands*. and no title can be obtained to them in any manner, excepting only the inceptive right of a pre-emption settler.

Unoffered Lands are lands which have been surveyed but have not been *offered*.

Offered Lands are lands which have been surveyed and also "offered" at public auction, pursuant to previous public notice by advertisement.

Minimum Lands are those which are not sold for less than one dollar and twenty-five cents per acre.

Double Minimum Lands are those which are not sold for less than two dollars and fifty cents per acre. The odd numbered sections only are granted to railroads, and the even numbered sections are *doubled* in price, becoming Double Minimum Lands. In Kansas the Missouri, Kansas and Texas and the Missouri River, Fort Scott and Gulf railroads have a right to even as well as odd numbered sections within the *indemnity* limits, that is, outside of the ten mile limit and within the twenty mile limit. Government does not double the price on the even numbered sections in the *indemnity* limits.

Land Warrants are assignable certificates issued by the government to discharged soldiers and sailors entitling the legal holder to either forty, sixty, eighty, one hundred and twenty, or one hundred and sixty acres of *minimum offered* public land, or as half pay for *double minimum offered land*, the other half being paid in cash. Warrants may be used in payment for *pre-emptions* with the same limitations as above, concerning Double Minimum Lands.

Agricultural College Scrip is assignable Land Scrip, issued to the several states to aid in the establishment of Agricultural Colleges.

First—The legal holder is entitled to a specified amount of *offered minimum* land, but he is restricted to quarter sections which have *two sides* bounded by a section line, or it may be located on any part of a quarter section where such part is taken in full for a quarter section, but not more than *three sections* can be taken with this scrip in *any one township*. The amount that may be located in any one state is also limited to 1,000,000 acres.

Second—This scrip is taken in payment of *pre-emption claims* without regard to the quantity located in any one township or state, but under the same conditions as land warrants, if used to pre empt *double minnimum lands*.

Private Entry—Offered lands only are subject to private entry. At private entry any person may purchase land to any extent by making written application to the register, describing the land he wishes to buy and giving its area. He pays therefor $1 25 or $2 50 per acre in cash, or with duly assigned warrants or scrip under above named limitations.

There are no lands in Kansas subject to private entry at $2 50 per acre and very little at $1 25 per acre.

PRE-EMPTION—By this process and no other, excepting by *homesteading*, a title can be acquired to public land which is *unoffered*, but *offered* may also be *pre-*

empted. Every head of a family, or widow, or single man or woman, over twenty-one years of age, being a citizen or having filed a declaration of intention to become a citizen, can pre-empt one hundred and sixty acres of either minimum or double minimum land by paying therefor and complying with certain regulations. The (qualified) party who makes the first settlement upon any public land by improving the same is entitled to the right of pre-emption, if the pre emption laws are subsequently complied with, including *filing* upon the same. His right dates from the time he performed the first work on the land.

Those who settle upon *unsurveyed* land must in order to pre-empt, within *three months* after date of receipt at the district land office of the approved plat of the township embracing their claims, file their declaratory statement of settlement with the register, and thereafter make proof and payment of the tract within *eighteen* months from the expiration of said three months. This gives *twenty one* months after the surveys are received by district land officers, within which pre-emptors must pay for land.

Upon *unoffered* surveyed land a pre-emptor must filed with the register his declaratory statement within *three months* from the date of such *settlement*, and must pay for the land within *twenty-one* months from date of settlement.

Upon *offered* land the statement must be filed within *thirty days* of settlement, and within one year from the date of such filing the land must be paid for.

By an act of Congress approved July 14, 1870, all settlers who had filed for pre-emption previous to that date, were required to pay for their land before July 14, 1871, but during the spring of 1871 Congress extended this time one year, that is, until July 14, 1872, but this extension applies only to those who filed *previously* to July 14, 1870.

The act of making any improvement of whatever character upon the land claimed, is recognized as a *settlement.*

A pre-emptor cannot pay for land until he has *actually resided* upon the same for a period of at least six months and before payment must swear or affirm:

"That I have never had the benefit of any right of pre-emption under this act; that I am not the owner of three hundred and twenty acres of land in any State or Territory of the United States, nor have I settled upon and improved said land to sell the same on speculation, but in good faith to appropriate it to my own exclusive use or benefit; and that I have not, directly or indirectly, made any agreement or contract, in any way or manner, with any person or persons whomsoever, by which the title which I may acquire from the Government of the United States should inure, in whole or in part, to the benefit of any person except myself."

This affidavit must be supported by at least one witness, who must appear with the pre-emptor before the district land officers in person. The settler can then secure the land by paying in cash, or by filing a warrant, or Agricultural Scrip duly assigned.

If a pre-emptor dies before perfecting the title, his or her rights descend to the "heirs." The executor or administrator may make proof of occupation, and pay for the land, and the patent will issue to "the heirs of the deceased settler."

Pre-emptors are entitled to lands at one dollar and a quarter per acre within the limits of railroad grants, provided they locate before the lands were "withdrawn" (that is withdrawn from settlement and sale to enable the railroad company to locate its li e after which the land is a ain open to se'tlement excepting that the *odd numbered* sections within a certain distance are donated to the railroad.) Kansas grants are all for ten miles on each side, but the limits are extended to so much land within twenty miles on each side as is necessary to replace the od num ered sections that may have been disposed of by the government before the grant was made to the railroad.

The *double minimum* lands are confiued to the limits of the original grant; and the even numbered sections outside of the original grant, but within the *indemnity* limits, are $1 25 per acre.

HOMESTEADING—The Homestead Laws permit a y person to acquire by occupation and the payment of commissions and fees hereafter noted, one hundred and sity acres of *surveyed* minimum land or eighty acres of double minimum land. Under this law the settler may file on the land he desires to obtain, and that filing holds good for *six months*, during which time the settler must take possession of the land by occupation and improvement. Affidavit must be made that he or she is the head of a family, or is twenty-one years of age, and that such application is made for his or her exclusive use and ben fit, and that said entry is made for the purpose of actual settlement and cultivation, and not either directly or indirectly for the use or benefit of any other person or persons whomsoever, and that the applicant has not heretofore had the benefit of the Homestead Act. If the applicant is actually upon the land and cannot by reason of dis ance, bodily infirmi y, or other good cause, personally go to the district land office, the affidavit may be made before the clerk of the court for the county within which the land is situated.

Officers, *soldiers* and *sailors* who have served ninety days, and remained loyal, may take under homestead laws, one hundred and sixty acres instead of eighty acres of double minimum land, but *no other* dis inctions whatever are made between these and any other persons. The applicant must make oath as to the company and regiment in which he served.

Within *seven years* from the date of the duplicate of entry given to the settler by the receiver at the district land office, the settler must *personally appear* at said office and make affidavit that he or he has resided upon or cultivated the same for the term of *five years* immediately succeeding the time of filing the affi avit of entry, and that no part of the land is alienated. The five years of occupation date, not from the date of entry but from the date of *settlement*. The affidavit of settlement must be corroborated by two credible witnesses. If by reason of physical disability, distance or other good cause, they cannot *accompany* the s ttler to the district land office, their testimony may be tak n before any officer authorized to administer oaths and who uses a *seal*. He must certify to the credibility and responsibil ty of the witnesses, and state the reasons of their inability to attend at the land office. The register and receiver endorse their opinion upon the testimony and affidavit, and transmit them to the General Land Office at Washington. If the proceedings are satisfactory to them they also give a certificate to the settler.

If a homestead settler *dies*, the widow, or if she die, the heirs, may continue the settlement and cultivation and obtain title. If both parents die, leaving a child or children under twenty-one years of age, the homestead may legally be sold by the administrator.

Homesteads are not liable for any debt or debts contracted prior to the issuing of the patent or deed therefor from the government.

COMMUTING A HOMESTEAD—Homestead settlers may *pay* for their land in cash or warrants at the government price, $1 25 or $2 50, upon making proof of actual residence and cultivation for a period not less than six months from the *date of entry* to the time of *payment*. This proof must be by affidavit of himself or herself and two witnesses, made before the district land officers.

Pre-emptors may change their filings into homestead filings, *excepting* that if a settler have a pre-emption filing on an odd section within a railroad grant (i. e. taken before the lands were withdrawn for the railroad) the railroad right would immediately attach to the land, if he attempt to make a homestead filing

Absence from a homestead more than six months at any one time before the expiration of the *five years*, if proven to the satisfaction of the register after due notice to the settler forfeits all right to the land.

To *cancel* a homestead entry, the grounds must be set forth in affidavit before the district land officers. They notify interested parties and after trial send the testimony and their own opinion to Washington, for final decision. If returned cancelled the land *thereupon* becomes open to the first legal applicant.

The fact that a person has had the benefit of the pre emption act does not *in any case* interfere with his right to *homestead*.

The fact that a person has had the benefit of the homestead act does not prevent him from pre-empting, but no one can leave his or her own land in the same state or territory to take the benefit of the pre-emption act.

Inasmuch as both homestead and pre-emption *require actual residence* upon the land claimed, no person can hold land under both acts at the *same time*.

No person can pre-empt more than once.

No person can homestead more than once.

No person can file a declaratory statement for pre-emption if he has legally filed before.

No person can make a second entry to a homestead unless the first entry was illegal

Pre-emption and homestead rights or claims can neither of them be legally *assigned*. Such claims may be sold, but the seller must abandon the claim or resign his right to *government*, and the purchaser must immediately proceed in all respects as if settling upon unoccupied land, excepting that he is permitted to occupy the house of his predecessor, instead of building another, but his right dates from *filing*, if on homestead, or *settlement*, if on pre-emption claim.

The right to a homestead dates from *entry*—that is, from filing, which holds the land six months, but improvements must be made within that time.

The right to pre-emption dates from *settlement.*

Adjoining Farm Homesteads.—Any person *owning* and residing on less than one hundred and sixty acres of land, may homestead so much adjoining land as shall, taken with his original farm, make a value of not more than two hundred dollars, computing in this estimate, the *original* farm at $1.25 per acre and the adjoining homestead at government price, whether $1.25 or $2.50 per acre, but if the original farm be *within a railroad grant,* then the original farm must be computed at $2.50 per acre.

Residence upon adjoining homesteads is not required, but in all other respect the law makes the same requirements as it does concerning other homesteads and cultivation is necessary.

Claimants upon unsurveyed land ought to designate in some manner the boundaries of the land which they propose to enter, else others might make improvements which would, upon survey, fall upon the same quarter section. If settlers locate at least a half mile north or south, and east or west from each other, they will each get a quarter section by the surveys. If two happen to fall upon the same quarter section it is usually divided between them, unless the first settler established the lines of his claim within which the residence of the other was afterwards located. In this case the second settler gets nothing.

Persons *buying* a claim on unsurveyed land should contract with adjoining settlers also, or the latter might claim the land thus purchased, from the fact that their settlement dates prior to that of the purchaser.

Entering Town Sites.—Whenever any number of persons not less than 100, without regard to age, sex or nativity, locate upon any public land, to which no prior claim exists, they may, any time *before* it becomes subject to "private entry," enter said land as a town site.

If there are 100 persons and less than 200, they may enter any amount not exceeding 320 acres. If more than 200 and less than 1000 inhabitants, they may enter not more than 640 acres. If more than 1000 inhabitants, 1280 acres, and for each additional 1000 inhabitants, not exceeding 5000, they may enter a further amount of 320 acres.

If incorporated, the corporate authorities must enter, otherwise the Judge of the county court may enter for the benefit of the occupants, and the land, or the proceeds thereof, shall be assigned to the persons interested, it being divided according to the share to which each is entitled under regulations to be prescribed by the Legislative authority of the State or Territory in which the land is situated.

In Kansas it is provided by law that a town site may be entered under above named law of Congress, by the corporate authorities, or the Probate Judge of the county. See General Statutes of Kansas, p. 1073.

Fees.—Pre-emptors must pay $2.00 for filing a declaratory statement of intention to pre-empt. For reducing testimony to writing when claimants establish pre emption and homestead claims, fifteen cents for each hundred words

Fees and Commissions.

For locating *land warrants* or *Agricultural College scrip* the following fees must be *paid at the time of location:*

For a 40-acre warrant or college scrip, 50 cents each to the Register and Receiver—Total $1 00

For a 60-acre warrant or college scrip, 75 cents each to the Register and Receiver—Total 1 50

For an 80 acre warrant or college scrip, $1 00 each to the Register and Receiver—Total 2 00

For a 120-acre warrant or college scrip, $1 50 each to the Register and Receiver—Total 3 00

For a 160-acre warrant or college scrip, $2 00 each to the Register and Receiver—Total 4 00

Homestead Fees.—On surveyed lands in California, Nevada, Oregon, Colorado, New Mexico and Washington, and in Arizona, Idaho, Utah, Wyoming and Montana, the commissions and fees are to be paid according to the following table:

Acres.	Price per Acre.	Commissions.		Fees.	Total Fees and Commissions.
		Payable *when entry is made*	Payable when *certificate* issues	Payable when entry is made.	
160	$1 25	$6 00	$6 00	$10 00	$22 00
80	1 25	3 00	3 00	5 00	11 00
40	1 25	1 50	1 50	5 00	8 00
80	2 50	6 00	6 00	10 00	22 00
40	2 50	3 00	3 00	5 00	11 00

For homestead entries on surveyed land in all other States and Territories including Kansas, fees are to be paid according to the following table:

Acres.	Price per Acre.	Commissions.		Fees.	Total Fees and Commissions.
		Payable *when entry is made.*	Payable when *certificate* issues	Payable when entry is made	
160	$1 25	$4 00	$4 00	$10 00	$18 00
80	1 25	2 00	2 00	5 00	9 00
40	1 25	1 00	1 00	5 00	7 00
80	2 50	4 00	4 00	10 00	18 00
40	2 50	2 00	2 00	5 00	9 00

Officers, soldiers and sailors, taking 160 acres of $2 50 land, must pay double the amount required as *commissions,* in either of the above tables, but the *fees* are not increased.

OSAGE TRUST LANDS.

That portion of the accompanying map marked "Osage Trust Land," was opened to settlement under two distinct laws and hence the northern two-fifths is frequently called "Trust Land," and the southern three-fifths, "Diminished Reserve," as it was held by the Osage Indians after the first mentioned.

was put in market. It is all sold by the government in "trust" for the Indians, and is all "trust land," and is to be disposed of in the same manner, under decision of the General Land Office, made March 29, 1871.

It is only to be sold to actual settlers at $1.25 per acre and not more than a quarter section can be taken by any one settler.

All settlers who were upon the land prior to the passage of act of July 15 1870, must pay for the land on or before July 15, 1871. All who settle after the passage of act (after July 15, 1870) and before the surveys, must pay within one year from the survey. (Government lands are considered to be surveyed when the plats are returned to the Local land offices and not till then. See page 199. The surveys upon this land will probably be completed by September or October, 1871.) Settlers after the surveys are returned, must pay within one year from date of settlement. Sections 16 and 36 are reserved for school purposes, as elsewhere in the State. Before making payment, all settlers must prove six months continuous residence on the land claimed, and actual improvement of some portion of the same.

Claims must be taken in the form of a square or of a parallelogram, and if they happen to be divided by sectional or township lines, this is still allowable, One, two, three or four forties (40 acre tracts) may be taken, but they must form a *square body*, or else all be *in a row*. If a settler found a square quarter section out of which one forty was already taken, he could not enter the three forties remaining, but might enter either one, or he might enter any two of them which lay "side and side." Under above limitations lands may be taken through which a "meandered stream" passes, or which is bounded on *one* side by a "meandered stream." Fractional forties may be taken, but the excess must be paid for, or allowance will be made for any deficiency in land. (See "Survey of Public Lands" for explanation of "fractional forties" and "meandered streams.")

All settlers must, within three months from date of settlement, file a declaratory statement, as in pre-emption cases, and must correctly describe the land they claim, which must conform in shape to above requirements.

Settlers, when they file upon the land, and also when they make proof of settlement and payment, must make affidavit that they have not, since July 15, 1870, sold their right to, or voluntarily abandoned any tract of Osage Lands, or settled upon, improved, or filed for any other tract of said land than the one designated in said filing.

After commencing a settlement upon these lands, *bona fide* settlers will not forfeit their claims by *temporary* absence, *provided*, the absence was for the purpose of bringing their families onto the land, or for the purpose of engaging "in their calling of 'herdsmen'."

Any person, male or female, native or foreign, 21 years of age, or the head of a family, can enter "Osage Trust" or "Diminished Reserve" land in Kansas under above limitations.

The United States laws relating to *town sites*, already explained, apply to these lands.

DISTRICT LAND OFFICES.

The area of public lands in Kansas remaining unsold and unappropriated on the 30th of June, 1870, was 41,499,081 acres. These lands can be obtained through the various United States land offices, which are located as follows:

Name of District.	Location of Office.
Topeka Land District	Topeka.
Humboldt Land District	Humboldt.
Arkansas Land District	Augusta.
Western Land District	Saline.
Republican Land District	Concordia.

In the Topeka Land District there is very little government land remaining.

The land north of the Osage Lands, in the Humboldt and Arkansas land districts, excepting that granted to railroads, is open to homestead and preemption, but is mostly taken up, except in Greenwood, Butler and Sedgwick counties, and the region west.

STEAM FLOURING MILL, POMONA.

Watson Stewart, register at Humboldt says, "South of the Osage lands lying along the south line of the State, and west of the Neosho River, is a strip about two and a half miles wide, known as the 'Cherokee

Strip.' It is unsurveyed and no provision is made for its sale."

In September, 1869, all the land in the Western and Republican Land Districts east of the 6th Principal Meridian was "offered" by president's proclamation, which made it subject to private entry, but it has been so affected by the withdrawals for railroads, that there is now no land here subject to private entry, but the most of the land in these districts is still open to pre-emption and homestead.

LAND SALES IN KANSAS.

The following figures give some idea of the real estate business in Kansas during the year 1870:

*At the Junction City Land Office:

Sold for cash	186,985	acres.
Entered as Homesteads	666,593	"
Entered with Agricultural College scrip	35,200	"
Entered with Land Warrants	38,760	"
Total	927,538	"

At the Humboldt Land Office:

Sold for cash	274,931	acres.
Entered with Warrants and Agricultural College scrip	19,571	"
Entered as Homesteads	62,257	"
Final Certificates to Homesteads	8,753	"
Total	365,512	"

At the Topeka Land Office:

Total sales	84,182	acres.

I have not at hand a detailed statement of the business at the Topeka, Augusta and Concordia Land Offices, but it was not as great as at the other offices, as the two latter are new offices, and as most of the public land is disposed of in the Topeka District. At Topeka there were sold during 1870, by private land firms, 276,750 acres, for the sum of $1,433,644. This is exclusive of large sales by private parties on their own account.

In these figures, which are all taken from the books of the agents, the sales by the extensive deal-

*The Land Office was removed from this place to Salina in April, 1871.

ers in Junction City and Humboldt are not included, but it is fair to suppose that the private sales in these two places are more than Topeka alone.

We then have the aggregate land sales in these three towns, for the year 1870 as follows:

Humboldt United States Land Office	365,512
Topeka " " " "	84.182
" Private Land Offices	276,750
Junction City United States Land Office	927,535
Junction City and Humboldt Private Land Offices	300,000
Total acres	1,953,979

The balance of private sales not reckoned in Topeka will make a grand total of at least TWO MILLION ACRES *sold in the year* 1870, *in* THREE TOWNS IN KANSAS.

It is needless to encumber these pages with more dry figures, and the book is too small to exhibit the entire land business of Kansas, including the enormous sales of six or seven railroad companies, and of land agents and land companies without number. The fact that land agents issue for free distribution more than thirty large and handsome real estate papers, certifies to the extent of their business.

But in order to give our eastern friends an approximate idea of the stupendous transactions here taking place in real estate, let us suppose that the sales in the remainder of the State are only equal to the sales in the three cities enumerated.

This gives a grand total of at least four million acres. Divide this amount by 640, the number of acres in a square mile, and we have 6,250 square miles of land sold in one year, and mostly to actual settlers.

Our minds more readily grasp the immensity of these transactions if we recall the fact that the State of Massachusetts contains but 7,800 square miles. *There was sold or taken up in Kansas, chiefly by actual settlers, during the year* 1870, *an area of land almost equal to the entire State of Massachusetts.*

RAILROADS.

There are now running in Kansas, (May, 1871,) according to the time tables before me, 1,393 miles of railroad, which has been almost entirely constructed within the last two years. These roads have been built in part by the aid of government bonds, but three-fourths of our railroad lines have been called into existence by the demands of commerce, and have been aided only by land grants and local subscriptions. Kansas is a grand battle-field for railroad kings, and this not as a matter of choice, but of necessity on their part.

While there are in the United States many thousand miles of railroad, it is apparent that most of the Northern lines are but parts of, or mere appendages to, four or five vast and powerful organizations which extend from the Atlantic seaboard Westward. These competing lines concentrate and contend at Chicago and St. Louis—the two great cities of the prairies—but the contest does not end in those cities. The trans-Mississippi region offers a vast business, which all desire, and it is the peculiar and fortunate situation of Kansas that she lies in the pathway of these lines. The competing railroads of Chicago come to Kansas through southern Iowa and northern Missouri, and the competing railroads of St. Louis come to Kansas through central and southern Missouri.

Here they do not concentrate at any one point, but by crossing each other, they establish points of competition in different sections of the state. Some run directly westward, to secure the trade of Colorado and the regions beyond; others, southwest toward New Mexico, Arizona and Mexico, while others push directly south for Texas and the Gulf.

If one were to rely simply upon a study of the map, it might appear difficult to assign any good reason why all these lines should come from Chicago and St. Louis to Kansas, especially some of those contending for the Southwestern, or still more those looking toward the Texas and Gulf trade.

There are various causes which produce this result, and without professing to be familiar with the hidden things of railroad magnates, we may discover some of these causes upon the surface.

The vast flow of immigration to Kansas was quite sufficient to induce the construction of several roads to our border, and it is believed, because it is evidently true, that this great tide of immigration is to continue southwest when Kansas prairies are all occupied, as occupied they soon will be. Besides, the people of Kansas earnestly desired railroads, and have given that local aid which is necessary to secure the attention of capitalists. Most of our railroads have land grants; but land grant roads in other States have been awaiting for years the advent of capitalists, and are yet unbuilt. Notably among these may be mentioned roads in Arkansas, and this brings us to other reasons why the roads of Chicago and St. Louis do not make a straight line through Arkansas to Texas and the Gulf, instead of coming around through Kansas.

The people of the former State have not been in a condition, and they are not altogether of the constitution to invite foreign capitalists to their State. Besides, there are engineering difficulties presented by the mountains of southern Missouri and Arkansas, and even if it was a level country, the cost of constructing railroads would be greatly increased by the heavy bodies of timber occupying those regions. Southeastern Missouri chiefly, and almost the entire State of Arkansas, is a densely wooded country, and emigration moves and will continue to move around those forests, following the fair and fertile prairie, which awaits only the plow, and corn-planter, and wheat drill; instead of the axe, and mattock, and grubbing-hoe. These prairies, diversified by convenient groves and beautified by bluff and stream, extend from Kansas through the Indian Territory, New Mexico and Texas to the Gulf, and into the adjoining Republic of Mexico; and while it is evident to men who build railroads that these prairies will soon be densely populated, the surface of the country is such that it is also actually cheaper to come through Kansas to the Gulf than to go directly across through Arkansas, while the vast mineral and agricultural wealth of New Mexico is to be developed by the aid of our Kansas railroads.

The time is not far distant when Arkansas, too, will be checkered by railroads; but she must await her time, and meanwhile two or three railroads will be built from Kansas to the Gulf and to New Mexico.

But the thought of these vast southwestern prairies brings us to the last, but, perhaps, the most potential reason for the chosen railroad routes via Kansas. Our State is the outlet for the vast cattle hive of Texas, because they can be driven here over the grass-covered and abundantly watered prairies which intervene, while they cannot be driven through the timbered regions we have referred to. The extent of this trade is enormous, and for this trade all these roads are competing, and they traverse regions which, as already shown, are to supply the beef markets of the world.

Concerning our Southwestern roads they evidently are the shortest route from the cities named to New Mexico and the great Southern Pacific Railroad, which, in a few years, is to be constructed by a short line to the Pacific Ocean, and in latitudes where the snow never falls.

Railroad building has but just commenced in Kansas. It is safe to say that within three years, two railroads will be constructed from Kansas to the Gulf, and one or two more into New Mexico, and one or two others across the State to Colorado. The means for travel and traffic afforded by railroads is a ncessity of modern life. Every county must have at least one railroad, and when the people get one they only become more anxious for another. Within the next few years thousands of miles of railroad will be built in this State, enabling every farmer to reach New York in three or four days from the time he leaves his own door.

Many of our friends in the East, and in particular, associations representing the laboring classes, have made great outcry at the land grants by which Congress induces the construction of railroads in the West. This honest but mistaken conviction is echoed by the political demagogues, who are ever on the alert for a popular party cry. The people who have lived any length of time on the frontier are not opposed to these grants. What would Kansas, or Iowa, or Minnesota be to-day without railroads? And yet we all know that without land grants there would not have been a hundred miles of railroad in Kansas to-day—nay, railroads would hardly have reached our borders, but for their encouragement by land grants in States east of us.

Instead of ceasing to make land grants, Congress ought to give hereafter more land than ever before, for the reason that all along our frontier, from the British Possessions to the Gulf, the settlements have reached the borders of the timberless plains. There are very few places to-day east of the Rocky Mountains where a pioneer can obtain for a homestead, timber and prairie on the same quarter section. Therefore, a railroad is to him a necessity. He must have timber and coal. Even where native hard wood timber is abundant, if people can have pine brought on a railroad, it is cheaper and better for building purposes.

It is nonsense to say the necessary roads will be built without land grants. Let the policy prevail that would stop all further land grants, and it will take a half a century to develop even the borders of our vast plain regions, equal to the growth and progress they will exhibit in ten years under a liberal land grant system. Even with land grants it is no easy matter to induce timid capitalists to build our roads, as those of us can testify who labored and waited many weary years for railroads in Kansas.

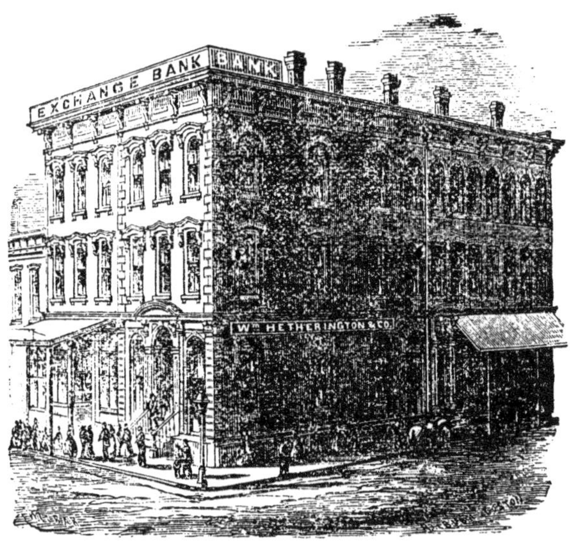

EXCHANGE BANK, ATCHISON.

THE K. P. R. AND ITS TOWNS.

First in order because the first road constructed in the State comes the Kansas Pacific Railway. This road has two eastern termini upon the Missouri river, one at the mouth of the Kansas river, and the other at Leavenworth, and meeting at Lawrence. The charter required the first named terminus to be at the mouth of Kansas river, on the south side thereof, which brings it to the State Line at Kansas City. This city is named from the Kansas river, but is not, as many suppose, in Kansas, but in the State of Missouri, and therefore does not demand our attention.

WYANDOTTE is on the north bank of the Kansas and the west bank of the Missouri river—handsomely situated upon the gently sloping bluff of these streams. A lively spring branch winds through the city. The trains of the K. P. R. are made up here, and the machine shops are here located, employing several hundred persons. The Missouri Pacific Railroad also continues through this city up the bank of the Missouri. The population is about 3,000. It is the county seat of *Wyandotte county*. About two-thirds of this county was originally timbered, but about one-half of it has been cleared. The county is noted for fruit productions. The State assessment for taxes is $3 per acre higher than in any other county in the State. Capt. Geo. P. Nelson, State Senator from this district, built and commanded the first steamboat ever built in Kansas. There were five steamboats built here for the Missouri river, of which but one is now running. The State Blind Asylum is located here, and numerous excellent business houses, residences and churches adorn the wide and graded streets.

The K. P. R. from Wyandotte to Lawrence follows the Kansas river, and the traveller sees broad bottom lands from which the timber is being cleared for domestic uses, leaving fertile farms, but disfigured with the unsightly stumps and logs of clearings. No towns of importance are to be found along this distance of thirty-eight miles, although there are growing villages, and a few miles distant on either hand, is inviting and well settled rolling prairie. The stations are *Armstrong, Muncie Siding, Secondine, Edwardsville, Tiblow, Lenape, Stranger and Fall Leaf.*

LEAVENWORTH is situated on the Missouri river, twenty-five miles by land above e mouth of the Kansas. It is the chief city in the State, having a population of about 25,000. It is the county seat of *Leavenworth county*. The site is unsurpassed for a large city, consisting of a series of gentle rolls and slopes, giving admirable building sites and drainage, and covering an area of six or eight square miles. This beautifully varied surface reposes in a vast amphitheatre, formed by the Missouri Bluffs, which rise to a hight of about three hundred feet, and sweep around it in crescent shape, each horn resting upon the river. With its paved levee upon the river bank—with its miles of graded and Macadamized streets—with its long rows of three and four story brick and iron blocks—with its numerous and well filled wholesale stores of all classess—with its banks, its hotels, its schools, its gas, supplying all parts of the city—

its princely residences and churches—with its four handsome daily papers—with its large machine shops and manufacturing establi hments—Leavenworth is entitled to be called the metropolis of Kansas. Photographic views, elsewhere presented, are sufficient evidence of the character of the buildings.

The largest and most ornate church edifice west of St Louis is the Catholic Cathedral of this city. As illustrative of the churches, a view is presented of the Baptist Church.

Leavenworth also has the honor of furnishing a United States Senator in the person of Hon. Alex. Caldwell, who was recently elected to serve a term of six years from the 4th of March, 1871.

Two miles above the heart of the city is Fort Leavenworth, from which the city derived its name and from which the inhabitants of the city have derived great gain by furnishing army supplies. This is not a fortified post, but a little city of handsome residences for officers, and commodious quarters for soldiers, with arsenals and depots for quartermaster's and commissary stores. It is the headquarters for the Department of the Missouri, and the base of supplies for all the vast region extending into and beyond the Rocky Mountains. It was located here because of the excellence of the site and of the river landing

Since the advent of railroads, the Missouri has lost much of its importance, but it served a good purpose to the cities upon its banks, and it is, in summer, a competitor in freights which reduces them to a much lower rate. The Missouri is navigable by large steamboats a distance of twenty-five hundred miles above Leavenworth, to Fort Benton, and four hundred and fifty miles in the other direction to its confluence with the Mississippi.

The elegant, substantial and expensive bridge which is soon to span the Missouri river at this point, is illustrated and described elsewhere. Lack of space prevents an extended description of the railroads concentrating at Leavenworth, and the reader is referred to the accompanying map for details upon this point, not only concerning Leavenworth, but all other towns and cities of Kansas.

The Missouri Pacific enters the city on the river bank, connecting northward with the Central Pacific at Atchison, with the St. Joe and Denver at Troy, and with the Union Pacific at Omaha. The North Missouri has its depot on the opposite shore of the Missouri where, at the east end of the bridge, concentrate also the Hannibal and St. Joe, and the Chicago, Rock Island and Southwestern. Other railroads west and south are projected and will soon be built.

Leaving this city by the K. P. R., we cross a country presenting the usual charming variety of Kansas landscape It has but lately passed from the ownership of the Indians, but already smiles with the fruits of labor, and supports promising villages along the railroad. This country, extending to the Kansas river, was the home of the famous Delaware tribe of Indians, who figured so conspicuously among the "Six Nations" of early American history, and who furnished from their Kansas home the guides and hunters who accompanied John C. Fremont in his "path finding" excursions across the Rocky Mountains. The stations between Leavenworth and Lawrence are: *Penitentiary, Fairmount, Big Stranger, Moore's Summit, Tonganoxie and Reno.*

LAWRENCE, thirty-three miles distant from Leavenworth, is situated upon the south bank of the Kansas River. Here is presented a good illustration of the formation of second bottom, with bluff and outstretching rolling prairie in the back ground, while on the north side of the river is to be found the bottom proper. A village of more than a thousand inhabitants—a city indeed—has in the latter location clustered around tne railroad buildings, and is known as North Lawrence. Hero it is that the K. P. Company are constructing their machine shops.

But Lawrence which was demolished and sacked—the Lawrence of which the world has heard, and which was named "the historic city," in a baptism of blood and fire—this city is on the south bank of the Kansas River. It covers two or three square miles of undulating and well drained second bottom, while an outskirt of elegant residences has crept up the bluffs and crown their hights. The main street, "Massachusetts," a name significant, as is "Lawrence" itself of the Yankee origin of its founders, is a mile long, and is built up with solid blocks of brick and stone business houses, two-thirds of that distance.

When Quantrell's rebel hordes burned the town in 1863, there were but three or four business houses left standing upon Massachusetts street. But while the smoke was yet ascending from the ruins, and the earth was still fresh upon the graves of seventy unarmed victims of the raid, the city council of this plucky town, by ordinance decreed that no wooden buildings should be built up n Massachusetts street. In consequence of this courageous edict hardly any other western street is so pleasing in the uniformity of its buildings. The population of Lawrence is about 10,000. It is the county seat of *Douglas* county. There are several elegant churches in Lawrence, two of which are herein shown. The crowning glory of the city is the State University, elsewhere illustrated and described. It stands upon the bluff in the southwestern portion of the city, called Mount Oread. Lawrence is supplied with gas, its main street is being paved with the Wyckoff wooden pavement, and a company is organized and will soon construct two and one-half miles o street railway through the principal streets.

The people of Lawrence pride themselves upon their patronage of schools, churches, lectures and libraries. Two large daily and weekly papers are published here

The Leavenworth, Lawrence & Galveston Railroad continues from this city southward, and the Pleasant Hill road will soon make direct connection with the Missouri Pacific, while other roads, endowed with land and local franchises are projected. Lawrence was the home of the famous General James H. Lane, United States Senator, now deceased. Here also reside Hon. E. G. Ross, late United States Senator, and Hon. Sidney Clarke, late member of Congress.

Continuing our journey westward over the K. P. R., we soon emerge from the timbered bottoms and enter upon open lands, with large, well cultivated farms and modest but thriving towns at the railway stations, which are

Buck Creek, *Williamsville*, *Perryville*, *Medina*, *Newman* and *Grantville*. Some of these stations deserve special mention, did space permit, being situated in a rich farming country.

Nearly opposite to this state, on the south side of the Kansas river, in Douglas county, is the village of *Big Springs*, situated on the old road which, before the days of Pacific railroads, lead to California. It has four churches, hotel, stores, etc. It is named from three large springs on the site. Here was held the first Free State territorial convention, and here encamped in the surrounding ravines, the men who had determined to make Kansas a free state.

Nearly opposite to Perry station is the town of *Lecompton*, which was the *Territorial* capital of Kansas. It has a population of about 400 people, and here is located a thriving institution of learning known as Lane University—which is under the care of the United Brethren Church.

TOPEKA.—At a distance of twenty-eight miles from Lawrence, and sixty-six miles from the Missouri river, we reach Topeka, the capital of the State and the county seat of Shawnee county. Its population is about eight thousand.

This city, like Lawrence, has a sister city north of the river—North Topeka, which, with its bank, wholesale grocery store and other establishments, gathers around the railroad depot considerable business. Crossing the Kansas over the handsome iron bridge, which is shown in the engraving, we enter Topeka proper.

This bridge deserves a passing notice, because it is at once so cheap, so elegant and so durable. It has six spans, each one hundred and fifty feet long and eighteen feet wide in the clear, with a sidewalk on each side. The height of the arches is sixteen feet. They are composed of boiler plate and cylinder iron, united together, so as to form a tube nine by thirteen inches in size. Each arch has two iron chords, upon which rest the joist and floor, and each of these chords are six inches deep and three-fourths of an inch thick. The chords and arches are connected by struts and braces, which distribute the strain uniformly. The entire structure is of iron, excepting the floor and floor joist, and it rests upon cut stone abutments and piers. This bridge was brought from the manufactory of Z. King & Co., Cleveland, Ohio, but so great is the demand in this country that extensive works for their manufacture have been established at Iola, Kansas, which are illustrated and described elsewhere.

It is interesting to note how extensively and for what a variety of purposes iron is now used in place of wood, and how admirably its imperishable substance is adjusted to these uses.

We have been so long on this bridge, that the turbid appearance of the waters beneath must have attracted our attention, and we are convinced that the Kansas is called the "Little Muddy" not less appropriately than the Missouri is named the "Big Muddy."

Topeka covers a wide extent of country. The portion towards the river rests upon a series of gentle rolls which run out into level land, while at the rear the site slopes southward to a creek which is skirted with timber. The main street—the broadest avenue to be found in the State—is well defined by adjacent business houses and residences all the way from the bridge across a bit of level ground, and over a prairie roll down to the creek above mentioned, nearly two miles from the river. This creek rejoices in the name of Shunganunga. It must not be inferred that streets are usually narrow in Kansas, but "Kansas Avenue" is one hundred and twenty feet wide, which makes it one of the broadest in the State. The buildings of Topeka are largely built of brick and stone, and it has many handsome business houses, one of which—the Kansas Valley National Bank—is represented by an excellent illustration. The Capitol, Episcopal Female Seminary and Lincoln School all speak for themselves by the illustrations presented. The Washburn College, a Congregational institution of promise, is located here. Topeka is supplied with gas.

The Atchison, Topeka & Santa Fe Railroad extends southwest from Topeka and is about to be completed northeast to Atchison. It is the intention soon to build railroads east to Leavenworth, and also lines extending north and south from the city.

Recrossing the bridge we are again whirled westward over the K. P. R., up the broad valley and across what was lately the reserve of the Pottawatomie tribe of Indians. *Silver Lake*, *Rossville* and *St. Mary's* are stations on this line, and at St. Mary's the Catholic Church, which had a prosperous mission here among the Indians, have erected two large school edifices. This is a thriving station with 600 or 800 inhabitants.

WAMEGO, the central station of the Kaw Valley division of the K. P. R., is one hundred and three miles from the Missouri River, and contains a population of about 1000 inhabitants. As a fresh engine is taken from the round house located here and the train stops "twenty minutes for dinner," we have time to notice that the town is commenced near the river, on a high and dry bottom, whence the main street ascends gently northward until it reaches the summit of the low bluffs. To speak of the scenery is to describe in advance the view that meets the eye at nearly all the towns along the Kansas, or its tributaries, or indeed any other stream in the State. Far-reaching bottoms or alluvial meadows, which are one, two, or three miles wide, winding river and stream, abrupt or sloping bluff and rolling prairies, which extend until they meet the skies in the distance. These constitute the views which one never tires of gazing upon in their endless variety, but of which the reader would weary if we attempted to describe them in detail.

LOUISVILLE, the county seat of Pottawatomie county, is located upon Rock creek, eight miles north of Wamego. It contains a number of business houses, mechanic's shops, and about four hundred inhabitants, and is on high bottom land, between two streams. A good flouring mill is run by a constant water power. There is also good unimproved water power on Vermillion Creek and on the Big Blue.

Beyond Wamego is *St. George*, with its excellent water power, and one hundred and eighteen miles from the Missouri is

MANHATTAN. This town is situated upon high bottom and sloping bluffs at the junction of the Big Blue River with the Kansas. Two of King's iron bridges are being thrown across these streams. Upon the former river, about three miles distant from the depot, is a splendid water power. Upon the rock bottom a stone dam is built, three hundred feet long, and over this pours in an unbroken sheet the bright waters of the "Blue." This furnishes a fall of twelve feet. A large flouring and saw mill is the only machinery to which this great power is at present applied. Near here resides H. C. and G. W. Chaffee, sons of Judge N. L. Chaffee, of Ohio, who have a herd of fifty-six head of thoroughbred Short Horn cattle. A life-like cut is given of one of these animals. Manhattan has a population of about 1500, with the usual number of business houses, churches, &c. The State Agricultural College, of which mention is made elsewhere, is located upon the commanding bluff which sweeps along the Blue almost into the town. The Adams House, built and owned by Maj. N. A. Adams, which we illustrate, is a building of which any young city may be proud, and its large, airy rooms and excellent appointments would do credit to an old city. We enter the region of the beautiful magnesian limestone at Manhattan, and this hotel, as well as other buildings, including residences and churches, is built of it. This gives the town a neat and substantial appearance. Railroads from the north are expected to follow down the Big Blue to Manhattan. This is the county seat of *Riley county.*

We must hasten westward, passing *Ogden* and *Fort Riley*, and reaching

JUNCTION CITY, one hundred and thirty-eight miles from the Missouri. It is situated near the confluence of the Smoky Hill and Republican Rivers, which unite to form the Kansas. This city has a population of about 3000.

It is built upon the crown of a low bluff or prairie roll, between the streams above mentioned. Its location, relatively to the surrounding country, is such as to command an extensive trade, even from the remote frontier. The Missouri, Kansas and Texas Railroad comes into this place, and will soon be pushed northwesterly, up some one of the attractive valleys in that region, while other roads will be built north and south. There are unimproved water powers in the vicinity, among which is reckoned a point on the Republican, adjoining the town, at which, by cutting a race way in bottom land, three-fourths of a mile long, the entire volume of the stream may be turned into the Smoky Hill with a fall of twelve feet. Five miles west of town is an excellent unimproved water power, but one mile from the railroad. Six miles east is a good flouring mill, run by Clark's Creek, which is fed by springs. Three Howe Truss bridges span the stream in the vicinity of Junction City. Extensive quarries of magnesian limestone have been opened here, which cuts with a cross-cut saw like wood, and large shipments are made of the blocks. It is largely used in building in the town. A beautiful little church has been erected of this material, of which I am glad to present a view, and also the following extract from a letter from Geo. W. Martin, dated Junction City, January 13, 1871. "We are having the finest job of frescoing done on that church to be found in the State." This is very high praise, for there are many elegantly frescoed churches, halls, etc., in Kansas. Junction City is the county seat of *Davis county*. The Republican and Kansas Rivers form the dividing line between Riley and Davis counties.

Fort Riley, but three miles distant, is the source of considerable business to this city. The residence and farm of His Excellency, General James M. Harvey, Governor of the State of Kansas, is a few miles north of Fort Riley, near Vinton P. O., in Riley county.

Leaving Junction City the K. P. R. follows up the broad valley of the Smoky Hill River and we pass the stations of *Chapman's Creek* and *Detroit*. We have hitherto been traveling through a country where unimproved land can be bought at from five to ten or fifteen dollars per acre, but we are now entering the vast homestead area of Kansas, where homesteads may be obtained within a few miles of the railroad. The Enterprise Flouring Mills, near Detroit, are asserted to be the "finest in Central or Western Kansas, drawing patronage from a half dozen counties and from a distance of nearly a hundred miles."

Abiline, one hundred and sixty-two miles west of the Missouri is pleasantly situated upon a small stream at a distance of two miles from the Smoky Hill, and is the county seat of *Dickinson county*. Its population is about 800. It is a thriving place, having made itself extensively known as the headquarters for the eastern shipment of Texas cattle over this road, although the trade is divided with other towns. The buildings are of a substantial character and everything betokens prosperity. In this county Hon. Ezra Cornell, the founder of Cornell Uuniversity at Ithica, N. Y., has established a large stock farm for the breeding of fine stock. His importations will be of immense value to that region. The "*Albany Cultivator*" states that he has brought 25 head of thorough-bred Short Horns to Kansas.

Proceeding westward we pass *Solomon City*, located upon the high banks of the Solomon River. This stream, after watering a broad and fertile valley in Northwestern Kansas, two hundred and fifty miles long, empties itself into the Smoky Hill, near Solomon City. This town seems to be so situated as to command considerable trade, and near it are located the salt works already alluded to.

Salina is one hundred and eighty-five miles west of the Missouri and was laid out by Col. Wm. A. Phillips. It did not make rapid progress until after the construction of the K. P. R. It is surrounded by a fine agricultural country, which is quite well settled. There are farmers near here who have averaged fifty bushels of corn per acre for the last ten years. The town has its usual quota of schools, churches and business houses, and its population is about 1300. There are shipped from here about 15,000 head of cattle annually. It is the county seat of *Saline county*, and commands the trade of extensive settlements to the southwest. In 1866 buffalo were killed within two miles of

Salina. They do not now come nearer than 75 miles to the west. There is a very good unimproved water power on the Saline river near Salina. The U. S. Land Office is located here.

Proceeding westward past *Bavaria* and its flourishing colony, we reach *Brookville*, at a distance of two hundred miles west of the Missouri. Here the Kaw Valley Division of the K. P. R. terminates and the Smoky Hill Division commences. The company are erecting expensive railroad buildings. For this purpose an excellent quarry of red sandstone has been opened beside the railroad track near here. We are now fairly within the region of buffalo grass, where all the uplands are covered with this nutritious herbage, although the wide bottoms to the extreme western part of the State produce tall grasses. As showing the demand for accommodations for shipping stock, it may be mentioned that the railroad company have stock yards at Brookville, at which seven cars can be loaded at once.

The stations of *Spring Rock*, *Elm Creek*, *Summit Siding* and *Fort Harker* are passed to bring us to

ELLSWORTH. This town is situated upon the Smoky Hill. We left this stream at Salina, and crossed the prairies a distance of thirty-seven miles, instead of following its wide southern detour. The town is surrounded by a fine farming country, and well adapted to stock raising. It is the county seat of *Ellsworth county*. It is of this region that Rev. J. Sternberg speaks in his excellent letter from Fort Harker, near which small military post his farm is situated.

The country intervening between here, *Fort Hays*, *Hays City* and *Ellis*, is little settled as yet, as the railroad has not been long completed. The latter place is three hundred miles from the Missouri River and is a division statione upon the railroad. Wide bottoms and fine farming lands are to be found here. This country cannot long remain unoccupied when there are so many people in the world without lands, which here are ready for occupation. We are now on the great buffalo range of the North American continent, where as many of this monstrous game as one desires may be killed at pleasure.

The State extends about one hundred and twenty miles west of Ellis. The western boundary line has not been established by survey, but it is on the one hundred and second degree of longitude west from Greenwich. The supply of timber gradually diminishes west from Junction City, and beyond Salina it is only found on this route in narrow belts and isolated greoves. The line of the K. P. R., by some mystery of engineering, was located upon the divide, or watershed, between the Smoky Hill and Saline Rivers, the entire distance of two hundred miles west from Ellsworth to the State line. The traveler sees for a good part of that distance a high rolling surface, pleasant to look upon, because of its gentle undulations, but comparatively destitute of running water and timber. But out of sight, at a distance of a few miles on each side, may be found an abundance of running water, sheltering bluffs for stock, and a small supply of timber.

The following description of this country written in April last, is extracted from the official report of a committee of the Chicago Colony, sent to Kansas to select a location:

"The climate here is very mild, vegetation being already several inches high. We experienced no inconvenience from lying on the ground for several nights, with nothing but a buffalo skin for a bed. We should call this the paradise of cattle and consumptives. Here swarmed countless thousands, the buffalo, elk, the antelope and deer.

"So far as the committee could discover, all the requisite conditions are here fulfilled. 1st. A climate of surpassing salubrity. 2d. Cheap lands, with a rich soil. 3d. Water and timber. 4th. An unsettled country, inviting to immediate county organization, where under our own auspices, all the initial work of education and civil and religious institutions could be commenced."

This report elsewhere speaks of coal in abundance, and explains the matter of timber by showing that it is found in limited quantities only. There is much more timber in Western Kansas than has been supposed until lately, but the amount is very small compared with Eastern Kansas. "The truth, the whole truth, and nothing but the truth," is what emigrants want, and what this book is intended to furnish, so far as space will permit.

The K.P.R. continues westward from the State line to the Rocky Mountains, or rather to Denver, which is twelve miles east of the mountains and six hundred and twenty-eight miles west of the Missouri River. From Denver the same company operate the Denver & Cheyenne R. R. to Cheyenne, one hundred miles north of Denver, on the Union Pacific R. R. The K. P. R. is also building branch roads into the mountains of Colorado, and will soon construct a line through the mountains towards Salt Lake City.

The Land Commissioner for the Kansas Pacific Railway is Hon. J. P. Devereux Lawrence, Kansas. The lands of this road are also sold by the National Land Company, who have offices along the line, and also in New York and Chicago with headquarters at Topeka.

THE C. B. U. P. R. R. AND ITS TOWNS.

ATCHISON is the eastern terminus of the Central Branch Union Pacific Railroad, and is situated at the extreme western elbow, made by the Missouri River in its windings along the eastern border of Kansas. It has a population of about 8000, and is lighted with gas. It is the county seat of *Atchison county.*

In the configuration of its surface the site presents every variety desirable in a town, whether of level low land, sloping rolls or towering bluffs, so that one may live on hill or in dell, as suits one's fancy. It is of course well drained, and a streamlet here enters the Missouri, after coursing through the town. This city is a place of extensive business and is headquarters for the railroad of which we are speaking. The Missouri Pacific terminates here, and the Atchison and Nebraska railroad continues northward, crossing the St. Joe and Denver Railroad at Troy, and is rapidly pushing north to connect with the Nebraska system of railroads. The Atchison, Topeka & Santa Fe Railroad has its northeastern terminus here, although not yet completed between this place and Topeka. Upon the opposite bank of the river is the North Missouri Railroad, connecting with the St. Joseph lines. Loaded cars cross the river on a steam ferry.

In its banks, business houses, churches, schools and residences, Atchison can vie with many cities in the east, which are fifty or a hundred years old. The people of Atchison point with commendable pride to their Central School building, which cost about $45,000. It stands upon a site where a similar structure was burned but about a year before this was erected. It contains ten school rooms, each 28x33 feet, with commodious wardrobes, and has an audience room 33x60 feet, with rooms for apparatus, etc. The first thing done in our live Kansas towns is to build a church and a fine school house. The C. B. U. P. extends one hundred miles west to Waterville, and on this line there are nineteen stations and towns. Many of them are but just started, as the road was recently completed, but there are about seventy or eighty stores on the line, dealing in groceries, notions, produce and dry goods.

The first station is *Farmington*, twelve miles west of Atchison, located in a fertile and populous farming region. This description applies to all the land along this road in fact, excepting as you proceed westward, the country is newer and more sparsely populated. *Monrovia*, upon the Stranger Creek, and *Effingham*, which is the R. R. station for Grasshopper Falls, being past we come to

Muscotah, which is one of the largest and prettiest towns on the road. It is located upon the banks of Grashopper river which here furnishes a fine water power. It is the home of U. S. Senator Pomeroy, who has here an excellent and well improved farm. Mjaor W. F. Downs, General Superintendent and Land Commissioner of the road, who resides at Atchison, also has a carefully selected farm at this place, and these gentlemen, by the introduction of stock of the best breeds and pure blood, and by the most improved system of cultivation, are making model farms. The town is within the borders of the late Kickapoo Reservation. Passing *Whiting* we arrive at *Netawaka*, thirty-six miles west of Atchison. It is a rapidly growing town, situated in a prosperous community. From here a daily line of stages run in connection with the trains to *Holton*, nine and a half miles distant, the county seat of Jackson county. The latter is a place of promise, situated on one of the chief tributaries of the Grasshopper. It has excellent prospects for a railroad from the north to follow down the latter stream.

Beyond Netawaka are *Wetmore*, *Sherman*, *Corning* and *Centralia*, the latter sixty-two miles from the Missouri. It is one of the largest and most prosperous towns on the road. Beyond are *Vermillion* and *Frankfort*, the latter having a fine water power on the Vermillion, close by.

Barretts, three miles beyond, also has water power, and at Elizabeth are fine magnesian limestone quarries. The rock with which the abutments of the Leavenworth bridge are built, were wrought from this quarry. *Irving* next beyond, ninety miles from Atchison, is located near the Big Blue River, and is the seat of "Wetmore Institute" of learning, which is under the charge of the Presbyterian Church. Irving is a thriving town, being surrounded by good farming country. Five miles beyond is *Blue Rapids*, located at one of the best water powers in the State. It is being extensively improved by an enterprising colony, at a heavy expense. The organization was known as the Genesee colony from Western New York, and they publish that they chose the site because of "facility of transportation, railroad station, fuel, excellent building stone, sand in the river, good land, picturesque scenery, and unfailing water power for the machinery of ten or twenty mills." They assert that "temperance, morality, education and religion are the bases and bulwarks of good society and permenent prosperity. The town was laid out February, 1870, and has been greatly prospered.

The claims of this colony, as to advantages of location, and the platform of membership, are published, not because of their novelty, but to illustrate why it is that settlers, singly and in colonies, are attracted to Kansas in greater numbers than to any other State, and also why it is that Kansas society is confessedly so excellent. If we except the water power—for I do not claim that all the towns in Kansas have available water power—I am confident that a considerable proportion of the towns in this State were started upon the same basis as that of Blue Rapids.

West of the latter place, and one hundred miles from Atchison, is the promising young town of

WATERVILLE. It is, at this writing, (January, 1871,) but about two years old. Lots which six months ago sold for twenty to seventy-five dollars each, are now selling at one hundred to three hundred dollars each. This rise in real estate is a fair average of the percentage of rise in Kansas towns at their most prosperous stage. Being the westernmost railroad town in the vicinity, Waterville commands the trade of an extensive frontier, and has about twenty-five or thirty stores, with banks, fine hotels, churches, etc. Its depot is one hundred and ten feet long. It is expected that one or two more railroads will center here.

Stages run to *Marysville*, *Washington*, *Clyde* and *Concordia*. The town has a fine water power, extensive quarries of white magnesian limestone, and large fields of gypsum are found in the vicinity.

It is proposed soon to resume work upon the C. B. U. P. R. R., pushing it westward in the neighborhood of the line as shown on our map. The country through which the road will be built, is among the most desirable in the State, being supplied with everything that is needed to support a dense population.

THE ST. J. & D. R. R. AND ITS TOWNS.

The Saint Joseph & Denver City Railroad commences on the west bank of the Missouri River, at Elwood in Kansas, opposite to the city of St. Joseph, Missouri. From the little village of Elwood the road runs across the Missouri River bottom, a distance of about six miles to

WATHENA.—This city, of about 1,500 inhabitants, is the largest town in Doniphan county. It is situated just within the valley of Peter's Creek, where the latter opens from the bluff on either side into the Missouri River bottom. The stream furnishes a good water power, which is improved by a flouring mill and woolen factory, while another mill is run by steam. The public school building is claimed to be one of the finest in the State. A railroad is projected down the Missouri bottom to *Doniphan*, in the southeast portion of the county, there to intersect the Atchison & Nebraska Railroad.

From Wathena our railroad follows up Peter's Creek to TROY, the county seat of *Doniphan county*. This place is situated on high rolling prairie, where the stream we have been following heads in numerous springs in and around the town. This place also boasts of its fine public school. The population is about 1,000.

About a mile southwest of Troy the road we are following is crossed by the Atchison & Nebraska R. R. Continuing westward we pass *Norway* and *Severance*, new and growing railroad stations, with a considerable grain trade.

Entering *Brown county* we pass the new town of *St. Francis* and reach HIAWATHA, the county seat. The town is pleasantly situated on high rolling prairie in the midst of a good country. It has the usual complement of churches and schools, and an enterprising population. At Padona, a few miles northwest a good mill is building to be run by water. Other mills run by steam are convenient for the people. Coal is extensively used for domestic purposes in this county, as well as in all the counties along this line, although timber is abundant.

Passing *Hamlin* station, we reach *Sabetha*, which is situated just in the edge of Nemaha county. A short distance to the north is Albany, and southward is Capioma, which are the post office centres for a thrifty farming population. It is proposed to run a railroad through this vicinity to connect the Nebraska and Kansas railroads. Passing another station, the name of which is unknown to me, we reach the thriving town of

SENECA, the county seat of Nemaha county. It has a population of about 1000, and is situated on gently sloping table land on the west bank of the Nemaha river, which runs northward into Nebraska. Seneca contains a fine stone school house, churches, etc., and is growing rapidly. Nine miles to the south is Centralia, on the C. B. U. P. R. R., and a daily stage connects the two places. A railroad will soon be built from the C. B. U. P R. R., from some convenient point southeast of Seneca to this place. It will be about fourteen miles long, and will make the distance from Seneca to Atchison sixty-four miles, while it is seventy-seven miles to St. Joseph.

The road over which we are passing was opened to travel since January 1, 1871, and stations are not established at all needful points, as yet. The next town, and the present terminus of the road, is

Marysville, the county seat of Marshall county. It is situated on the east bank of the Big Blue River, on high sloping bottom, and the adjacent bluffs. It has a population of 800 or 1000 people, and is rapidly growing. The river affords an excellent water power. Upon its rocky bed a dam is built of stone, whence the water is conveyed several rods through a tunnel in the solid rock, to the mill below. A good bridge spans the river. The counties through which this road, as well as the C. B. U. P. railroad passes, are among the most desirable in the State for farming purposes. A large amount of wheat is raised in these counties, and probably more spring wheat than in any other portion of Eastern Kansas, although winter wheat succeeds admirably here. These counties are quite well settled, as will be seen from the census returns. Timber is abundant, and the climate is healthy, but of course a little more hay is required to carry stock through the winter, than in Southern Kansas.

This Railroad is to be built northwest, striking the Little Blue, and following up that stream into Nebraska and to Fort Kearney, where it connects with the Union Pacific Railroad.

THE A. & N. R. R. AND ITS TOWNS.

The Atchison & Nebraska Railroad commences at Atchison, as its name indicates. although there is talk of connecting it with the Leavenworth, Lawrence & Galveston road, at Lawrence, both being chiefly under one ownership.

From Atchison this road runs on the Missouri River bottom lands to *Doniphan*, a town of several hundred people, with a large grain trade, whence it climbs a considerable grade, following Rock Creek and passing *Brenner Station*, crossing the St. Joseph & Denver road near Troy. Beyond is down grade to the stations of *Fanning* and *Highland Station*. The latter is connected by stage from the trains with *Highland*, a village of 300 or 400 enterprising people, situated on high rolling prairie, in a densly settled farming community. The place is the seat of Highland University, an excellent school for both sexes. A shaft is being sunk at this place for coal, which crops out in several places in the county. *Iowa Point*, a small village on the Missouri River, is the next station.

White Cloud is the last station on this road in the State of Kansas, and is the northeastern town of the State. It is well situated for business on the Missouri River, and has an extensive trade with that part of Kansas, as well as the adjacent portions of Nebraska and Missouri. The population is about 1,200. On the opposite or eastern side of the Missouri River runs another railroad, from which a branch or spur is building, or about to be built, to White Cloud. The town has good churches, &c., and is surrounded by a rich country and an abundance of timber. It has several saw mills in the vicinity, and manufactures more lumber than any other town in the State.

This road is now building into Nebraska, to Brownsville, and on up the Missouri River.

I am informed that the elevations furnished me on this road and inserted upon my map, were incorrect, and that the figures should be as follows, showing the elevations of depots in feet above the ocean level: Atchison, 800;

BANCROFT BLOCK, EMPORIA.

Doniphan, 835; Brenner, 947; Troy Junction, 1,121; Fanning, 888: Highland Station, 871; Iowa Point, 852; White Cloud, 864.

THE MISSOURI RIVER RAILROAD.

This railroad commences at the State line, near Kansas City, and passing through Wyandotte, follows the Missouri River, with unimportant stations, which are shown on the accompanying map, to Leavenworth, thence up the river to Atchison. The road is chiefly owned in Leavenworth, but is leased to and run by, the Missouri Pacific Railroad.

M. K. & T. R. R. AND ITS TOWNS.

Commencing at Junction City, the Missouri, Kansas and Texas Railroad, was constructed across the divide between the waters of the Kansas and the Neosho rivers and down the valley of the latter into the Indian Territory. It was formerly known as the Neosho Valley Railroad, and still later as the Southern Branch Union Pacific. Leaving the depot at Junction City, which is common to this road and the K. P. R., we follow up the considerable grade which leads us across Clark's creek to *Skiddy*, and across the divide to Parker, on the upper waters of the Neosho River. Extensive settlements have recently been made in this region by colonies from various localities, and especially from Chicago, Illinois, and another from Cincinnati, Ohio. At Parkersville, which is a new place, preparations are making for a speedy enlargement of the business facilities. This place is 1,339 feet above the ocean, its elevation being but a trifle less than that of Brookville on the Kansas Pacific, seventy miles west.

COUNCIL GROVE is situated on the Neosho, and was a well known trading post upon the old Santa Fe wagon road. It is the county seat of *Morris county*, and contains a population of about 1000. It is situated just outside of the boundary of the Kansas or Kaw Indian Reserve, which is about to be opened to settlement. Coal mines of fair quality are opened in this county, and in Lyon county adjoining. This enterprising place is expecting another Eastern railroad to be soon constructed.

Going down the widening valley of the Neosho, we pass the growing station of *Americus*, which is situated in a very desirable farming region and is the promising business centre for a thriving country. Here as in Kansas style, is a good stone school house, and a cheese factory is located here, which uses the milk of about 350 cows. The village has 300 or 400 inhabitants. A valuable unimproved water power on the Neosho river is near Americus.

EMPORIA is distant 60 miles from Junction City and 61 miles from Topeka, with which it is connected by the Atchison and Topeka and Santa Fe R. R. It is located on an undulating prairie between and near the Neosho and Cottonwood, and a few miles from the junction of these streams. It is the county seat of *Lyon county*, and contains a population of about 3,000 people. The valleys about Emporia are famous for their well tilled farms, and the town commands a very extensive trade, owing to its advantageous position relative to the vast and rapidly growing region laying south and west. The citizens also look with confidence for the speedy construction of another railroad from the direction of Ottawa. Many fine business houses, private residences with churches and school houses of like character adorn the streets of this city. It has also added greatly to its otherwise fair fame by rigorously prohibiting the sale of intoxicating liquors. The State Normal School is located at Emporia and is in a very prosperous condition, owing partly without doubt, to the interest manifested by the citizens in regard to its welfare. Both the Neosho and the Cottonwood furnish water power with fine mills, and there are other unimproved water powers in the vicinity.

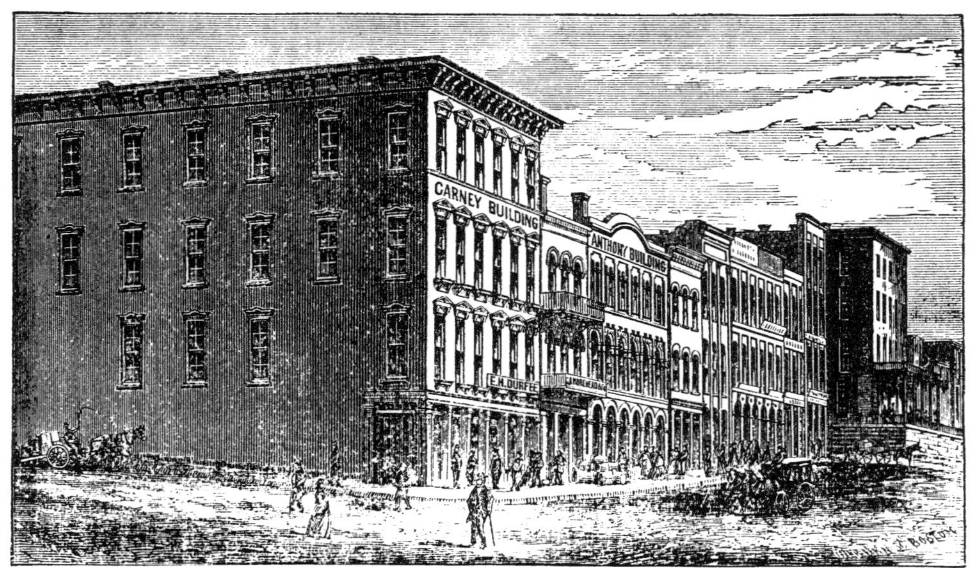

CORNER LEVEE AND DELAWARE STREETS, LEAVENWORTH.

Eight miles below Emporia is *Neosho Rapids*, it being the station for a town a mile or two distant on the north side of the Neosho, below its junction with the Cottonwood. Here is an excellent water power, awaiting improvement. It is not improbable that the new railroad from the northeast will enter the valley at this point.

Hartford, next below, has the commencement of a school under the M. E. Church, which will doubtless grow to meet the requirements of this populous region.

The station of *Strawn*, a newly established town of some promise next is met in our trip down the "far famed Neosho valley," bringing us to

BURLINGTON, situated in the centre of *Coffey* county, of which it is the county seat, and has a population of about 1,400. The town is located immediately on the south bank of the Neosho River, down which we have now followed until we find it to be a large stream. A dam has been thrown across it at this point, and a valuable water power secured, by which a woolen factory and two flouring mills are operated. The dam, just above the town, is 300 feet long, and by a canal one-half mile long, an excellent power is obtained in the town, with sixteen feet head. A small run, fed by springs, winds its way through the town, giving variety to the rolling town site. Burlingtonians expect to be blessed with two more railroads at no remote day, one from Ottawa and another from the north.

Continuing on the south side of the river for miles, we reach Le Roy station, which is two or three miles away from Le Roy, the town it represents. The latter is immediately upon the north bank of the Neosho, in the heart of a prosperous community of farmers, and it contains some hundreds of inhabitants. A steam flour mill is in town, and a flour mill run by water near by, while two other excellent mill sites are awaiting development.

I have not hitherto spoken of saw mills, for it is to be understood that they are abundant in all parts of Kansas.

NEOSHO FALLS is the next town which attracts our attention upon this route. Among the many claims it presents to immigrants is its pleasant site on the south bank of the Neosho. The volume of this river has been so much increased by the numerous tributaries that enter it upon both sides, that it is no longer the modest creek we found soon after leaving Junction City. It has swollen to a river of importance, and upon its smooth and solid rock bottom a dam is constructed at Neosho Falls, which extends across the river. It is 200 feet long, and gives eight feet head of water. The power is estimated by engineers as sufficient to drive machinery to the extent of twelve hundred horse power the greater part of the season. At present it is only improved by a saw and grist mill, of large capacity, but power will be furnished to those desiring it for other purposes. About eight hundred feet above the dam stands one of King's wrought iron bridges, 200 feet span, crossing at Main street. Its two approaches, of forty feet each, as well as the bridge proper, stand upon stone abutments and piers. An excellent view of the water power and bridge beyond, from a photograph, is presented elsewhere.

The depot of the M., K. & T. R. R. is located conveniently to the business part of town. Neosho Falls is the division headquarters for the road, with round houses, etc., and the office of the Land Commissioner, Professor I. T. Goodnow, is located here. The population of the town is 800 or 1,000. It doubled in six months after the railroad offices removed here. The buildings are of such a character as is to be expected in an enterprising Kansas town. Concerning additional railroads, the city has its great expectations. It is looking for a railroad from the northeast, and another from the east; but the road which is expected first is one extending directly to Fort Scott, saving fifty miles, or half the distance now traveled. Neooho Falls is the county seat of Woodson county. In the southwest corner of this county is a valuable water power, on the Verdigris, which should be improved by a mill, for the benefit of the rich and rapidly improving surrounding country. It is situated at Toronto. Coal is developed, and used for domestic purposes and blacksmithing.

Continuing our route southeast 15 miles, we reach HUMBOLDT. The Land Office for Humboldt Land District is located here, adding greatly to the business of the place. We have reached that portion of the Neosho which runs nearly south, and the depot for Humboldt, on the M. K. & T. R. R., is on the west side of the river, while most of the town is on the east side. The Leavenworth, Lawrence & Galveston Railroad also enters the town on the east side. The latter road keeps upon that side of the river for some distance, and the two roads cross each other ten miles below Humboldt. The attractive town site is near the junction of two creeks, with the Neosho river, giving to the support of the town extended and fertile valleys. Coal is found in abundance in this county. This town was laid out in 1861, but being twice pillaged and burned by rebels during the war, made little progress for several years. But of late its growth has been vigorous and healthy. Its inhabitants number about 2000. There are a number of good buildings here, churches, schools, etc. One of King's Wrought Iron Bridges connects east and west Bridge street, a beautiful avenue a mile in length. In addition to the two roads mentioned, another east and west road connecting eastward at Fort Scott, it is confidently believed will be constructed very soon. A view is given of the bridge and two business blocks in Humboldt. Following our M. K. & T. R. R. down the east bank of the Neosho, we reach

TIOGA and NEW CHICAGO, two towns recently located side by side, at the crossing of this road and the L. L. & G. R. R. These towns, situated on the lowland and bluffs of the Neosho, are growing so rapidly that they must soon find it for their interest to adopt a common purpose and a common name. Our friends in the remote east have little idea of the amount of business transacted in one of our towns. In good weather, the principal street of all our towns is crowded with teams, and the sidewalks thronged with a busy, and oftimes a motley throng. A friend informed me, for instance, that he recently counted two hundred farm wagons in one day in the streets of New Chicago and Tioga, which were drawn thither by ordinary business demands.

Near here lives W. S. Irwin, who represented in the State Legislature last winter a more numerous constituency than any other member of the House of Representatives. He has been five years in Kansas in the nursery business. He has fruited the Concord, Iona, Israella No. 1, Delaware, Ives Seedling, Rogers' Hybrids No's. 4, 9 and 15, and the Rebecca, all of which he commends for his region. He discards the Catawba and Isabella on account of mildew. He mentions particularly, what all have observed who have eaten grapes in Kansas, that the Concord and other common varieties are far superior in flavor to the same varieties grown in Eastern States. The first house was built in New Chicago June 27, 1870. Now, in less than one year, it numbers many hundred. The combined population of these two places probably reaches about 2000.

Southeast of these towns is *Erie*, on the east side of the Neosho river, a town which has been very rapidly built. It is on high bottom land, and is said to contain more than a thousand inhabitants.

About eight miles southeast of Erie is OSAGE MISSION, a thriving town on the line of the road from Fort Scott to Parsons, called the Sedalia Branch of the M. K. & T. R. R. I have not visited this place, and have not received much reliable information about it, but it is said to contain more than 1500 inhabitants, with all the elements of progress common to Kansas towns of this size. Beyond New Chicago the road leaves the immediate vicinity of the Neosho (although still in the broad valley when miles away,) and makes a cut-off by crossing into the headwaters of the Labette. After passing for a few miles over a rolling prairie of easy grade, as is shown by the elevations on our map, it again approaches near to the Neosho. The character of this entire valley has hardly been alluded to, but it is unsurpassed for the extent of its well tilled bottoms, for the abundance of timber and water power, and for the rapidity with which it has been filled with an active thriving population.

Passing the station of *Ludore*, we reach PARSONS, beautifully situated on a prairie roll, between the Labette and one of its tributaries. There the eastern branch of the M. K. & T. R. R. comes in from Sedalia, Mo., *via* Fort Scott. By this route through trains now run to St. Louis. At Parsons are to be erected offices, machine shops, round houses, etc., such as will be commensurate with the importance of a railroad, which, with its various branches, will in time embrace little less than 1000 miles of track.

Labette City is a village of about 400 people on the east bank of the Labette river, in a well settled country. Seven miles more brings us to

OSWEGO, the county seat of *Labette county*. A recent traveller who has been often over the route, describes Oswego as "the same substantial good town, improving steadily, surely." It has a population of about 1500. It is located a short distance from the Neosho on a bluff which comes abruptly to the river on its west side. Never failing springs abound and an excellent water power is improved with flouring and saw mill. The village of *Montana*, a few miles distant, has mills, etc., and about 250 inhabitants. All this region is plentifully supplied with coal. Ten miles from Oswego is

CHETOPA. This thriving young city is situated on the west bank of the Neosho river and near the south line of the state. Chetopa is southwest of, and distant seventeen miles from Columbus, on the Missouri River, Fort Scott & Gulf Railroad, from which point the latter road will probably soon be extended to Chetopa. It is also on the line of the projected South Pacific R. R., which I am informed is under contract to Baxter Springs, eighteen miles distant to the east. Being so situated as to command an extensive southern trade it is rapidly growing. Its four neat and tasteful church edifices entirely completed, bespeak the character of the inhabitants, not less than the school houses, stores, hotels, etc. Near here are the valuable coal mines, from which in January, 1870, when but recently opened, ten car loads per day were shipped north. Adjacent are the heavily timbered bottoms of the Neosho, affording the finest quality of oak and walnut, while forty miles south are the extensive pineries of Grand River. Planing mills at Chetopa use lumber shipped from the latter region, while flouring mills, foundry, etc., make up the complement of improvements. The trade in Texas cattle is very considerable at Chetopa as well as at all the towns along the southern line of the state. From Chetopa we look south upon the Indian Territory, whose solitudes are already awakened by the battle cry of modern civilization—the steam whistle. By this sign do we conquer the wilderness.

The Missouri, Kansas & Texas Railroad is already constructed to Fort Gibson which is on the Arkansas River, eighty-seven miles south of the Kansas State line, and it is proposed to build nearly as much farther during the year 1871, leaving but fifty or sixty miles to reach the northern boundary of Texas. The Indian Territory is 210 miles across—it being of the same width as the state of Kansas. It may not be generally known that it is no farther from Topeka, the Capital of Kansas, to Galveston, on the Gulf of Mexico, than it is to Columbus, the Capital of Ohio. This road will reach Galveston in conjunction with the Texas Central, and another line will be pushed southwest to Camargo, in Mexico. The Kansas line will also be extended northwest to Fort Kearney on the Union Pacific in Nebraska. The General Manager of this road is Robert S. Stevens, a Kansas man, whose talent for pushing a railroad is being backed by a company which appreciates the importance of improving opportunities. This road is to be of great importance to Kansas, not only in giving access by means of branch lines to the pineries of that region, but by opening an avenue of trafic, whereby the tropical productions and fish and oysters of lower Texas, and the cotton as well, may be brought here in exchange for apples, pears, butter and cheese, hay, bacon, fine blooded stock, etc.

THE L. L. & G. R. R. AND ITS TOWNS.

The Leavenworth, Lawrence & Galveston Railroad, as it name indicates, commences at Leavenworth, and it received its land grants upon that condition. But the railroad bridge is not completed across the Kansas river at

Lawrence, and trains are therefore made up at the latter place. Passing south across the broad bottoms of the Wakarusa and up Coal Creek, we pass near to Blue Mound, an isolated hill about one hundred feet above the Wakarusa, and upon whose summit, in the early Kansas troubles, stood a tall flag-staff. Whenever armed forces or suspicious parties were seen by the scouts approaching from Missouri, the Free State men were warned by running up a flag on this staff, which could be seen in Lawrence and all the surrounding country.

The first station is *Vineland*, where there is no village as yet, but where is the fruit farm, nursery and vineyard of Mr. W. E. Barnes, who furnished our essay on grape culture. From Vineland the road climbs by a sharp grade to *Baldwin City*, which is situated on the high prairie, and on the old Santa Fe wagon road, which wound its serpentine course on the divide between the waters of the Kansas River on the north and the Marias des Cygnes on the south. Baldwin City is a village of a few hundred inhabitants, and is the seat of Baker University. The M. E. Church has here erected a fine edifice, with boarding houses, and smaller building for preparatory department, and the institution gives promise of great usefulness. At this place and at *Prairie City*, the next station near at hand, are good flouring mills. Passing the flag station of *Norwood*, we reach the city of

OTTAWA. This place is situated on both sides of the Marias des Cygnes (River of Swans) but is chiefly built on the gently sloping and undulating surface of the portion south of the stream. Across the stream is thrown the beautiful wire suspension bridge shown on another page. Having spent two years before any other white man lived in this immediate vicinity, in preparing to lay out and build this town, it would be an easy matter to fill a considerable book with its history; but having promised the public an impartial sketch of Kansas, I will only say that Ottawa has steadily grown from the erection of the first house, in April, 1864, to this time, when it numbers about 3,500 inhabitants. Its two principal streets are paved, and the town contains many fine buildings. Some of its buildings, including Ottawa University, are shown elsewhere. It is a live town, surrounded by a good country, and is still improving. Its churches, schools, etc., are a credit to any town. The site of Ottawa is a beautiful one; its situation, relative to a great region of country, is central and commanding, and its people are intelligent, enterprising and public spirited.

A few miles north of Ottawa, near the L., L. & G. road, are the Franklin county coal mines, employing about fifty men, and delivering a large amount of coal daily.

Arrangements have been made for the location at Ottawa of the machine shops of the Leavenworth, Lawrence & Galveston Railroad, which will give employment to a large number of men, as this road is to be continued south through the Indian Territory, and so long a line with its many branches will require extensive works.

The L. L. & G. R. R. has another line coming into this place from Kansas City, and the Missouri, Kansas & Texas Railroad is also building a branch leaving the Missouri Pacific at Holden and coming through Paola to this place, whence it will proceed westward through Pomona.

Pomona.—This new but promising village is ten miles west of Ottawa, in the valley of the Marais de Cygnes. It is an original conception, being located upon the border of a tract of 12,000 acres of excellent land owned by Messrs. J. H. Whetstone and S. T. Kelsey, which tract is entirely surrounded by a well constructed wire fence. Within the fence more than 100 miles of hedge and forest tree rows have been plowed and planted, and a large amount of nursery stock set out by Mr. Kelsey, (whose essay is elsewhere given.) Within five years this entire tract will be divided by hedge rows and forest trees into small tracts, and settled by a prosperous and independent community. In such hands, and with such prospects, I need hardly say that the village is prospering. It is not yet a year old, but it has about 50 houses and a fine mill and school house, of which illustrations are given elsewhere. Coal underlies the entire site and surrounding country, and is delivered at the town for about 15 cents per bushel.

I have spoken particularly of this enterprise, because it illustrates what may be done in Kansas and how by energy and sagacity a good deal may be made out of a little. This entire tract, then unoccupied land, was purchased two years ago for $4.50 per acre. There are still opportunities for other such enterprises in Kansas.

In the southeastern part of this county, is Lane post-office and settlement near which stands the John Brown cabin elsewhere shown. Here is also a steam flour mill.

To the southwest of Ottawa, about sixteen miles is the French settlement and Silk Factory of M. de Boissiere, who was expelled from France on political grounds by the late Emperor. He is a socialist of great wealth, who has purchased three thousand acres of fine land and has erected a good building, and is intending to erect others, where will be attempted a practical solution of some of the knotty problems of social science, and industry. Whatever may come of the theories, the seed of the Mulberry tree sown in large quantities, have made excellent returns, the trees growing fifteen to thirty inches the first year. They are grown to furnish food, by their leaves, for silk worms.

Near by is a fine steam flour mill located at Williamsburg. Both these settlements are underlaid, at a depth of ten to thirty feet, with excellent coal.

But we loiter too long in this vicinity, and must hasten southward, by the stations of *Princeton* and *Richmond* to

GARNETT, the county seat of *Anderson county*. This town of about 1000 inhabitants is situated on rolling prairie, and is nearly surrounded by timber. The first house was built in this town by Capt. John J. Lindsey. Being the only town in the county, it has lately grown rapidly, having churches, hotels, mills, etc; its prospects are good, especially when a railroad is constructed through this place from Paola, as is contemplated.

Leaving Garnett, we pass the stations of *Welda*, and *Divide*, and crossing the high divide known as Ozark Ridge, pass *Carlyle* station, and striking into the Neosho Valley, we enter the town of

IOLA, which is the county seat of *Allen county*. The town is located on high bottom, gently rolling to the river, which runs on the west of the town. The most important event which has lately happened to this place is the location at this point of the large manufacturing establishment of the King Wrought Iron Bridge Company. A view of these buildings, and more particular description of them is given elsewhere. Iola has about 1000 inhabitants, and is growing rapidly. The river is bridged at this place by one of King's Iron Bridges. About two miles above the town is said to be an excelient water power on the Neosho River.

Northwest from Iola is *Geneva*, a village between Elm and Indian creeks. It is 6 miles from Carlyle, and 3½ from Neosho Falls, between which places runs a daily stage. At Geneva is located a Presbyterian Academy.

The next station is *Humboldt*, the road passing on the east side of the town. As we described the place in treating of the M. K. & T. R. R., we hasten on across the Neosho, and through the towns of *New Chicago* and *Tioga*, already described, and out on to the prairie again to the new town of

THAYER, which is the present terminus of the road. This town has grown as only Kansas towns can grow, or at least, as only towns in a new and fertile country, with low priced lands, can grow. I don't dare say how many people there are in this town, for I have not visited it. The first house was erected last fall, and there are now hundreds of people there, while, as in all our new towns, "the cry is still they come." The Railroad is in process of construction to the south line of the state, where a town will be located. The direction of this extension is unknown to me, excepting that it is to be southwesterly. The south line of the State is to be reached in July, 1871, a distance of 45 miles from Thayer.

This road has a few hundred thousand acres of valuable land for sale. I have not the name of the newly appointed land commissioner, but letters will reach him if sent in the care of M. R. Baldwin, general superintendent, Lawrence. Retracing our course to Ottawa, we leave the north and south line and go northeast to Olathe, passing the stations of *Ferguson*, *Wellsville*, *Martin*, and *Gardner*, all new places, but in a well settled region. This line of road is called the *Kansas City and Santa Fe Railroad*, but it is controlled and run by the L. L. & G. R. R. Company, through trains passing over the Missouri River, Fort Scott and Gulf Road, from Olathe to Kansas City.

THE M. R. FT. S. & G. R. R. AND ITS TOWNS.

The Missouri River, Fort Scott and Gulf Railroad commences at Kansas City, Missouri, where it makes direct connection with eastern trains. A bridge crosses the Missouri river at this point. From the Missouri river bottom, on which the depot is situated, the road follows the windings of Turkey creek until it reaches the summit on open prairie.

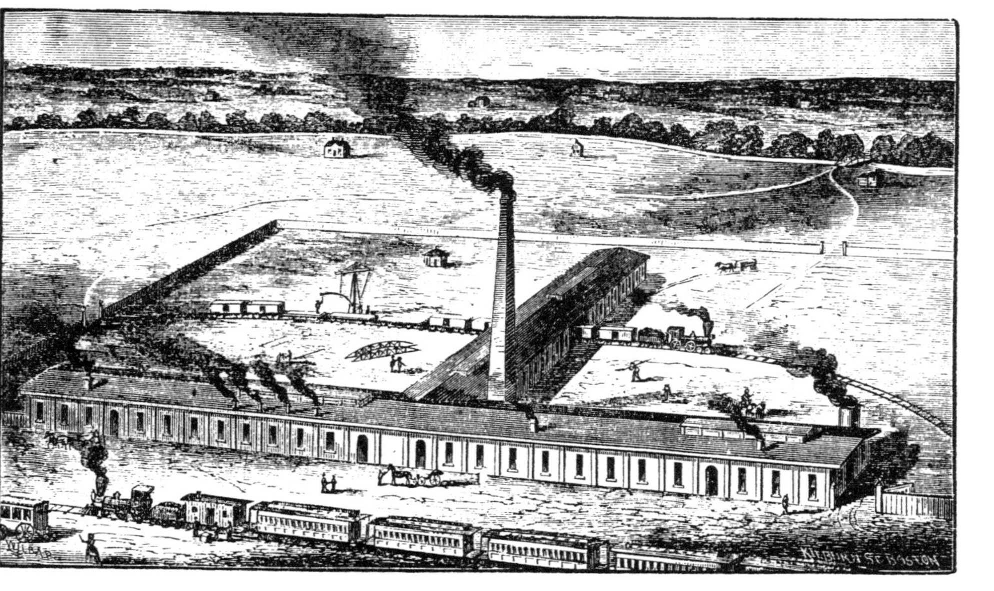

KING IRON BRIDGE MANUFACTORY AND IRON WORKS, IOLA, KANSAS.

Shawnee Station, is near a small town of the same name which contains a few hundred inhabitants. All the land in this vicinity is enclosed and divided into farms. Near hére is the old Shawnee Mission, and this gives me opportunity to say what I intended to say in its proper place, that Col. Johnson, who lives here, thinks the quickest and most satisfactory way to raise fuel on the open prairie, is to plant peach stones a few feet apart each way. He planted a bushel on three or four acres, and the grove yielded an incredible amount of fuel. Peach wood is hard and makes an excellent fire. It grows rapidly, bears peaches in three or four years from the pit or stone, and one good crop will pay for the trouble. The object of growing a thicket of peaches is not fruit however, but fuel, but if peaches will insist on growing who will object to it? Hoping the reader will excuse this digression, we continue our route over a very fine country with fine farms on every hand, past the station of *Lenexa* to

OLATHE, the county seat of Johnson county. This thriving town of almost 2500 inhabitants is situated on rolling prairie, between the head waters of Cedar and Indian creeks. The Deaf and Dumb Asylum is located here, with a good sized three story stone building. An east and west railroad is now being constructed through Olathe, which we will describe in the next division.

From Olathe our railroad commences a down grade, passing *Ocheltree* and *Spring Hill* stations in Johnson county. The latter station is the depot for a thrifty little village of the same name, situated a mile or two west of the road. Passing *Hillsdale*, a few miles over the county line, we follow down a considerable stream called Bull Creek, and on its east banks we find

PAOLA, the county seat of *Miami county*. This town was laid out in the early settlement of Kansas, its pioneers being attracted by large springs of pure water, and also by the excellence of the surrounding country. It contains good buildings, mills, hotels, etc.

The branch railroad from Holden, Missouri, tapping at that place the Missouri Pacific, is soon to be completed to Paola. On this road, near the state line is *New St. Louis*, a new place of promise, and yet nearer to Paola is *Somersett* where a mill, stores, etc., are now building. The northeast corner of this county has settled very rapidly during the last three years.

Six or eight miles southwest from Paola is *Osawatomie*, situated at the confluence of the Pottawatomie and Marias des Cygnes Rivers, and between the two streams, which are bridged at this point. A good water power on the first named stream is being improved by the erection of a dam and mill. The place contains, perhaps, 500 people. The State Asylum for the Insane is located here, and large buildings are now being erected in addition to the old ones. The little village is chiefly noted for the fight which took place in 1856, between old Captain John Brown, with a handful of Free State men, and a considerable force of Pro-Slavery Border Ruffians. The town was eventually sacked, after a gallant resistance, and Brown was from that event called *Osawatomie Brown*. The proposed railroad from Paola to Garnett and Neosho Falls, is to run through Osawatomie.

MISSOURI VALLEY LIFE INSURANCE BUILDING, LEAVENWORTH.

In the southeast part of Miami county is the village and post office of *New Lancaster*. Near by is one of the oil springs which abound in the border counties of Kansas, and from which oozes a thick black substance which in summer dries down to the consistency and appearance of thick tar.

Following on railroad from Paola, we pass the town of *Fontana*, which is located in a good country, and reach

LA CYGNES. This new town was lately made the county seat of *Linn county*. The site was surveyed and staked for a town in the fall of 1869, and now, in less than two years, it claims 1200 inhabitants. There is good water power here, as well as in various places lower down on the Marias des Cygnes. Of course the town is thrifty and ambitious, and it is supported by an excellent country around it.

Passing *Barnard* station, we reach *Pleasanton*, a town of about 800 inhabitants, which has also grown very rapidly. It has an improved water power, two flouring mills, and does a good business with the surrounding country. A vein of coal two to three feet thick is opened here.

Seven miles west of Pleasanton, and connected with it by a daily stage, is *Mound City*, situated on the south bank of Little Sugar creek. It is partially enclosed by the arc of one of the highest mounds in Kansas, called Sugar Mound, from the Sugar Maple trees which cover its side and a portion of its summit. From this Mound flow the constant waters of several excellent springs. A surface vein of coal fifteen to thirty inches thick is opened here. A railroad is in contemplation to pass through Pleasanton and Mound City. Six miles from Mound City is a good flour mill, run by water on Big Sugar Creek.

Continuing a southward course from Pleasanton, we cross Little Osage River and reach the station of *Osaga*. Near by is a good water power, well improved, and also at *Fort Lincoln*, a few miles westward, up the stream.

FORT SCOTT is the next station and the county seat of Bourbon county. It contains about 5,000 inhabitants. It is the chief town in this portion of the State, and has no rival within less than about thirty miles in either direction. Besides the road upon which we entered the eastern part of the town, the Sedalia branch of the Missouri, Kansas & Texas Railroad runs through the southern portion of the city. Besides this road is the La Clede and Fort Scott, another road soon to be completed from the east, while still another is projected, and likely to be built, southeast, into the timber regions of Arkansas. A road will also soon be constructed from here directly west to Humboldt, with a line via Iola to Neosho Falls. Fort Scott is located on rolling prairie, chiefly on the south side of Marmaton River, which flows eastward into Missouri. A small stream, fed by springs, winds through the northern part of the city. The place does an extensive business, and has a woolen factory, a foundry, mills, etc., and is about to be supplied with gas. It would seem only necessary to tap the gas reservoir beneath the city for the latter purpose, as there issues from a drill hole, made in testing for oil, a constant stream of gas, which burns with a ready blaze. One of the most valuable coal mines in the State is opened near the city, and its shipment is an important item.

Passing successively the stations of *Godfrey*, *Pawnee* and *Drywood*, we reach GIRARD, the county seat of CRAWFORD COUNTY. This new town has about 800 inhabitants, and confidently looks for the construction of an east and west railroad. This entire country is underlaid with promising coal veins.

Cherokee station is a growing place. A large amount of coal is mined here from a vein said to be four feet thick. It sells at the banks, loaded on cars, at nine cents per bushel. A kind called red coal is in thinner veins, and sells higher, for blacksmithing purposes. *Monmouth* is a village of about 300 inhabitants, six miles west of Cherokee station, pleasantly located near timber.

Coalfield is another coal mining town, and station on the road.

COLUMBUS is the county seat of *Cherokee county*. The first house was built a little more than a year ago, and the place now numbers about 1000 inhabitants. It is situated on gently rolling prairie, and has a prospective Railroad from the East.

The next station, and the terminus of the road is *Baxter Springs*, a thriving business place claiming about 2000 inhabitants. Being upon the border of the Indian Territory, it is the last town in this direction, and is a place of extensive business. It is located on the west bank of Spring River, which furnishes excellent water power here and elsewhere. At *Lowell*, a village three miles from Baxter Springs, and connected with it by daily stage, is a very fine water power with mills. Spring River has a succession of water powers throughout its entire course. A promising grindstone quarry has lately been opened in the southeastern portion of this county. The Atlantic and Pacific Railroad from St. Louis is about to extend its line westward through Baxter Springs.

A few miles south from here are located my old friends, the Ottawa tribe of Indians, formerly the owners of a good share of Franklin county, and from whom the town of Ottawa was named. It is reported that upon their new reservation an excellent vein of *pure white marble* has been discovered, and a company is about to open the quarry and test its value.

This Railroad will undoubtedly soon be pushed on southward, but I think its precise course has not been determined upon. Major B. S. Henning, of Kansas City, Mo., is the efficient General Superintendent of this road. The lands are sold by John A. Clarke, Land Commissioner, of Fort Scott.

THE ST. L. L. & D. R. R. AND ITS TOWNS.

The St. Louis, Lawrence and Denver Railroad is commonly known as the Lawrence and Pleasant Hill Railroad. It commences at the former place and runs by *Eudora*, a town of several hundred inhabitants at the junction of the Wakarusa and Kansas rivers. Thence the road continues down the bottom lands of the latter stream to De Soto, whence it strikes into Cedar Creek and follows it up to *Olathe*. Thence it passes eastward to *Pleasant Hill*, on the Missouri Pacific Railroad, 20 miles beyond the eastern boundary of Kansas. The road is not yet running, but it is under contract to be completed during the summer, and it will considerably shorten the distance between Lawrence and Olathe, and the city of St. Louis. Gen. G. W. Deitzler of Lawrence, is President.

THE A. T. & S. F. R. R. AND ITS TOWNS.

The Atchison, Topeka and Santa Fe Railroad commences, by the terms of its land grant, at Atchison, but the portion between this city and Topeka is not yet completed. It is however under contract, and is to be constructed within a year's time.

At ATCHISON, which we have already described, this road connects with the roads running in every direction from that city. The Chicago and Southwestern is also to build a road directly west from Plattsburg, in Missouri, 35 miles to Atchison. This will necessitate the construction of a bridge across the Missouri river at this point. The A. T. & S. F. R. R. will use the track of the C. B. U. P. R. R. for a few miles, as shown on our map, and will strike across the divide and southwest down a tributary of Grasshopper river, which it will cross at, or in the vicinity of, *Grashopper Falls.* This village of about 800 inhabitants is pleasantly situated, chiefly on the west bank of the stream. It has a very good water power, while but a mile distant is another, and they furnish power to run two flouring mills, and a woolen factory. The town contains five or six church buildings, which fact tells its own story about the character of the people. Six miles above the village is another water power now being improved, while three miles down the stream from the village is another mill, and at *Osawkee*, 10 miles below Grashopper Falls, is a flouring mill run by water. All these water powers are on Grasshopper River. In the south part of this county on this stream, are the towns of *Medina* and *Perryville*, on the K. P. R. R. The latter has a population of about 500.

About 14 miles southeast of Grashopper Falls is OSKALOOSA, the county seat of *Jefferson county.* It is built on high rolling prairie, at the head of several streams, which flow from numerous springs in and around the town. The place is nearly surrounded with timber. Firewood sells at three dollars per cord. The population is about 900. No liquor saloons have ever been permitted in the town. A large court house and public school house built of brick, with trimmings of Junction City stone, and an elegant Protestant Episcopal Church, also built of brick, adorn this highland village.

From Grasshopper Falls to Topeka there are as yet no towns, although villages will soon spring into existence, after the railroad is completed.

The A. T. & S. F. connects on the north side of the Kansas River, at North Topeka, with the K. P. R. Crossing the Kansas river on the railroad bridge built by the former company, we arrive at the depot, machine shops and general offices of the road, located on the eastern border of the city of Topeka. This city was fully described in the article relating to the K. P. Railroad, and we continue on our way southward. *Wakarusa* station is located in the fertile valley of the river of that name, and is the natural centre for a good country. About six miles to the westward is the village of *Auburn*, pleasantly located in the Wakarusa valley. The next station is *Carbondale*, where extensive coal mines are opened, and a large amount of coal delivered. From this point a railroad is projected to follow down a creek which heads near by, and upon reaching the Wakarusa, its valley will be followed to Lawrence, there delivering coal, and giving the A. T. & S. F. R. R. connection with the railroads which run eastward from that city.

The next town is BURLINGAME, one of the county seats of *Osage county*. At an election recently held, a majority of the votes were declared to have been cast in favor of LYNDON, but the election was contested, and meantime the county offices are held partly at one place and partly at the other. The population of Burlingame is about 800. The attractive town site is located on a small stream, and a large and elegant public school house stands upon a conspicuous eminence. There is now being erected a woolen factory, in which new and excellent machinery will soon be placed. It will be run by steam, as the coal mines near at hand supply cheap fuel. The elegant stone building is 130 feet long, with Mansard roof. An extensive wagon manufactory is in operation here.

Passing the station of *Peterton*, located in the rich valley of Dragoon's creek, we reach *Osage City*. Here are also extensive and valuable coal and other mineral deposits, which are described under the heads "Stone Quarries," and "Paint." This town has not long been in existence, but it appears to be flourishing.

Following eastward from this village, by stage, down the valley of Salt creek, a distance of eight miles, we reach the new and enterprising town of LYNDON, already referred to. This town was laid out March 7, 1870, by a company of which Hon. L. D. Bailey, late Judge of the Supreme Court, is president. Six months afterward, the Judge informed me in as delicate a manner as possible, evidently a little fearful lest he might hurt my feelings—that his town had beaten the first six months growth of Ottawa. Of course (in my view) language would fail to express higher encomium upon their success. The town now contains about 700 inhabitants. Coal is easily obtained, and the country has filled up rapidly with actual settlers.

East from Lyndon, near the county line, and near the confluence of Salt Creek with the Marias des Cygnes, is the town of *Quenemo*, formerly the agency of the Sac and Fox Indians. The celebrated warrior, Black Hawk, was a chief of this tribe, and a son and namesake of Ke-o-kuk, the equally celebrated friend of the white man, is now a chief of the tribe in the Indian Territory, where they recently removed. Mr. Wm. Whistler, a remote descendant of the tribe, who lives at Quenemo, and last winter represented Osage county. in the State Legislature, informed me that the last buffalo killed east of Council Grove met their death in June 1848, when a Sac and Fox hunter killed three, near the present town site of Quenemo.

In returning to the Atchison, Topeka & Santa Fe Railroad, we will diverge southward from the route by which we came to Quenemo, and pass up the broad valley of the Marias des Cygnes, a distance of about twenty miles to the

MINISTER, NO. 6,363. THE PROPERTY OF ANDREW WILSON, TOPEKA.

town of *Arvonia.* This place was founded as a Welch settlement by J. Mather Jones and others, but includes people of various nationalities, and has become a village of considerable size.

Proceeding a few miles further up the valley, we enter the new but promising town of *Reading*, lately laid off as a town and railroad station. The surrounding lands are largely in the hands of eastern capitalists, who have the ability to build a good town at this point. There are a few things however, which are in general absolutely necessary to success in town building. There must be displayed, among other things, *liberality*, *energy* and *printers' ink.* Eastern capitalists are not infrequently totally oblivious of these necessities. They general expect to "keep the cake and eat it too." I am glad to be informed, however, that Reading is in the hands of parties who are disposed to do the fair thing for immigrants.

Continuing our journey by railroad we pass the station of *Horton*, cross the Neosho River and arrived at EMPORIA. As the city has been fully described herein, we hasten westward up the broad and beautiful valley of the Cottonwood, and pass the new station of Toledo. As the cars have been running but a few weeks, there is but little to indicate where the stations are to be.

COTTONWOOD FALLS, eighty-two miles from Topeka, is nearly in the centre of *Chase county*, of which it is the county seat. The rapid stream affords an excellent water power, which is improved by a saw and flouring mill. The stream is crossed by one of the King Wrought Iron Bridges. The town is pleasantly located, chiefly on the south side of the river, upon an undulating prairie roll which overlooks the valley. It contains about 500 inhabitants, and with the advent of the railroad is growing rapidly, as it is the shipping point for a great extent of fertile country to the southward. Westward from Cottonwood Falls, up the river a few miles, is a good mill at an excellent water power, and also another water power eight miles below the town.

The stations of *Elmdale*, *Hunts* and *Cedar Point* occur in succession as we pass up the valley. The latter village is a short distance from the depot, nestled under a bluff on the south side of the Cottonwood upon which are growing a fringe of Red Cedar trees. The river affords at this point a good water power, which is well improved.

Florence is a new town in Marion county, laid out about six months ago and now numbering in population some hundreds. It is built upon bottom land at the junction of Doyle creek and the Cottonwood, and promises to be a place of considerable business. There is an excellent water power here, waiting to be improved, as are many others on this excellent stream.

The Cottonwood valley is, I think, among the most picturesque in the state. The bottoms are from one to three miles wide, and on either side excellent magnesian limestone crops out, at the top of the steep bluffs which wall in the valley. The stream is moderately well timbered, and abundant creeks and rills break through the bluffs and enter it from the north and south. A marked characteristic of the scene, is the regularity with which the bluffs and projecting strata of rock lessen in height as we ascend the stream, until at Florence they are but a few feet above the level of the bottom lands. Huge rocks are laid in the abutments and culverts along this road, almost as they came from the quarry, with little use of hammer and chisel. For the most part they project themselves from the bluff, or have fallen part way down its side, and are ready to be transported to their near destination.

Northwest from Florence, and in the Cottonwood valley, at the mouth of Clear Creek, is the village of MARION CENTRE, the county seat of *Marion county*. It is in the midst of the best farming land in the county. Two fine and constant water powers are here awaiting capital for their improvement.

The railroad leaves the Cottonwood at Florence and follows up Doyle Creek to the new village and colony of Conesburg, now Peabody, which was first opened to settlement in December, 1870. It is located on the north side of Doyle Creek. A splendid tract of country lies around and to the south of this place. There is very little timber in this region, but the soil is good and water abundant.

From this place the road continues its southwest course over the divide, separating the waters of the Cottonwood and the Arkansas rivers. At a distance of fifteen miles from Peabody is *Newton*, the last station yet located on this road. It is on a tributary of the Little Arkansas river, called Sand Creek, where said creek is crossed by the old Texas cattle trail. At this writing, May 10th, the cars only run to Florence, but they will run into Newton about July 1st, and the will road immediately be continued westward. The first house was built in Newton during the last ten days, but there is already a good deal of excitement in that vicinity as to its prospects.

To the south and a little west of Newton, near the Little Arkansas, is the small village of *Sedgwick*, while still farther in the same course, on the banks of the Arkansas River is *Park City*, located where the new Texas cattle trail crosses the river.

WICHITA, the county seat of *Sedgwick county*, is situated on the east bank of the Little Arkansas, at its junction with the Arkansas River, and is twenty-five miles south of Newton. It contains about 800 inhabitants and is a very active, thriving business place. The settlements in this county have nearly all been made within the last year, and there are yet thousands of beautiful claims to be taken under the pre-emption and homestead laws. Until this country was awakened by the speedy prospect of a railroad, very few were inclined to locate there. I visited Sedgwick county for the first time during this spring, and I think the Arkansas Valley the finest valley in the State, so far as the lay of the land, and excellent soil and water are concerned. It is not better than the Kansas valley perhaps, excepting in extent. The Arkansas valley is here from ten to twenty miles wide, and instead of being absolutely flat, is varied by very *gentle* rolls. The soil is a deep, rich loam, and is very quick and warm, and it contains considerable black sand. By digging three or four feet through this soil one enters, in places, a composite layer of clay and gravel of irregular thickness, while in other places near by, the subsoil is entirely a compact bed of gravel or coarse sand. Beneath the composite strata referred to, one also strikes upon the gravel and sand subsoil. Here is displayed a striking system of sub-irrigation. The Arkansas River rises in the Rocky Mountains, and its banks are full during the growing season, owing to the melting snows in the mountains; but, although apparently ready to carry desolation all around by overflowing, it never does overflow, but *underflows* instead in the porous subsoil of the valley. By capillary attraction, it is evident that a portion of this water is drawn up within reach of the roots of growing vegetation. It is to be noted however that the roads are excellent, mud drying quickly after a rain. Throughout this entire region, water is obtained by digging a few feet on the uplands, as well as on the bottoms, and small flowing streams are common on

OXFORD WILEY, NO. 8,753.

[Owned by N. L. Chaffee, at Manhattan.]

the prairies. The water is pure and soft. There is in this vicinity but little rock, magnesian limestone and gypsum being found in the eastern portion of Sedgwick county, and red sandstone in the western portion. There are indications of coal, and the Lignite variety will undoubtedly be found in this valley; but coal will be transported on the cars from the mines in Osage county, so as to retail for twenty-five to thirty cents per bushel. Timber is found in limited quantities, but the people have adopted the herd law, by which every man cares for his own stock, and little fencing is needed. The law stands for five years, during which time hedges will be grown. Iron ore has been discovered in the northwest portion of the county.

All things considered, the Arkansas valley is probably among the most attractive portions of the state for settlers at this time. This valley grows particularly fine vegetables. In short it is unsurpassed for the production of all tilled crops, while the region but a few miles southwest, described by Mr. Honeck on page 109, will furnish illimitable stock range summer and winter for many years, as it is not adapted to dense settlement, but almost every square mile in Sedgwick county will furnish excellent tillage land.

Captain Henry Booth, who is favorable know to many Kansas men, having been a resident of Western Kansas for fifteen years, and for some time Post Trader at Fort Larned, thinks more rain falls on the Arkansas bottoms in that vicinity than falls generally in Kansas anywhere west of Junction City. The river is wide and being at a higher stage of water in the summer season, he thinks it causes rain in its immediate vicinity. He has been familar with that region for ten years, and has full confidence that these wide bottom lands will prove to be very productive. The small streams of that region he says are fed by springs (which flow out so near the bed as to be out of sight in high water) and the streams are never dry. The stock range is the best he ever saw. Messrs. Beal and Boyd and others, took 1,500 head of Texas cattle into the vicinity of Ft. Larned in October last, and out of the lot about 20 died, the remainder wintering in good order on the grasses, with no other feed excepting salt. Of the rough land south of the Arkansas River, in the vicinity of the Big Bend, he speaks very highly as a pastoral region. The water is good and abundant, and the grass of excellent quality. The Buffalo killed there in April of this year were, fat after wintering on these grasses. He confirms the account of abundant and delicious wild fruits. All these statements are also confirmed by J. M. Steele, Representative from Sedgwick county, who is familiar with that country

The Atchison, Topeka & Santa Fe Railroad has not been pushing its line very rapidly until this season, but its valuable land franchises are now in the hands of a powerful and enterprising corporation, and the road will speedily be constructed up the broad valley of the Arkansas River and one of its tributaries to New Mexico. Passing through the boundless grazing and tillage lands of that territory, awakening to life the solitary places, and developing the untold mineral wealth of that region, it will pass on by the shortest and best line to the Pacific Ocean. It will also have such branch lines as the varied interests of its tributary regions may demand. The most valuable salt deposits in the United States are on the immediate southern border of Kansas, and will be developed by this road. The general direction and the excellent country for the most part, through which this road passes, must make it a very important route.

—Since writing the foregoing I have had the pleasure of an interview with several of the officers and directors of the Atchison, Topeka and Santa Fe Railroad, who have recently (May, 1871,) explored the country on the line of their road, through Sedgwick, Rice, Barton, Rush and Pawnee counties, extending their trip *via* Fort Zarah, to Coon creek, 18 miles beyond Fort Larned. They followed the bottom lands of the Arkansas on their outward trip and returned on the upland prairies, 15 to 20 miles from the river. They report excellent grass and good soil throughout the entire route, even the uplands through the counties of Barton, Rice and McPherson as well as Sedgwick, showing a smooth even sod of blue stem—the most valuable of our prairie grasses—over almost the entire face of the country. Good building rock was also found in many places, abundant indications of coal were noticed, scattering groves of timber were seen, many running streams were crossed, and *everywhere* the settlers have found pure soft water at a depth of six to fifteen feet on the bottoms, and from twelve to thirty feet on the uplands. They saw and heard of numerous wells, and in but one instance did they learn of a well deeper than twenty-five feet. The water is uniformly found in gravel and is *soft*—(good for washing clothes) although the surface soil appears to contain an abundance of lime.

Mr. W. O. B. Peabody, Resident Engineer of the road, informs me that the genuine Kentucky Blue Grass was seen by him in many places, especially in the vicinity of the old Santa Fe wagon road. This road having been traveled for many years, as already explained, by teams from the Blue Grass regions of Missouri and Eastern Kansas, these teams have scattered the seed along the roadside for many miles to the westward. But Mr. Peabody assures me that he saw many thickly set and thrifty patches of blue grass at a distance from the Santa Fe road, which he is confident have sprung from seed conveyed by buffalo. He has spent many months in the best blue grass regions of Kentucky, where the exercise of his profession called him across a succession of fields set to grass, and he is confident that this grass in the Arkansas valley is the identical Kentucky Blue Grass. This testimony is vastly valnable, for it settles the question, "will blue grass grow in Western Kansas." I have already shown how rapid and certain is its growth in Eastern Kansas, but I have supposed that we must await experiments before attempting to answer the above question. It is true there is every indication that it would succeed on the best lands in Western Kansas. It is also true that I have been repeatedly informed by persons of apparent reliability that they had seen Kentucky blue grass in Western Kansas. The evidence is conclusive that some kind of blue grass grows in many places in those regions, but not understanding how the Kentucky Blue Grass could get into that country, I have called it the Kansas blue grass. The explanation of Mr. Peabody is, however, entirely satisfactory, as the buffalo would naturally transport to a considerable distance the blue grass seed they would crop in their ramblings across the Santa Fe road. In Eastern Kansas, cattle will in two or three years seed the prairies, in places, for miles around a blue grass pasture. I am now satisfied that the farmers in Saline, McPherson, Lincoln, Ottawa and other counties, were correct in their conclusions that they had discovered small patches of Kentucky blue grass in that region, which were annually spreading and driving out the buffalo grass.

The General Manager of the road is T. J. Peter, and its lands are sold by Land Commissioner D. L. Lakin, of Topeka This road sells on long time, as do all Kansas Railroads, but this Company has also devised a plan whereby a liberal deduction of about one-third is made to actual settlers in consideration of improvements upon the lands. The road bed, the masonry and all the appointments of this line are most excellent, furnishing in themselves a satisfactory guaranty, aside from the high reputation of the officers of the road, that this company will construct a first class through line.

TOWNS NOT HERETOFORE DESCRIBED.

All the villages and cities of any importance, situated upon a railroad, or within a county through which a railroad passes, have already been described.

It is deserving of notice, for the benefit of Eastern readers, that by the word "town" we mean a village or a city. Subdivisions of land, each six miles square, are called *townships*, but every collection of houses is called a town in the West, and occasionally, the inhabitants call their place a city before there are many houses to be seen.

Wabaunsee County contains no towns with more than a few hundred inhabitants. ALMA, the county seat, is situated on Mill Creek, which stream furnishes excellent water power toward its mouth. Near the stream, below Alma, is *Newbury*, and in the central portion of the county is *Eskridge*. In the northwestern portion of the county, on the Kansas River, is *Wabaunsee*, a village laid out by the Connecticut colony, which came to Kansas, under the management of C. B. Lines, in 1856. The colony was called "Beecher's Sharp's Rifles," from the fact that Henry Ward Beecher presented to each male member a Sharp's rifle and a Bible.

This county, as well as Pottawotomie county, and a large portion of Jackson and Shawnee counties, was largely in the possession of the Pottawotomie Indians until recently, and therefore the land thus held is but sparsely populated.

Washington County is on the north line of the State, and Little Blue River runs through its northeastern portion, affording excellent water power at *Hanover* and *Ballard's Falls*, both awaiting development. The county seat is WASHINGTON, a town of about 500 inhabitants, situated on the north side of Mill Creek, on undulating second bottom. There is here a water grist mill and saw mill, and also others six miles down the stream. Coal has been little developed, as wood is delivered at $3.50 per cord; but there is coal in abundance, and it is used by blacksmiths, which tests its quality.

Republic County, next west of Washington, is abundantly watered, the Republican River running across its western portion, which is described by the letter from Mr. Warner. New Scandinavia is situated on the east bank of the Republican, and has fine unimproved water power. BELLVILLE, the county seat, is situatdd centrally in the county, on high table land a very little rolling. It is between Riley and Salt Creeks. This central portion of the county although high, is said to be good tillage land, while the valleys are excellent.

Jewell County, is but sparsely settled, the first emigrants going in the spring of 1870, but many hundred families have gone there and into the region beyond. JEWELL CITY is the county seat. It is very favorably spoken of.

Mitchell County south of Jewell, has in its limits two thriving towns. Cawker City is situated in the northwest portion of the county on the north side of the Solomon, at the confluence of the North and South Forks of that stream. Other streams also enter near here, making this place the centre of a number of valleys and giving a good supply of timber, much of which is hard wood. There is here a good steam saw and grist mill. Fast of this place, and nearly in the centre of the county, is BELOIT, the county seat, beautifully situated on the south bank of the Solomon River, which is also thriving apace. The surrounding country is highly spoken of.

Osborne and other counties to the west of Mitchell, are watered by the South Fork of the Solomon and its tributaries. Settlements are just beginning to extend into this attractive country.

Lincoln County lies south of Mitchell. The Saline River runs through its entire length, furnishing one or two water powers. The county is well watered and is highly prized by its citizens for stock purposes. A good deal of blue grass is said to grow upon the bottoms, furnishing winter feed. *Abram* has recently been laid out near the centre of the county as county seat. Another town is being laid out by the side of a water power in the western portion of the county. Magnesian limestone rock extends entirely across the bottom of the river. Messrs. Ira C. & H. S. Buzic, Schemerhorn, Green, Powers, Lyden Barrett, Penny Freebon and others, each wintered from 500 to 1,000 head of cattle upon the native grasses, and they came out in very good order, with small loss. Others did this all thorugh Western Kansas, but I mention these names because they were furnished me by a friend who is acquainted with the parties. The *Lincoln County Gazette* was established at Abram since my list of papers was put in type.

Ottawa County is a fine county of land, both for farming on the wide bottoms of the Solomon and Saline and tributaries, and for farming and grazing on the uplands. The county seat is MINNEAPOLIS, situated on gently rolling prairie on the east side of the Solomon River near the mouth of Pipe Creek, a considerable stream of constant running water. A dam 120 feet in length extends across the Solomon, built on rock bottom, and a flouring and saw mill is constantly running by water power. *Lindsay*, two miles below, also has a water power not yet improved, a short distance below the town. At Delphos, on the Solomon in the north part of the county is a water power, and also on the Saline in the southwestern corner of the county. T. E. Scott keeps about 700 head of sheep in this county, with profits that are entirely satisfactory to himself. Jacob Campbell and many others keep large droves of cattle.

Cloud County, situated north of Ottawa, is watered both by the Republican and Solomon Rivers and their tributaries.

CONCORDIA is the county seat, and also contains the United States Land Office for the Republican Land District. The town was located in 1870, on the south side of the Republican River, on second bottom and bluff land. The site is a beautiful one, and the town is growing rapidly. *Clyde* and *Shirley* are thriving villages on the Republican, in the northeastern part of the county, and

Glascoe was lately laid out on the Solomon, in the southwestern part of the county. It is in the region of the Republican River that are found the salt marshes described by Professor Mudge. I am informed by B. H. McEckron, Representative from this county, that there flow into the Republican in this county, three timbered streams on the north side of the river, and thirteen on the south side. A few miles north of Concordia a valuable coal mine has recently been opened, from which coal is carried forty miles, to Waterville, and there used for blacksmithing. The eastern half of this county is red sandstone formation, and the western half Magnesian limestone.

Clay County lies eastward of the last mentioned county, and the Republican River runs through the county from the northwestern to the southeastern corner, with numerous tributaries, while Chapman's Creek winds through the southwestern part of the county.

Clay Centre is the county seat, and is situated on the north side of the Republican. The site slopes gently to the southwest, and a stream, fed by living springs, courses through the lower portion of the town. They have erected a stone school house and Baptist church. A flouring and saw mill stores, &c., also are to be found here.

Republican City is situated near the river of that name, and is in the centre of the county. It was recently laid out, but has stores, a hotel, drug store, &c. Bituminous(?)coal is found in this county, of very good quality; and lead ore has recently been discovered in the northern portion of the county, which, by analysis at St. Louis, yielded ninety per cent. of lead. A company is organized to test its value. On the Republican, in the southeastern portion of the county, is *Wakefield*, a thriving village, in an excellent country. It was laid out by an English colony, under the charge of Rev. Mr. Wake. This county contains fine lands, both for cultivation and grazing.

We have thus rapidly glanced at the northwestern counties of Kansas. All that this region needs for its thorough development is railroads. There are no land grants yet made for that section of the state, but if by granting every other section, two or three railroads could be constructed through that region, it would be vastly better for all. Eighty acres, five miles from a railroad, is better than 160 acres, fifty miles from a railroad. Railroads will soon push into this country, as the attractions of these valleys are too great to remain much longer unawakened by the whistle of the locomotive. But if no land grants are made, local subsidies will be necessary, and these can only be made available in the form of county, township or city bonds.

Crossing the Kansas Pacific Railway, the only organized county in Central or Western Kansas, of which we have not spoken, is *McPherson*. This county is watered in the north part by the Smoky Hill River and its tributaries, and the Little Arkansas passes through the southwestern portion, receiving Turkey Creek, which rises in the central portion of the county, and is timbered with hard wood. The wide bottoms along these streams, are excellent agricultural land, and the county is well watered, affording fine range for stock. LINDSBORG, formerly known as Sweedale, is situated on the north bank of the Smoky Hill River, and is the county seat. It was located by the "1st Sweedish Agricultural Colony," organized in Chicago, under the direction of Rev. O. Olsson and others. In the eastern part of the county is another Sweedish colony from Galesburg and Berlin, Illinois, Rev. A. Dahlsten pastor. These gentlemen have organized two large and flourishing Lutheran churches. The country is excellent, and some large stock farms have been opened. A Kentucky colony is located on the rich lands of Gypsum Creek, in the eastern part of the county, and there are good settlements in the south portion of the county and excellent land.

Of the country west from this county, I have already spoken sufficiently in detail. This entire Arkansas Valley region, with the valleys of its numerous tributaries, will soon be noisy with the hum of busy multitudes, who will be making homes, planting crops, trees and hedges, and building railroads and towns. The town of *Atlanta* was lately located centrally in Rice county, by an enterprising company.

Crossing the fine county of Sedgwick, already described under the head of of the A. T. & S. F. R. R., we enter *Sumner County*, which is on the south line of the state, and entirely within the "Osage Lands," which we have already shown are for sale to actual settlers only at $1.25 per acre. The Arkansas River passes through the eastern portion of this county, and this, with other streams, sufficiently waters a very excellent country. The first settlers went into this country during the spring of 1871, but it is rapidly being occupied. It is not yet organized, and I do not know where its principal towns are situated. Sumner is a magnificent county.

The country west of Sumner county has been but little explored. Its valleys are highly spoken of for cultivation, in the letter published from Mr. Honeck, while its uplands are evidently unsurpassed for grazing, and it must be a good fruit region.

COWLEY COUNTY lies east of Sumner, and is watered by the Arkansas, which flows along the western line of the county a distance of 25 or 30 miles, and also by the Walnut, a fine stream which runs through the central portion of the county and empties into the Arkansas River near the State line. Near the confluence of these streams is *Arkansas City*, which was laid out in the fall of 1870, and contains several hundred inhabitants, and is rapidly improving. A pontoon bridge is about to be built across the Arkansas River at this place. North of this place, and at the junction of Timber Creek with the Walnut River is WINFIELD, the county seat of Cowley county. It is situated on second bottom and overlooks the broad and beautiful valley. Two water powers are here found, and there are numerous water powers in the county. This county has timber, stone, coal and as good land as lies out of doors. Winfield was laid out by E. C. Manning in January, 1870, and contains 500 or more inhabitants. This entire county is within the Osage Trust Lands.

Butler County—Moving northward up the Walnut we cross the county line and soon reach the village of *Douglas*, which has a valuable unimproved water power. Twelve miles up the Walnut is *Augusta*, which is the seat of the U. S. Land Office for this district. It is a new place, but is rapidly improving, and is said to contain more than 500 inhabitants. It is situated at the confluence of the Whitewater and Walnut rivers, with a water power on both streams. Twelve miles above Augusta is ELDORADO, the county seat of of Butler county. It is a thriving and substantial town, with about 600 inhabitants, built on gently sloping second bottom, at the junction of the main Walnut with the West Branch. It has an unimproved water power. There are many other water powers in this county, as the streams are all rapid and fed by numerous large springs. The Walnut valley is one of the finest portions of Kansas Its railroad facilities are yet undetermined, but it is probable that a road will soon be constructed from some point on the Atchison, Topeka & Santa Fe Railroad, down this rich valley through Butler and Cowley counties, while other roads will penetrate this region from the east.

Eastward from Butler is *Greenwood county*, also a very valuable county of land, and with an abundance of timber, stone, water and water power. The Verdigris and Fall River course through this county from north to southeast, furnishing water power every few miles, and receiving numerous tributaries. Two mills are now run by water. Good coal has been opened in various parts of the county. EUREKA is the county seat, and the only town of importance in the county. It is centrally located, on Fall River, and contains a population of about 800, and is a town of substantial growth and character. *Greenwood City* has been recently laid out near the eastern line of the county in an excellent farming region. Eureka will undoubtedly be connected with the world by rail at no distant day by a line running eastward, but probably the first railroad she obtains will be a branch from the L. L. & G. R. R. at Ottawa *via* Burlington.

Wilson County lies southeast of Greenwood, and is also well watered by Fall River and Verdigris, which run through the count , receiving many tributaries, and unite near the southern border. At their confluence is *Neodosha*, a thriving town with a population of about 800. It has water power and three good mills, a grist mill and a three foot vein of coal, one mile from town. At FREDONIA, the county seat, and Fall River, above *Verdi*, on the Verdigris, and at *Guilford*, *Altoona*, *Coyville* and *Jackson's Mills*, are improved water powers. Fredonia and Altoona are towns of importance. *Buffalo* is a post-office and village in the northeastern portion of the county.

Montgomery County is south of Wilson, and like that county, is almost entirely within the Osage Trust Lands. It is the eastermost county on these lands, and has settled with great rapidity, and its lands, especially the valleys, are highly esteemed by the settlers. It is watered by the Verdigris River and its tributaries. INDEPENDENCE, on this stream, and in the center of the county, is the county seat. It is a thriving place of nearly a thousand inhabitants. The Leavenworth, Lawrence & Galveston Railroad is now being completed diagonally through this county to the south line of the State, but at this writing I am not informed as to its route. The county is well supplied with coal, timber and stone. *Parker* is the second largest town and is located in the southeastern portion of the county. There is an abundance of water power in the county, and a number of mills run by water. There are also several villages, among which are *Radical City*, *Elk City*, *Coneyville*, *Ennisville* and *Liberty*.

Howard County lies to the west of Montgomery, and is also entirely within the Osage Trust Lands. It is watered by Elk River, Big Caney, Middle Caney, and many other smaller streams. The county has an abundance of water power. There is a great deal of fine bottom land in the county, but perhaps it has not so large an amount of tillage land in comparison with the grazing land, as the adjoining counties. It is rapidly settling, but there are many choice farms yet to be taken at $1.25 per acre. I am not able to say what is the county seat, as the question has been in dispute. *Longton*, *Elk Falls* and *Peru* are the principal towns in the county. The first settlers went into the county but a few months ago, but the population is rapidly increasing.

IRRIGATION.

I think the only stream in Kansas from which water can ever be used to any considerable extent for irrigation, is the Arkansas River. The benefits of irrigation are in demand only during about three months of each year, while crops are growing, and at that time the streams in Kansas, as everywhere else, unless fed by mountain rivlets flowing from perpetual snows, are at their lowest. It is true that upon small streams, dams may be made, and by erecting windmill pumps at wells, reservoirs may be filled, but for extensive operations in irrigation, the Arkansas is the only stream that can be relied upon. Not only is this stream at its highest stage during the summer, but its banks are everywhere low, so that water may be taken from it without difficulty. The fall of the Arkansas River in the Indian Territoy is estimated by Mr. O. Chanute at two feet per mile. In Kansas, the country rises much more rapidly to the west, and the fall of the river is probably two or three times these figures. In Colorado, main irrigation ditches are given a grade of from two to five feet per mile, accroding to that excellent authority, the *Rocky Mountain News*. The Arkansas therefore has fall enough for irrigation purposes, especially when we take into consideration its numerous windings.

Another important element in this discussion is the character of the soil to be irrigated. I have not made anything like an exhaustive investigation of this subject, but it appears that a sandy soil is essential to success in irrigation. It is probable that a clay soil would retain the water so long as to bake the surface and injure the roots, and from a few experiments made in this State I think the same thing true, but to a less degree, of our prairie loam.

It is questionable whether there is much land in Kansas, excepting in the extreme western portion, that is adapted to irrigation, and I am quite confident that with *deep tillage*, there is little land in the State that needs irrigation, excepting in the extreme western portion. Some however have supposed, not from experiment, but from the appearance of the soil, that the Arkansas River region, above Fort Dodge, would be benefitted by irrigation. If this be true, we may look to that vicinity for magnificent irrigation operations within a very short time.

While in Colorado recently, I obtained a few items upon this subject which may interest the reader. The city of Denver is irrigated by a ditch which is carried along a gentle eminence, rising at the eastern outskirts of the city. The water is conveyed in a common ditch, which is about three feet wide and three feet deep, although usually of greater width than depth. At convenient distances, conductors made of four, 2 inch pine plank, 6 to 12 feet long, are placed in the lower bank of the canal. The lower end, or mouth of all these troughs, extends beyond the embankment to prevent washing. At the upper end is a gate, which may be opened to any desired hight, indicated upon it in inches, and when in place it is fastened with a strong padlock. The water is conveyed from the largest ditch to a set of smaller ones, from which it is distributed through troughs with gates, as above described, to still smaller ditches, which run through the city at the edge of the sidewalks, and from which it is taken into the yards and gardens. The ditch gates in Denver vary from 8x8 inches to 16x16 inches in size. The price for water was formerly $5.00 per year for a single lot of 25x125 feet. Farmers above the city are supplied from this ditch at the rate of $3.00 per square inch. That is, a gate is opened to such a hight as to make an opening, say 32 inches square. The gate is then locked, and the water flows through the opening during the entire season, which the farmer conducts upon his land in such manner as suits him. For this he pays $96.00 for the season. When a company owns a ditch, the price varys from $2.00 to $3.00 per inch. Usually, however, the farmers co-operate to construct and own a ditch themselves, when the cost is considerably less. It is ordinarily calculated that from one-half an inch, to one inch of water is required through the growing season, to each acre irrigated. One farmer told me he irrigated 35 acres with 20 inches of water, and that it required one man to attend to the irrigation during three months time. The water was applied to every portion of the ground about once a week, running in one set of small ditches ten or twelve hours, and then turned onto another part of the field for the same period. The engineer of the Greeley colony reports the completion of a canal 26 miles long. The cost of excavating was $22,669, there being 107,949 cubic yards at 21 cents per yard. It would seem that there is some mistake in the figures, for a ditch of the above size would only convey about water enough to irrigate 3,000 acres, allowing one-half inch per acre. This would be quite expensive irrigation. Frequently water is taken from streams at a trifling expense, but ordinarily it may be said that the *cost of water* for irrigation, varies from 50 cents to $3.00 per acre, each year.

ALTITUDES.

No pains have been spared to obtain the correct elevations of different places in Kansas above the ocean level for use on the accompanying map. The Superintendents and Chief Engineers of the various railroads kindly furnished me the levels of their respective lines, but no two were from the same base. In order to arrive at the altitude above the ocean, I applied to Mr. O. Chanute, of Kansas City, Chief Engineer of the M. R., Ft. S & G., the L. L. & G. and the A. & N. R. Railroads, and whose scientific accuracy is well known.

Mr. Chanute informed me that by the levels of the Mobile & Ohio R. R, high water of 1849 at Columbus, Kentucky, was 308¼ feet above tide water at Mobile. The levels of the Illinois Central and Ohio & Mississippi R. B. from Columbus *via* Cairo to St. Louis, corrected by test levels over the Iron Mountain R. R. from Columbus show the St. Louis Directrix to be 403 feet above the Gulf. Mr. Chanute has not been able to obtain what he considers entirely reliable figures showing the elevation of the mouth of the Kansas River above St. Louis, but according to the best data at his command, the bottom land at State Line and Kansas City, on which is situated the Union Depots, is 748 feet above tide water at Mobile. The fall of the Missouri River he reckons at 0,664 feet per mile, making St. Joseph, 109 miles up the river, 820 feet above the ocean.

Denver at the foot of the Rocky Mountains in Colorado Territory, 638 miles west of Kansas City by the K. P. K. is 6,100 feet above the ocean level.

NOTE.—The elevation of Newton on the A. T. & S. R. R. is not correctly shown n the accompanying map. It should be 1,445.

PRODUCTIONS OF KANSAS.

It would seem that enough had been said about the productions of the State, but I am in receipt of such questions as these: Can you raise vegetables in Kansas? Can you raise sorghum in Kansas? Is it a good country for hogs? etc., etc. Perhaps some of these questions have not been directly answered in the preceding pages.

Kansas is an excellent country for vegetables and vines. Mellons grow in profusion. The best Irish potatoes grow on land which has in it the most sand, and a crop should be planted for summer use as soon as the frost is out of the ground, and then a crop planted in June for winter use. Some persons cover their potatoes with straw instead of earth, at planting, dropping the seed in a furrow. Potatoes are always of good quality, and produce a good crop if planted in this way. This is an excellent country for sweet potatoes, and by packing them in dry sand in tight boxes or barrels, they are kept through the winter nicely, in a cellar of moderate temperature. Cellery and asparagus also thrive. A gentleman in Leavenworth blanched his cellery successfully, by letting it grow thickly together on rich land, instead of heaping earth about the stalks. The leaves shaded the stalks so completely that they grew tender and white. Sorghum is a crop which has never failed. Even during the famous "dry season" its long roots found sufficient moisture below the surface—another proof of the value of *deep* cultivation. Peanuts are easily grown here on our lightest lands. In short, *anything* that grows in the States east of Kansas in this latitude, or farther north, can be produced, cheaply in profusion here. *Sod corn* is grown by planting corn on newly turned prairie sod, cutting through it with an ax or spade. The seed is put in this opening, and the planter presses the sod with his foot as he walks along. No after culture can be given, as the sod is too tough to be cultivated, but weeds do not appear the first year, and from 20 to 40 bushels of corn may be grown if planted before June. The sod rots the first year, and afterward plows easily.

HOGS.

Concerning fattening pork, a large number of our best farmers lately gave their opinions through the *Kansas Farmer*, that they can grow corn at the present prices for labor, etc., at 40 cents or less per bushel. They agreed, as do farmers generally, that corn fed in the ear, will produce ten pounds of pork for each bushel of corn. This refers to fattening hogs after they are grown to proper size, and means that a hog in fair condition and of decent stock, weighing 250 pounds, can be made to weigh 350 pounds by feeding 10 bushels of corn. In raising hogs, our farmers have but recently commenced upon what is to be a system extensively practiced, and that is to graze them on red clover, winter rye, sorghum, etc. Some farmers pasture sheep or young cattle on winter rye during the winter, and then let it grow and ripen, and turn hogs in to harvest it. The object is save labor and thereby increase the profits.

Perhaps it is out of place, but I must protest against the notion of some people that it will not pay to use fertelizers. Deep plowing, and rotation of crops, will keep our lands in good heart for generations probably, yet it will *pay* to apply all the manure that is made on a farm. Farmers in Illinois, Iowa, etc., have found this out, and Kansas farmers are also beginning to learn it.

MANUFACTURES.

While it is true that Kansas is to be pre-eminently renowned for stock raising, agriculture and fruit growing, it is not less true that with our water power and cheap coal, certain branches of manufacturing will prove very remunerative. Aside from flouring mills, the demand for which is apparent and is not half supplied, there should be many more agricultural implement manufactories. It is needless to say that the demand is extensive and incessant and constantly increasing, and it is evident that such material as is not to be found in this State, can be shipped here for a less rate than can cumbersome machinery after it is put together. The same is true of wagons, carriages, etc. In the manufacture of woolen fabrics of coarser grade, there certainly will be great profit, as the material is at hand, and the market is extensive both here and in the newer regions south and west. Cotton can be obtained cheaply also, as it is grown successfully in the Indian Territory which lies immediately south of us, and our railroad lines, will within a year, penetrate the vast cottonfields of Texas, which are less than three hundred miles distant from our southern State line.

The following extract from the *Bulletin of the National Woolen Manufacturers' Association*, furnishes conclusive testimony as to the adaptation of the West to the business of manufacturing goods of common grade:

"The advantages legitimately claimed by the western manufacturers are, the saving of transportation on both raw material and fabrics; the facility of sending directly to customers—no commissions being paid to middlemen in the large cities—and the public sentiment of the consumers in favor of the products of their own region, which is encouraged by the confidence that the goods are honestly made. It is evident from facts observed by us, that the West will hereafter rely to a large extent upon the products of its own mills for ordinary cloths, and that the East must relinquish this market, or compete by cheaper productions, or a higher class of fabrics."

FREIGHTS.

The following table, furnished me by Messrs. Ridenour & Baker, Wholesale Grocers, at Lawrence, shows that freights between Kansas and the East are very reasonable. Goods from New York are delivered at the Missouri River cheaper than at most of the towns in the interior of Illinois. The strife between the various through lines, which compete for the increase trade of Kansas and the west and southwest, is sufficiently dwelt upon under the head of Railroads, and it is there shown that this competition is no inconsiderable item in the long list of causes which bring so many people to Kansas and make them so prosperous after they get here:

TABULAR STATEMENT of the rates of freight per hundred pounds, between the various cities mentioned, and the State of Kansas at the Missouri river January 1, 1871. Prepared by Messrs. Ridenour & Baker, wholesale grocers, Lawrence, Kansas.

	FIRST CLASS.	SECOND CLASS.	THIRD CLASS.	FOURTH CLASS.
New York	$2 60	$2 03	$1 69	$1 14
Boston	2 60	2 03	1 69	1 14
Philadelphia	2 60	2 03	1 69	1 14
Pittsburg	1 70	1 20	1 00	85
Columbus	1 40	1 05	85	60
Cincinnati	1 00	75	75	50
Indianapolis	90	75	65	45
St. Louis	60	40	40	30
Buffalo	2 40	1 85	1 50	1 05
Cleveland	1 70	1 20	1 00	85
Toledo	1 70	1 20	1 00	85
Detroit	1 70	1 20	1 00	85
Chicago	1 00	75	75	50
Quincy	60	40	40	30

The above are winter rates. Summer rates are about 30 to 50 per cent less. First class rates from New York and Boston to the Missouri River are now, May 1, 1871, $1.84 per hundred.

First class includes household goods well boxed; and on some roads, second had furniture, well boxed, accompanied by passengers, but most railways charge double first class rates on these articles, except by special contract. Agricultural implements, by special contract, and farm wagons in pieces, are first class. Also, dry goods, boots and shoes and general merchandise. Classified lists showing in what class any particular article will be rated, can be seen upon application to any railroad, or freight express agent. There are many articles, especially in the fourth class, upon which special rates can be obtained by shipping full car loads. *Immigrants to Kansas* are also enabled to make contracts for greatly reduced rates per hundred on their household goods, furniture, farming implements, farm stock, etc.

Messrs. Ridenour & Baker estimate that the rates of freight of the same class going east are about one-third less than they are coming west. Wool, sacked, is classed by all roads between here and the eastern cities, at one-and-a-half times first class rates. At the present rate of $1.84 cents per hundred from New York, freight on wool would be $2.96 per hundred. Deduct one-third for eastern bound freight, and it leaves $1.98 per hundred. In shipping by the car load, less rates can be obtained. But it is safe to calculate that the wool grower not only raises his fleeces at the trifling cost already described, but he can then *ship them to New York or Boston for two cents per pound.* How can eastern wool growers compete with these advantages?

WHEN TO COME TO KANSAS.

There are many evident reasons why it is better to come to Kansas *now*, than to come a few years hence. The census of 1880 will show the prediction of Horace Greeley to be true, "that ten years will give to Kansas a population of one million of inhabitants." The increase of the last five years has been at a much higher proportional rate than this, and emigration is likely to increase rather than diminish. It needs no argument to show that it is better to be in advance of, rather than than to follow, this tide of human beings. In a few years the railroads will all be built; the towns established; the water powers improved, and high prices for land and lots will prevail. Lands which can now be brought for five or ten dollars per acre, or taken as homesteads, will then be worth thirty to one hundred dollars per acre. Mill seats with good water power can now be had without expense, by those who will improve them. Coal mines that are to yield enormous profits may now be purchased at a nominal cost, and land can be bought for a song, upon which busy villages and towns are speedily to be established.

One takes a sleeping car in New York and reaches Kansas in three days fresh, vigorous and ready for business. He finds towns already established with as good churches, schools and society as in any eastern town, but which are soon to double or treble their population. If he prefers fresher fields for enterprise, or cheap lands for tillage, the railroads will take him in a few hours where he can purchase at low rates and on long credit—or, by continuing his travels a day's journey from the depot he can find free Homesteads and "Land for the Landless."

Nor is this all. It is quite unnecessary to take risks in founding towns, and making valuable improvements. Town building has come to be a legititimate and important part of railroading in the west. It is quite useless for private companies to attempt to rival railroads in this line, and so town building is no longer a doubtful and dubious business. The railroad system is now so well established in this state that it is not difficult to tell about where the lines will run, and to select localities where good towns will find support, but where there are now limited improvements and low prices. So also, to one who seeks a farm in the interior, there is not the uncertainty as to the future which prevailed a few years ago. It is now settled that every county must have, and soon will have, one or more railroads within its boundaries. As the counties are about twenty-four miles square, it follows that every farmer will soon be so near a depot, that he can drive to it and back again in one day.

HOW TO COME TO KANSAS.

Having determined to come to Kansas, the first necessity is to sell out where you now are. In this you will probably find trouble at once. You have put a certain price upon your property and say you must have it, but there are many others who want "to go out west," and there is much property on the market.

First you must determine the question absolutely, do *you* want to go west? Having decided that you would on the whole prefer the west, *sell out for just what your property will bring.* Have no fear that you will loose anything by selling at a low price, because the purchase you make in Kansas is certain to compensate you for such losses in a short time. Besides, if you are a farmer, you can carry on that business with such profits in Kansas, that you ought nct to be detained a single month by the low price at which you must sell. While you are hesitating there, land is doubling in value here. Do not doubt that people eat and drink—sleep and wake—live and die—in Kansas very much as they do elsewhere. Have no fear but that you will find a plenty of people here who are much like those you leave behind. Make up your mind for hardships and privations—for sickness and sorrow—because these are inseparable from humanity. Finally, remembering that home is as sweet and that heaven is as near, in Kansas as in any other country, with a stout heart prepare for your journey.

WHAT TO BRING.

It is not difficult to determine what to bring with you in coming to Kansas. First ascertain how much money you can get for various household articles. Then by learning the weight, you can, with the help of the chapter on freights in this book, determine what it will cost to bring each article to Kansas. With the assistance of the subjoined list of prices, you can then readily determine what articles to bring. Generally speaking, you will bring all bedding, table linen and carpets, and in these carefully wrap, separately, crockery and table furnishings, because they will not sell for much at auction. There are numerous but indescribable articles for use and ornament, which cannot be sold at any price, and hardly given away, yet they will help to make things comfortable and cozy, and you will probably be sorry if you leave them. In such cases the test is simply: "This article weighs so much, and it will cost so much to take it to Kansas; will it be worth as much when I get it there?" In this council the ladies should have a decisive vote, for upon them will devolve the greatest privations in "going West." Bring high priced furniture if you have any, and expect to want any here, but the less the better, unless you can reach Kansas with your pockets full of greenbacks. Common furniture, mirrors and agricultual implements you will sell. It does not pay to bring any but good stock to Kansas, unless it be sheep, and that matter is treated under its appropriate head.

One of the best things "to take" is a lunch basket filled with roast chicken, sandwiches, bread and butter, pickles, or a tumbler of tart jelly, a Washington pie, etc. For a small sum you can buy a lamp-heating tea-pot or "Ætna," thus making yourself quite comfortable wherever you are. Three meals a day can be obtained on all principal routes, for seventy-five cents per meal. If you start for the table as soon as the cars stop, and when there, without being boisterous, make yourself entirely at home, there is always a plenty of time. Take a sleeping car. It pays, no matter what penurious people say. These cars are clean, ride easier than other cars; are better ventilated and the company is more select. By this means you arrive at your journey's end vigorous and clear headed, and ready to see things just as they are. The cost is one dollar and fifty cents to two dollars per night, for double birth. Leave out a plenty of extra clothing, and prepare for the necessary exposures of travel.

The following are the prices for the *cheapest* furniture at Ottawa, Kansas, which shows about the average prices for the State:

Item	Price	Item	Price
Bedsteads	$4 00@ 4 50	Cribs	4 00
Tables, fall leaf	5 00	Wardrobes, black walnut	15 00@18 00
Tables, extension, ℔ foot	1 75	Lounges	3 50
Chairs, ℔ ½ dozen	4 50@ 5 00	Lounges with mattress	6 50
Tin safes, 3 shelves and drawer	7 00	Cook stove No.7, complete	20 00
Bureaus, full size	15 00@18 00	Cook stove, Charter Oak, complete	27 00
Bureau washstand	8 00	Cook stove, Concord, complete	27 00
Washstands	4 00	Heating stoves	$6 00@10 00
Mattresses, husk	5 00	Stove pipe ℔ joint	30
Mattresses, moss	10 00@12 00	Sad irons ℔ ℔	08
Rockers, arm	4 00	Milk pans each	25
Rockers, cane seat	4 50	Fruit cans, q'ts ℔ dozen	1 00
Rockers, sewing	1 50@ 2 50		

Toilet sets, grates, mantels, table cutlery, and house furnishing goods at eastern prices.

AGRICULTURAL IMPLEMENTS.

Plows, 12 inch Moline Breaker, rolling cutter, guage wheel, two shares 30 00
Plows, stirring, German steel 14 00
Plows, stirring, caststeel, double shin 18 00
Nearly all plows scour in this soil.

Plows, Robinson's Gang and Trench 100 00
Corn planters, best two horse .... 70 00@75 00
Mowing machines 130 00
Combined mowing and reaping machines 175 00 200 00

The above prices are only ten dollars above factory prices for freight.

Wagons, two horse, with brake, top box, neck yoke, stay chains and whiffletrees .... $95 00@100 00
Pitchforks, 3 tines .... 75@ 90
Shovels, Ames' caststeel 1 75
Hoes .... 50@ 75

Harrow teeth ⅌ lb........ 07@ 08
Axes, best 1 50
Grindstones ⅌ lb........... 03
Nails ⅌ keg, 10d........... 5 50
Saws, cross-cut ⅌ foot... 75
Well buckets, each...... 75
Horse shoes, ⅌ keg...... 7 00

Hardware, putty, etc., as cheap as in Illinois or Ohio.

PINE LUMBER.

Flooring ⅌ M .... $37 50@$50 00
Siding ⅌ M.................. 22 00@ 30 00
Ceiling ⅌ M.. .... 27 50@ 30 00
Shingles ⅌ M.............. 4 00@ 5 50
Finishing inch ⅌ M. .... 40 00@ 50 00
Framing stuff ⅌ M 35

Common boards and fencing ⅌ M............. 32 50@ 35 00
Lath ⅌ M.................... 6 50
Windows (glazed) 8x10.. 1 75
Doors, 4 panel............. 2 00@ 3 00
Paper (building) ⅌ lb... 5½@ 06½

MECHANICS WAGES.

Carpenters ⅌ day............ $2 50@$3 50
Boss carpenters ⅌ day..... 4 00
Painters ⅌ square 1st coat 15
Per square additional coat 10
Masons common stone work ⅌ foot, laid in wall 16
Best rubble ⅌ foot, laid in wall 20

Best hammer dressed range ⅌ foot, laid in wall 30
Brick work ⅌ M, laid in wall 16 00
Fine cutting ⅌ square foot 1 00
Plasterers ⅌ square yard, 3 coats and lath........... 40

Farm laborers command $25 per month and board.

Work horses cost $75 to $150 each. A yoke of oxen can be obtained for $125 to $150, and good milch cows are worth $35 to $60 each.

THE COST OF LIVING.

If one brings a family to Kansas intending to live upon a salary, hiring a house and buying at retail, he will not be likely to save more than he would upon the same salary in the East, provided he lives in the same style. Of course the matter of style is what *costs* in all families and ruins many, but the apparent necessity for keeping up with our friends and neighbors, is not so pressing here as in old communities. In this therefore, there can be a saving. The item of rent is a heavy one here. The uses to which money may be put are so various and so profitable, that people who build houses reeeive large returns for their investments. For instance, a neat house with a cellar, three or four rooms on the first floor and two chambers above, with a garden of a quarter or a half acre, will rent for from $20 to $30 per month. Cottages with two or three rooms rent for $12 to $15 per month. Rents are payable monthly in advance. Few people rent for any considerable period. They soon "run up a smoke of their own," if it is but a humble domicil. He who lives in his own house, and buys when articles are plentiful and cheap, can live cheaper here than he can in the East, as the tables given below will testify:

RETAIL.

Article	Price	Article	Price
Flour, ⅌ cwt	$2 50 @ $4 00	Rice, (Carolina) ⅌ ℔	12½
Flour, graham, ⅌ cwt	3 50 @ 4 00	Salt ⅌ bbl	3 50 @ 3 75
Corn meal ⅌ cwt	1 40 @ 1 50	Vinegar, ⅌ gallon	35 @ 50
Potatoes ⅌ bushel	50 @ 60	Dried apples ⅌ ℔	10 @ 12½
Hams ⅌ ℔	14 @ 20	Dried peaches ⅌ ℔	15 @ 18
Bacon ⅌ ℔	14 @ 16⅔	Raisins ⅌ ℔	30
Shoulders ⅌ ℔	10 @ 12	Prunes ⅌ ℔	18 @ 20
Pork, pickled	13 @ 15	Currants ⅌ ℔	18 @ 20
Beef, dried ⅌ ℔	20 @ 22	Blackberries ⅌ ℔	18 @ 20
Mackerel ⅌ kit	1 64 @ 4 25	Cherries, pitted	30 @ 40
White fish ⅌ kit	1 65 @ 2 00	Raspberries ⅌ ℔	50
Cod fish ⅌ ℔	12½	Corn ⅌ bushel	45
Halibut ⅌ ℔	16⅔	Oats ⅌ bushel	40
Cheese, N. Y. factory ⅌ ℔	20 @ 22	Coal oil ⅌ gallon	50
Cheese, Kansas, ⅌ ℔	18 @ 20	Rope, manilla, ⅌ ℔	25
Butter ⅌ ℔	25 @ 35	Tobacco, best Navy, ⅌ ℔	80 @ 1 00
Eggs ⅌ doz	18 @ 20	Tobacco, G. I., ⅌ ℔	80
Beans, Med. Navy ⅌ ℔	05 @ 06	Tobacco, smoking, ⅌ ℔	35 @ 1 00
Sugar, N. O, ⅌ ℔	12½ @ 15	Tubs, No. 1, each	1 25
Sugar, Coffee, ⅌ ℔	15	Tubs, No. 2, each	1 10
Sugar, hard, ⅌ ℔	16⅔	Tubs, No. 3, each	1 00
Coffee, choice Rio ⅌ ℔	23 @ 25	Washboards, zinc, ea	30
Coffee, fair, ⅌ ℔	20 @ 22	Buckets, 2 hoops, ea	25
Coffee, Java, O. G	30	Buckets, 3 hoops, ea	30
Molasses, Sorghum, ⅌ gallon	75 @ 80	Beefsteak ⅌ ℔	12½ @ 15
Molasses, N. O. ⅌ gal	90 @ 1 10	Mutton chops ⅌ ℔	12½ @ 15
Syrup, ⅌ gallon	60 @ 1 40	Pork steaks ⅌ ℔	12½ @ 15
Teas, ⅌ ℔	90 @ 2 00	Veal Steaks ⅌ ℔	12½ @ 15

The foregoing table was prepared for this book in January, 1871, by my friends Messrs. Ridenour & Baker, long established and favorably known grocery merchants of Lawrence. They also have large branch houses at Topeka, Emporia and Tioga, all under the firm name either of Ridenour or of Baker, and these figures may therefore be relied upon as representing the average retail prices in this state at the time they were made.

HORSES.

The breeding of fine horses has come to be so important an interest in Kansas, that I desired to treat the subject in a considerate manner, and therefore applied to various "horse men" for such data as was needful, but have received very little assistance in this direction.

Through Mr. B. F. Akers, of Leavenworth, I learn that there are *more than sixty* thoroughbred horses and mares in this state, and among the former he quoted from memory the names of "Newry," "Chicamauga," "Veto," "Express," "Leinster," "General Mitchell," "Derby," "Orlando," "Prairie Boy," "Blondin," "Escape," etc.

Among the dealers and breeders who have contributed most largely to the horse stock of the state by valuable importations of thoroughbred and trotting horses and mares, are Mr. B. F. Akers, Col. C. R. Jennison, H. D. Bunch, Steiner & Tough, and F. C. Buckley, all of Leavenworth; Dr. W. L. Challis, of Atchison; Mr. G. W. Greaver, of Wyandotte; A. M. Eastman, of Topeka, who bred "Henry," a famous trotting horse which has been taken East, and lately trotted a mile in 2:22½, on Flatwood Course, N. Y.; Mr. Conn, of Council Grove; J. Reynolds, of Howard county; a gentleman who has recently brought several fine horses from Kentucky to Wyandotte county; and many others, also have horses of great value. The moneyed value to the state, of these efforts to establish the reputation of Kansas for thoroughbred and trotting horses, is probably not fully appreciated by the most of us, and the writer confesses to a very moderate degree of enthusiasm upon the subject. Whether a horse trots a mile in 2:29½ or 2:30, seems a matter not of very great importance to the world, and if he will carry me safely sixty miles a day, I am not particular as to his pedigree. But this is not the way horse fanciers regard these questions, and speed and blood command fabulous sums in the market. Farmers and breeders raise horses for the money there is in them, and there is certainly a great deal of money in the business of raising fine horses. In this regard the reputation of a state is of great importance. A Vermont horse will command a better price, with most buyers, than one of equal value from Maine, because of the reputation gained by the former state in this direction, and if any Western man wants a thoroughbred, he goes to Kentucky for it. The breeders in our state are confident that Kansas will soon have an enduring reputation for its fine horse stock. There are many young horses in this state which will soon be upon the market. Mr. Akers, above alluded to, introduced to the Eastern public three noted trotters, bred in this state, which be named "Kansas Chief," "Kansas Queen," and "Kansas Pet," and after a series of successes with them upon various courses, he disposed of them for the handsome sum of *fifteen thousand dollars.* The same gentleman also brought to the state the trotting stallion "Comas," of which a cut is given herewith.

In this connection it gives me pleasure to state that the well known Amasa Sprague of Providence, Rhode Island, will soon open a large farm in this State, to be devoted principally to the breeding of fine horses and cattle. He is already the owner of some of the best stock in New England, which will be immediately removed to this state to a farm purchased near Leavenworth for this purpose. Mr. Akers is associated with Mr. Sprague in this enterprise, and it is their purpose to fit up a farm of about 40,000 acres in the interior of the state, seed it to blue grass, divide it into suitable fields by osage hedges, erect substantial and commodious buildings, and put upon the place the best stock that can be procured. The enormous wealth, enterprising spirit and business sagacity of Mr. Sprague, combined with the thorough practical knowledge possessed by Mr. Akers, who has acquired a competency in this business in Kansas, renders the brilliant success of this scheme a foregone conclusion. In five year's time these gentlemen will have the best stock farm in the world.

"COMAS."

This well known trotting stallion was brought to Kansas by B. F. Akers being selected after a visit to the best breeding studs in the country. He was foaled in 1863, and was bred in Iowa. Like "Kirkwood" and "Bashaw, jr.," he was got by Green's Bashaw, dam Topsey, by Prophet, by Hill's Vermont Black Hawk, by Sherman Morgan, by Justin Morgan, by True Britton.

Green's Bashaw, by Drake's (Vernol's) Black Hawk, 1st dam by Webber's Tom Thumb; 2d dam, "The Chas. Kent Mare," (dam of Rysdyk's Hambletonian, sire of Dexter,) by imported Bellfounder; 3d dam, "Old One Eye," by Hambletonian, (son of imported Messenger; 4th dam, by imported Messenger.

Drake's (Vernol's) Black Hawk, by New York Black Hawk; dam by Kentucky Whip, son of Cook's, or Blackburn's, Whip.

New York Black Hawk, by Andrew Jackson, dam the celebrated Sally Miller, by Mambrino, by imp. *Messenger*.

Andrew Jackson, by Young Bashaw, dam by Whynot, son of imp. *Messenger*.

Young Bashaw, by imp. Barb Grand Bashaw, dam by imp. *Messenger*.

Mr. Otto Holstein, correspondent of the *Field, Turf and Farm*, in describing this horse, says, after giving his pedigree: "Here is blood enough on his sire's side to insure trotting qualities in his progeny. But this is not all. While the paternal house furnished to the trotting world 'Dexter,' 'Lady Thorn,' 'Goldsmith Maid,' 'American Girl,' 'George M. Patchen,' &c., the maternal side has scarcely been a whit behind, for, from it. sprang the celebrated 'Lancet' and the wonderful 'Ethan Allen,' the sire of 'Honest Allen,'

Pocahontas, &c. *Comas* is, therefore, one of the best bred trotting stallions in America, being a combination of the two most successful trotting families in the United States, the Bashaw and the Messenger, with the additional excellence of the Black Hawk.

"His general excellence of color is that he is a rich chestnut, and of form is that he is a pony-built horse, fifteen hands and two inches high, revealing the great speed, elastic step and wonderful endurance for which the family is so noted. His carriage is lofty, consequently his head and neck are well set upon his shoulders. His back is apparently short, owing, measurably, to the strong arches of muscle over the loin, so necessary for enduring strength in the trotter. His legs are clean and flat, his withers and shoulders inclined, chest deep, and capacious enough for excellent respiratory action, main and tail fine

"COMAS."

(The property of B. F. Akers, Leavenworth.)

and long, his eyes are good, as also are his joints and feet, the great and necessary adjuncts to a successful stock horse. *Comas*, comparatively speaking, has been bred with more than an ordinary degree of care, and a foundation has been formed for future excellence, which is now fully substantiated by the appearance and wonderful trotting action displayed by his produce."

"KANSAS BOY."

[The property of B. F. Akers, Leavenworth.]

I am indebted to Mr. Otto Holstein for the following description of this horse. "The stable companion of Comas is his son, 'Kansas Boy.' This fast and fashionable bred three year old stallion is a blood bay, fifteen hands and three inches high, was sired by Comas, dam by Gauglion Gangle, son of Bertrand, son of Sir Archy, son of imported Diomed. Large as he is there is no waste timber in his make up, but is well and compactly built, not leggy, possessed of a gamey head, rangy neck, splendid shoulders, deep, roomy girth, well ribbed on the barrel, with grand quarters like his sire, a set of legs as hard and clean as polished ivory. An analysis of his breeding is conclusive as to his future worth. Through his dam he traces back to the stoutest and most fashionable blood known to the American racing turf, as well as throwing his descent down the line of the winning trotting blood to 'Andrew Jackson,' who, in the characteristic words of the late Hiram Woodruff, was 'Rough to look at, but king of trotters.' *Kansas Boy*, will in all probability not be offered to public patronage until his trotting abilities are thoroughly developed. He has been in training but a short time, and with Comas can trot close to '40 to pole."

"NEWRY."

(The property of Dr. W. L. Challis, Atchison.)

As among the most noted of thoroughbreds in Kansas, we present herewith a cut of the splendid stallion "Newry." He is a bay horse, foaled 1864, bred by the late Robt. A. Alexander, of Kentucky, from whom he was purchased by Col. C. R. Jennison, and by him sold to Dr. W. L. Challiss, of Atchison. He was got by the illustrious race horse and stallion, LEXINGTON, dam Novice, (dam of Norfolk,) by imported Glencoe; thence through seven uncontaminated crosses of pure blood. His produce give ample evidence of a brilliant future for him. Upon the race course, he defeated the fast "Fanny Cheatham," both in their two year old form, a first mile of a heat race, in 1:46¾. The celebrated "Norfolk," his full brother, in a race of three mile heats, defeated "Lodi" in the unprecedented time of 5:27½–5:29½, both heats standing out in bold relief against the world.

DESCRIPTION OF ILLUSTRATIONS.

State Capitol, Topeka.—Frontispiece.

The east wing of the elegant design made for the capitol of Kansas is completed, excepting the pillars and portico. This wing is 114 feet long, 78 feet wide, and 95 feet high to the apex of the roof. It is divided into three stories, with basement under ground for steam heating apparatus, fuel, etc. The upper story is divided into two legislative halls, with committee rooms, while the two lower stories are divided into convenient offices for the use of the Executive and Judiciary Departments of the State Government. The exterior walls are four feet thick, and are constructed of Junction City magnesian limestone. The building is of the corinthian style of architecture. The partition walls are of limestone, with brick arches, upon which rest heavy wrought iron beams and joist. The iron suspension roof is covered with tin. The expense of the building thus far, has been about $375,000, and with the completion of the portico and some minor additions, it will answer all needful purposes for many years. Mr. J. G. Haskell, of Lawrence, is the architect. It is impossible that in all respects this *wing* can give entire satisfaction as a capitol building, but it is a thoroughly built, substantial and elegant structure, and a credit to the State.

It stands upon twenty acres of ground, donated by the city of Topeka to the State, near the business part of the place. These grounds are now being laid out, and preparations are making to ornament them with trees and shrubery.

Old University Building, Lawrence.—Page 11.

This building is 50 feet square and two stories with high basement. It was erected by the people of Lawrence, and by the contributions of friends in the East. It stands upon an eminennce overlooking the city, and is built in a substantial manner of stone and brick,

State University, Lawrence.—Page 16.

This cut is an accurate representation of the new University Building. It is 246 feet long, 98 feet wide in the middle, 63 feet wide in the wings, and 95 feet high to the observatory balcony. Its chapel hall, in the centre of the building, is 94 feet long, 56 feet wide and 35 feet high. The building contains more than 50 rooms for the various branches of instruction. For all the Physical Sciences, the rooms are arranged *in suits of four rooms each*, as follows Lecture Room 23x45 feet, 1st Labratory 19x52 feet, 2d Labratory 21x45 feet, Library and Aparatus Room 10x35 feet, Professor's Room 11x13 feet. The building throughout is built of limestone, and the water table, corner stones, window arches and sills, etc., are of magnesian limestone from Manhattan. The shade of the latter contrasts gratefully with the limestone, which is taken from the edge of Mount Oread, upon which the building is situated. The interior is now being finished, and when completed it will be heated with steam, ventilated by the most approved method, and supplied throughout with water and gas, and in all respects will be one of the best arranged University buildings in the land. The entire cost will be about $150,000, and I venture to say that it is one of the largest and best public buildings ever erected in the United States for that amount. Mr. J. G. Haskell is the architect.

The educational work of the institution was commenced September, 1866. The President and Chancellor is Gen. John Frasser, L. L. D., assisted by a corps of eight accomplished professors. The University is a child of the State and crowns the public school system of Kansas. Forty thousand acres of land has been set apart by the State for its endowment, and annual appropriations are made for tuition, as all State pupils are admitted free of tuition charges. Its scientific apparatus is extensive and valuable, and altogether it is one of the most promising educational institutions in the United States.

John Brown's Cabin. Page 20.

A description of this Cabin follows the cut.

Humboldt Bridge. Page 25.

This structure of 190 feet span, crosses the Neosho river at the narrowest place occurring within a distance of many miles. It connects the principal portion of Humboldt, which is on the east side of the river, with that portion around the Missouri, Kansas and Texas Railroad Depot on the west side.

Adams House, Manhattan. Page 31.

This Hotel was erected and is owned by Maj. N. A. Adams of Manhattan. It contains large, airy rooms, and is a well kept house and an ornament to the place. It is constructed of magnesian limestone at a cost of about $30,000.

Topeka Iron Bridge. Page 36.

For a complete description see page 217. The view is taken from the north side of the river.

Drouthy Kansas. Page 41.

This humorous sketch serves to tell its own story, although I have heard people profest, with solemn earnestness, that such a sweet potatoe, watermelon and Irish potatoe, such corn, pumpkins and wheat, never grew in Kansas.

People of so lugubrious and solem a turn of mind, are not expected to look at our "Drouthy."

The charcoal sketch from which this picture was copied, was dashed off by Prof. H. Worrall of Topeka, to enliven a party of Cincinnati tourists who came to visit this dry country, but were detained in Topeka several days on account of a severe rain storm which flooded all the country.

Ludington House, Ottawa. Page 47.

This commodious and substantial block was erected in Ottawa by D. W. Zimmerman, and is now owned by citizens of Ottawa. It contains in its farther portion a spacious public hall, which is now being fitted up for concerts, exhibitions, etc., by H. F. Sheldon. The well kept Hotel is situated on Main street and is convenient to the depot.

The Leavenworth Bridge. Page 54.

One of the most important works that has been undertaken for the benefit of the city of Leavenworth, and the State of Kansas, is the great railway and highway bridge now being constructed over the Missouri River. This bridge is intended to connect the several railroads centering on the west side of the river, at Leavenworth, with those centering on the opposite side; and also to facilitate the intercourse between the metropolis of Kansas and the rich and thriving section of Missouri adjacent to the border.

The extreme difficulty of bridging the Missouri River, together with the novelty of the design adopted here, have invested this bridge with peculiar interest, and its successful completion will go far to revolutionize the method of placing foundations in similar streams. The piers are each composed of three large cast iron cylinders, sunk by the "pneumatic process," from fifty to seventy feet, not simply resting upon, but actually *penetrating* the solid rock a distance of about twelve feet. These columns are then filled with masonry, and above water they are braced and tied in a substantial manner, forming a great iron pier. The bridge proper is composed of three iron spans, each 340 feet in length, and the bottom chord will be 50 feet above extreme high water. This great hight makes the approaches long and expensive. The cost of the whole structure, including nearly one mile of approaches, will be about $750,000, and this capital is mainly furnished by the citizens of Leavenworth county. The foundations and approaches are completed, and it is expected that by November, 1871, the superstructure will be in place, and ready for the passage of trains.

The cut herewith given, drawn for this book from the engineers' working plans, shows the bridge as it will appear when completed. The bridge was designed by Gen. W. W. Wright, engineer in chief, under whose supervision it is being constructed.

Congregational Church, Lawrence. Page 61.

The Plymouth Congregational Church, at Lawrence, has been erected during the past two years. It is 115 feet long, and 68 feet wide, in addition to which are the entrance and stair case wings. The auditory is 87 feet long, 60 feet wide and 30 feet high. It is furnished with solid Black Walnut pews and pulpit, upholster d and carpeted throughout, and has one of the largest and best organs in the west. The building also contains a lecture room 20x60 feet, two parlors, each 20x22 feet, and a pastor's study, Sunday School Library and infant class room, each 13x20 feet.

The edifice is built of brick, with limestone dressing and is of the most substantial character. The cost, inclusive of foundation, was $45,000. J. G. Haskell, of Lawrence, was the architect.

Corner Main and Second Streets, Ottawa. Page 65.

This view of four or five buildings in Ottawa, is given to illustrate the manner of growth in a new town. Some of the cheapest buildings on the street are shown, but the thoroughly constructed stone and brick bank building, is typical of those which will soon take the place of the wooden structures around it, and the modest sign of the "Great Western Hotel de Horse," is characteristic of the genuine, unpretentious, and retiring Western man.

Morris School, Leavenworth. Page 70.

This large public school building was erected in 1866, and 1867, Mr. E. T. Carr, of Leavenworth, being the architect. It is built of brick and is a very convenient and imposing structure. It seats 850 pupils and cost about $50,000. The upper story is used by the State Normal School, of Leavenworth.

Kansas Valley National Bank, Topeka. Page 77.

This beautiful building stands on the corner of two principal streets in Topeka, and the Kansas Valley National Bank, occupies the principal rooms on the main floor. The Atchison, Topekaand Santa Fe Land Office, telegraph office and State Superintendent of Insurance, who also occupy rooms. The building is constructed of brick and stone, and cost $27,000. The Bank commenced business October 8, 1866. Its authorized capital is $500,000, Daniel M. Adams is president and Chas. N. Rix, cashier. Its business has steadily increased, and it reports having annually paid its stockholders 20 per cent. per annum, besides setting apart a liberal surplusfund.

Street Scene, Humboldt. Page 82.

This life-like cut tells its own story, without the necessity for explanatory remarks. Like all other cuts in this book (with exceptions named) it is from a photograph.

New Episcopal Female Seminary, Topeka. Page 88.

This elegant structure is now being erected of limestone, with contrasting magnesian limestone trimmings. It is situated upon a beautiful square of 20 acres presented by the city of Topeka, two blocks east of the capital square. The view given is from a perspective plan by the architect, Mr. J. G. Haskell. It will be completed during the year 1871.

The building is 100 feet long and 74 feet wide. Its well lighted basement is 10½ feet high in the clear, with three high stories above, and airy rooms next to the roof. It contains complete accommodations for boarders, and private apartments for the principal and his family. A beautiful studio with a north light will be a valuable feature, while the music rooms, reception rooms, parlors, dispensory, infirmary and dormitories will be spacious, and provided with all conveniences for ventilation and to promote health.

The south wing containing the gymnasium, the main school room and the chapel, bears the name of *Wolfe Hall*, after Mr. John D. Wolfe of New York, who has very generously contributed about $20,000 to the institution.

This is to be, in all its appointments, the most complete girls schools this side of the Mississippi, and perhaps we should say this side of the Alleghanies Rev. J. N. Lee, A. M , is principal, and the school is under the supervisory care of Rt. Rev Thomas H. Vail, D. D., Bishop of the Diocese of Kansas, who is President of the Board of Trustees for the institution. The catalogue for last year shows an attendance of 148 pupils, five pianos in use, etc., during which time the school was in session in the old building. All the varied advantages of this institution, including a home with its care and culture, are to be obtained for about $300 per annum.

Baptist Church, Leavenworth. Page 95.

This church is 57x96 feet from outside to outside, including towers. The audience room is 53x67 feet. The hight of walls to commencementof roof is 28 feet, and the hight from floor to apex is 62 feet. This room is carpeted and each sitting cushioned. The sittings, including gallery, number 700. Each tower has two finished rooms entered from gallery. In the basement are five rooms. one of which is a session room that seats 300 persons. The church is built of brick, and finished in the most thorough and elegant manner. The entire cost has been about $65,000.

Wire Suspension Bridge, Ottawa. Page 100.

This beautiful structure was erected in the year 1867 at a cost of above $14,000. Its span is 150 feet, and it rests upon abutments of rough dressed limestone each being founded upon the rock bottom of the river bed. They are 10x20 feet at the base and about 30 feet high. It connects the north and south portions of Main street in the city of Ottawa, which here crosses the timber skirted Marias des Cygnes.

Ottawa University. *Page* 106.

This building was erected in 1866 of limestone walls faced with cut sand-stone, and with limestone cap sills, corners, etc. It is 40x65 feet in size, and with three high stories, including basement, and is elegantly finished. It stands upon one section of 640 acres of choice land, adjacent to the city of Ottawa, and through the land winds a small stream fringed with timber. This section is divided by Osage Orange hedges into fields of convenient size, and adorned with forest, fruit and ornmental trees and shrubbery.

Poole's Building, Lawrence. *Page* 110.

This fine building is the property of Samuel Poole, of Lawrence. It is built of brick and occupies one of the most prominent corners on Massachusetts street. It is 51 feet wide and 110 feet long. The lower story is used for business purposes, and the upper story is occupied by Liberty Hall. This fine room seats 1,000 persons, and is 25 feet high. The walls and ceiling are freecoed, and the stage is arranged with scenery and foot lights complete. The stage is 48x20 feet.

Block in Humboldt. *Page* 115.

This block is erected of stone on the main square in Humboldt, and is devoted to general business purposes.

Public School, Pomona. *Page* 122.

This commodious and convenient school house was erected in Pomona within a year after the first house was built in the village. It contains a graded school, with a large attendance, and illustrates the modern methods by which we transform. in a brief space of time, a spot of open prairie, to a crowded town, with all the conveniences of modern civilization.

S. W. Cor. Second and Delaware Sts., Leavenworth. *Page* 126.

The elegant four story building, represented in this picture, will be recognized by Kansans as standing on one of the principal streets in Leavenworth. These stores are constructed of brick and stone, with iron fronts, and are finished in the most thorough and workmanlike manner, and are occupied by substantial and reliable bussness firms.

Universalist Church, Lawrence. *Page* 130.

I take pleasure in calling attention to this beautiful little church, not only from its harmonious proportions and graceful parts, but from the peculiar adaptation of the plan to a new country.

Everything attempted to be done in a new country, from the least to the greatest, whether the construction of a stable to to the erection of a Cathedral; whether the laying out of a new town, or the completion of a continental railroad, should be so planned that it shall answer the immediate purposes for which it is intended, and at the same time be capable of *expansion*, by additions which shall not mar the *unity* of the design.

The lecture room at the rear of the main portion of this church, is 22x46 feet, forming a complete little church for a new settlement, capable of seating two hundred persons. It is intered through the lobby, which shows in the cut, while the end door may be thrown open for egress. The audience room, which can be added at any time, is about 34x45 feet, with a tower 12x12 feet, and a lobby in front. The larger room seats 300 persons, and the interior is nicely finished with Black Walnut and Hard Pine. This church is built of pine, braced and tied together in the most substantial manner, and the entire cost is within ten thousand dollars. I think it would be a valuable improvement, so to construct the partition between the rooms, that it could be removed at pleasure, forming one large audience room for extra occasions.

Kansas Fruit Medals. Pages 139–143.

In the year 1869 an appropriation of $500 was made by the Kansas State Legislature, to defray the expenses of an exhibition of fruit before the American Pomological Society, to convene in Philadelphia during the same year. Dr. Wm. M. Housely, George T. Anthony, C. B. Lines and S. T. Kelsey, were appointed a committee by the Kansas State Horticultural Society to collect fruits for the purpose of this exhibition. They obtained about 20 barrels of apples, pears and grapes, and proceeded with them to Philadelphia. There they found the American Pomological Society convened with the Pennsylvania Horticultural Society, and the exhibition of fruits was held under the auspices of the latter society. Notwithstanding the large display of fruits there made, and the extraordinary exertions of other states to carry off the coveted first prize, the award of the great gold medal was made "to the Kansas State Horticultural Society for a display of fruits unsurpassed for beauty and excellence." Such was the size, beauty and flavor of the Kansas fruits, that none but experts could recognize in the specimens, the varieties which they were accustomed to raise in the east.

Neosho Falls, Woodson County. Page 148.

This view of the valuable water power on the Neosho river at the town of Neosho Falls is accurately copied from the photograph, excepting that both of the long approaches to the bridge are constructed of iron, with arched supports, which the artist has not inserted in the approach which is shown. This water power was improved by Col. N. S. Goss, the founder of the flourishing town of Neosho Falls. The length of the dam is 220 feet, and the power is sufficient to carry a large amount of machinery. Being situated upon the railroad which is penetrating the best cotton fields in America, this would be an excellent site for a cotton factory. The enterprising town is hidden by the trees and river bank, at the left of the picture.

Plan of Highland Cemetery, Junction City. Page 156.

This plan sufficiently explains itself, while it bespeaks the taste and public spirit of the people of Junction City, who have thus laid out and adorned the city of the dead. The above plan was but recently adopted, but the work o growing trees and shrubbery is progressing as rapidly as possible.

Presbyterian Church, Junction City. Page 166.

I regret to acknowledge that the data I had received concerning this tasteful edifice, is not at hand at the moment of sending this matter to press. The cut is from an accurate photographic view, and sufficiently shows the excellent appearance of the structure. It is built of magnesian limestone, and is thoroughly finished inside and out. All must concede that it is a very good building to stand where buffalo were pursued by the wild Indian, but a short fifteen years ago. E. T. Carr of Leavenworth was the architect.

Lincoln School, Topeka. Page 179.

This is one of the most graceful and complete structures in the State. It forms a harmonious picture from whatever point of view it is approached. It is in the form of an irregular Greek cross, and is 74x91 feet in size and three stories high, exclusive of basement. Its largest tower is 15 feet square and 104 feet high. The smaller tower forms the ventilating shaft, with a smoke stack in the centre. The walls are limestone faced with brick, and the openings are trimmed with an excellent quality of limestone. It contains seven school rooms, each about 24x33 feet, three recitation rooms, a sufficient number of wardrobes and dressing rooms, and a hall in the third story 36x51 feet. The building seats 704 pupils, or 528, if all occupy separate desks. It was erected in 1870 at a total cost of about $50,000 including furnishings.

The Challis Ferry Boat, Atchison. Page 186.

The ferry boat "S. C. Pomeroy," at Atchison, is propelled by two powerful engines, and is capable of carrying across the swift waters of the Missouri a large number of loaded teams. The ferry boats which ply between the opposite banks of our western rivers, as well as the steamboats which carry freight and passengers up and down these rivers, are all so constructed as to take on or discharge passengers, freight, teams, cattle, etc., at the side of the boat, instead of the end. This is necessary, from the fact that the strength of the current in these rivers is so great as to oblige the boats to tie up with their bows headed up stream, when their sides drift against the bank. As the rivers are constantly rising and falling, the ferry boats tie up to a wharf boat, which is moored along shore, and which is reached by a bridge from the land. When this ferry boat is crowded, teams pass entirely around it on the open space shown in the picture.

Steam Flouring Mill, Pomona Page 206.

This substantial stone building was recently erected and fitted up with the most approved mill machinery, at a total expense of about $18,000. Kansas now has many excellent flouring mills, but she needs many more, especially in the newly settled portions of the State.

Exchange Bank, Atchison. Page 213.

This fine brick block is situated on the principal street in Atchison, and was built and is owned by the Banking House of Wm. Hetherington & Co. This is the oldest Banking House in Atchison, having commenced in 1859, and continued with a constantly increasing business. The building is built of brick and stone, with iron trimmings, and is an elegant and durable structure.

Bancroft Block, Emporia. Page 227.

This building is 50x80 feet in size, and three stories high with basement. It is built of stone and brick, with iron front, and is completed in the most substantial and tasteful manner. The lower story is used for stores, the second story for business offices, including the real estate office of E. P. Bancroft, who erected and owns the building. The third story is thrown into one large hall, well lighted and ventilated, which will seat 600 persons. It is considered by speakers and singers one of the best halls in the state. It has two good entrances, and is situated in the centre of business and near the hotels.

Cor. Levee and Main Street, Leavenworth. Page 229.

This magnificent block of buildings is constructed of brick and iron. It has been erect d at different times and by various parties, during the last twelve years, and is devoted exclusively to wholesale merchandising, and is occupied by wealthy firms who carry heavy stocks of goods. In the distance is the Planters House, one of the best known hotels in the West.

King Iron Bridge Manufactory and Iron Works, Iola. Page 237.

The main building shown in the picture is 50x350 feet, and the addition is 40 x200 feet. Both buildings are 18 feeet high, and built of limestone. They have capacity for about 300 workmen. The main track of the Leavenworth, Lawrence and Galveston Railroad passes in front of the building, and a side track passes across the middle of the rear building. Coal from the vicinity is now furnished at 20 cents per bushel, and a shaft is being sunk, from which coal is to be delivered to the works at 12 cents per bushel.

This company was organized since January, 1871, and its manufactory will soon be in motion. The company consists of Z. King, president, T. B. Mills, vice presiden, Jas. A. King, secretary, and B. M. Smith, treasurer, and it has control of all territory west of the Mississippi river, for the manufacture and sale of the celebrated King's Wrought Iron Bridges. (See page 217.)

Missouri Valley Life Ins. Building, Leavenworth. *Page* 239.

This building is now in course of erection by the Missouri Valley Life Insurance Company, of Leavenworth, and when completed will be one of the finest and best appointed buildings in the country. It is 73x125 feet on the ground, is to be faced with dressed stone, the basement blue limestone and the superstructure with a fine quality of magnesian limestone. The basement is to be 5 feet in the clear above the sidewalks, and will be divided into offices, coal room, boiler room, etc. These offices are to be well lighted and pleasant, and are designed for first class business offices. The first floor is to be fitted up entire for offices, and approached from the corner entrance will be the principal business offices of the company with the minor offices in the second story, and so arranged as to be approached by a private stair case. Besides the numerous rooms in the second story for the use of the company, there are several splendid offices, designed for renting. In the third story the Free Masons propose to have their Lodge rooms. These when completed, will be the finest in the West. The building is to be heated by steam, will be thoroughly ventilated and supplied with all the modern improvements, and from its central location and the admirable adaptation to the uses for which it is intended, it will undoubtedly be a profitable investment. The architect is E. T. Carr of Leavenworth.

Minister, No. 6,363. *Page* 244.

This splendid animal is of red color. He took the first premium at the fair of the Kansas State Agricultural Society in 1870. He was got by Lord Derby, 4, 949, and was calved September 23, 1863, and was bred by the late R. A. Alexander of Kentucky. He is now owned by Andrew Wilson of Topeka, Kansas. His pedigree is to be found in the American Short Horn Herd Book, vol. 7. His weight on 17th August, 1868, was 2,310 lbs.

Oxford Wiley, No. 8,756. *Page* 246.

Oxford Wiley was calved August 13, 1866, was bred by A. J. Alexander of Kentucky, and is now owned by N. L. Chaffee of Ashtabula county, Ohio. He is kept by the sons of Judge Chaffee at their farm near Manhattan, Kansas. His color is red roan. He was got by imported Royal Oxford, 1,877 and is a very fine animal.

"Comus." Page 302.

(The property of B. F. Akers, Leavenworth.)

Described on same page.

"Kansas Boy." Page 303.

(The property of B. F. Akers, Leavenworth.)

Described on same page.

"Newry." Page 304.

(The property of Dr. W. L. Challis, Atchison.)

Described on same page.

INDEX.

www.ingramcontent.com/pod-product-compliance
Lightning Source LLC
LaVergne TN
LVHW010220110826
845151LV00004B/1152

* 9 7 8 1 4 2 5 5 2 6 0 7 8 *